Denton Jacques Snider

The Shakespearian Drama

A Commentary

Denton Jacques Snider

The Shakespearian Drama
A Commentary

ISBN/EAN: 9783337055103

Printed in Europe, USA, Canada, Australia, Japan

Cover: Foto ©ninafisch / pixelio.de

More available books at **www.hansebooks.com**

THE
Shakespearian Drama.

A COMMENTARY,

BY

DENTON J. SNIDER.

THE TRAGEDIES.

BOSTON:
TICKNOR & CO.
1887.

TABLE OF CONTENTS.

INTRODUCTION, - - - I to LXIV

NATURE OF TRAGEDY, - - - 1

TIMON OF ATHENS, - - - - 11

ROMEO AND JULIET, - - - 36

OTHELLO, - - - - - 79

KING LEAR, - - - - 125

MACBETH, - - - - - 210

HAMLET, - - - - - 286

INTRODUCTION.

SECTION I. PREFATORY.—ORIGIN AND SCOPE OF
THE PRESENT WORK.

The present is the third shape in which the material of this book has been given to the public. It was first written in the form of detached essays, and printed in various periodicals, without the author's having any intention of composing a work upon Shakespeare. But the essays continued to increase, through a number of years, till they at last embraced all of the poet's dramas. They originated in the room of the instructor, whose simple principle was to study each passage, scene, and act by itself, then to unite them into the entire play, and finally to unite the plays by the common fact underlying all of them. Thus the work grew, without pre-conceived theory or plan, without even a thought of its own existence at the start.

The second shape was the collection of the essays into a book, with revision and additions. This book has been out of print for some time, and as it is still asked for, it would seem to have a fair claim to a new lease of life. It has, accordingly, been revised once more, probably for the last time, and in parts re-written. Its title has been changed, in order that it may take its place as an integral, but independent, portion of a larger work upon the four Great Books of Occidental Literature— Homer, Dante, Shakespeare, Goethe—which are gradually coming to have the meaning and name of Literary Bibles, and upon which the work alluded to is a commentary.

The present is, however, but one of a thousand books which have been written, and will continue to be written upon Shakespeare. This increase of Shakespearian literature has been looked on as something appalling; and so it would be if everybody were compelled to read it all. But it is no more to be regretted than the increase of Shakespearian study, from which it evidently springs. Nearly every High School, (and sometimes the humbler Common School) throughout all Anglo-Saxondom, in Europe, America, Asia, and perchance Africa, has its teacher of Shakespeare, who will, in a large or small way, have his own ideas, his own point of view derived from study and instruction. From the school he passes to the community; grown-up people also wish to know about Shakespeare, and gladly take a guide; thus each village has, or is likely to have in the future, its own expositor of Shakespeare. He, in the course of nature, must write down his results; then the printing press is always at hand; the modest,

INTRODUCTION. III

shrinking manuscript is drawn forth into day, and is rapidly metamorphosed through newspaper, magazine, review, into a book finally, which challenges the whole world, and which may become a light-point for several dozens, or, by good luck, for several hundreds, who show their faith or goodwill by giving their cash to help pay off the printer's bill. Whoever deals much with the great poet will, of necessity, be filled with new ideas; Shakespeare will fertilize even a barren brain and make it produce some kind of a crop. The present book sprang from a High School, and was fostered in a community by a few dozens of sympathetic people. The same process is going on wherever the English tongue is spoken; is not that the poet's girdle round the earth? In the next fifty years it is not hard to foresee that more will be written on Shakespeare than the entire Shakesperian literature now extant; all the machinery is in place and at work for an enormous production in this line. Certain authors who have written their book on Shakespeare, have been horrified at the prospect of such a deluge sweeping over their little writ in the near future; but it is clearly in the divine order of things, and these writers show a touch of egotism, as if they thought that their view and their book were the grand finality and culmination of Shakespearian Literature. Still the world goes on writing and printing other books of the kind, in spite of the fact that they have written a book.

The point of view in the present edition is not materially changed from what it was before. The book has been subjected to some refutations, but with the best intention to profit by them, they have failed to convince. Refutations seldom refute; they are usually but different ways of looking at the same object, and they are apt to take for granted the very thing at issue. Nothing is plainer than that Shakespeare can be regarded from the most diverse points of view; different minds will fraternize with different sides of the universal poet. Let them not think that their way is the only way; the Shakespearian arena ought to be ploughed up and sowed with charity. Calling names can do no good, and though a sarcasm may be more effective than an argument, it is never an argument.

Knowing how little I have been convinced by refutations, I shall not try much to refute others who may differ from me. I shall endeavor to unfold my point of view, and there let the matter rest. I must refuse, therefore, to enter into the many controversies which have sprung up around Shakespeare. Besides, I have noticed that it is very dangerous to assert what Shakespeare is not, for example, that he is not an idealist, not a realist, not conscious of his plan, above all that he is not himself, but somebody else. The writer who puts a limit upon Shakespeare, is usually revealing his own limit. Far safer and better is it simply to state what you find in the poet, than what you do not find, lest it be there too, and you not see it. Negative criticism is of small account at best, and is apt to be a criticism of the critic, of whom nobody wishes to hear. I have seen so many fatalities of this kind, particularly among writers who have intended murder, but committed suicide, that I must be allowed to throw away the weapon. Very little controversy then, and that little nameless.

It may be reasonably required of an author to save his readers, as far as he is able, from disappointment. The study of Shakespeare has developed into numerous specialties; many who pursue one branch of it with zeal disregard, or even despise, its other branches; such persons generally do not want to be troubled with any work which lies outside of their particular direction. The present book undertakes to give a special phase of the Shakespearian Drama. Lest the reader should expect something not contained in it, at the beginning I wish to tell him what he need not look for, and also to give a general statement of its purport.

That realm of learning which pertains to the language of Shakespeare—the philological element—has been entirely omitted. Grammatical, metrical, textual, and other similar researches, have accumulated to an enormous extent around the works of the poet; this is a great field of erudition by itself. Now, it is absolutely necessary to have such a literature; linguistic study, up to a certain point, is the foundation of all solid knowledge of Shakespeare. Still, language itself is only a means for a higher object; hence these researches must be regarded merely as instrumentalities—important, but not final.

INTRODUCTION.

The historical side of Shakespearian criticism is but little dwelt upon. Dates of the plays, sources of the plots, allusions of contemporaries, facts of the poet's life, books that he read, editions of his works, everything down to the most insignificant historical details, have been already diligently collected, and the field seems pretty well gleaned. At least in this western part of the world there is little prospect of discovering any new Shakespearian documents. There remains the choice between oft-repeated repetition and silence; of the two, the latter seems preferable.

Nor is there to be found here any indulgence in that favorite pastime of erudite leisure which may be called the sport of probabilities. Upon a very small fragment of an historical fact there is reared a colossal air-palace of conjecture—perhaps a harmless, but certainly a very insubstantial, edifice. What difference does it make, in the judgment of Shakespeare's work, whether he was a Catholic or Protestant; whether, indeed, he was called Shakespeare, or by some other name? His book remains the same, and must be judged as it is; any argument to the contrary implies that our view of Shakespeare is to be determined by our view of something else, or of somebody else.

The purely literary element of Shakespearian criticism—that species of criticism which points out the beauties of the poet, and glows over them in rapturous exclamations and figurative convulsions—may now and henceforth be reasonably omitted. Indeed, the poetry of Shakespeare must be left largely to the reader, for it appeals to the emotions and the imagination, while criticism ought rather to address the understanding. The poetical sense is immediate, natural; it cannot be conferred, though it may doubtless be aided by pointing out for it the beautiful passages of a poem. At least this phase of criticism does not fall within the scope of the present undertaking.

In general, the aim of this book is to show each drama as a Whole, in its thought, organization, and characters; then to group cognate dramas into a higher Whole by their common fundamental principle; at last, to behold all the dramas of the poet as one Whole—in fine, to sum up Shakespeare. Such a plan, if successful, will unfold the inner meaning as well as the outer structure of the Shakespearian Drama.

To a work of this kind neither too great nor too little value must be ascribed. If we make it a substitute for the beautiful poetic form of which it is hardly more than a skeleton, we misapply it totally. Criticism is not poetry, and cannot take the place of poetry. On the other hand, an utter resignation to the sensuous glow of passion is not the true poetical habit. Mere gratification of the senses is bestial, and Art may, in this way, be degraded into an instrument of sensuality. The inner spiritual essence must always be felt through —nay, be seen through. Then there is a genuine appreciation; then, too, the senses are lifted up into the realm of beauty, and become angels of purity, by means of the indwelling spirit. Poetry has both sides—a sensuous and an intellectual; it is not in itself a philosophy, but, without a philosophy, it is in danger of being turned into a temple of the grossest passions.

It will doubtless be disagreeable to some very ardent admirers of the poet to descend into the depths of his spiritual being, and there behold the foundation of his Art. They say that his procedure is unconscious and instinctive; why, then, foist upon him an order and a law? So is the procedure of nature unconscious; still, it is the great spiritual vocation of our age to discover nature's law. Take Shakespeare merely as a wonderful phenomenon of nature, is it not reasonable—indeed, is it not necessary—to seek for his law also? Be assured the human mind enjoys no repose in ignorance. Then, too, Shakespeare was not the unconscious baby that babies would make him out. He thought; he planned; he mostly knew what he was doing. It is an absurdity to declare that, in a world where thought alone is greatness, its greatest man was an unthinking prodigy.

Still, the protest of the poetic temperament must be heard, and in a due degree heeded, for it seeks to call the mind back to beauty, away from excessive abstraction. A one-sided pursuit always warps the power of just discrimination; any Shakespearian specialty has a tendency to unfit its follower for a full enjoyment of the poetry. A man who is in the habit of centering his attention solely upon the grammar, upon the meter, or upon the figures, will certainly fail of the total impression. It is well known that some of the acutest verbal critics, and most learned commentators on Shakespeare, have shown an utter want of all poetic sense. The same fate must overtake the person who too exclusively looks for the abstract thought of an artistic product. As the work of beauty springs from the happy interpenetration of spirit and sense, so the true appreciation must conjoin the two elements—must both feel and know in one. Still, criticism has to give expression to the side of intelligence, since the side of feeling can only be uttered adequately in the realm of poetry. Let it not be forgotten, then, that Art is Thought in a sensuous form; that it is not a system of Pure Thought on the one hand, nor is it an embodiment of Pure Sensuality on the other.

SECTION II. HISTORIC ELEMENTS OF THE SHAKESPEARIAN DRAMA.

The origin of the Drama is supposed to lie in an inborn tendency of human nature. Aristotle, the oldest, and still one of the best, writers on the Art of Poetry, ascribes to man what he calls *mimesis*, or imitiation, from which he deduces the Drama as well as other forms of Art. In antiquity, the most perfect Drama, that of the Greeks, originated in religious festivals, from which its influence passed into the Christian world. The Mass of the Church is essentially a drama, showing an abridged history of man, in his fall and redemption.

From the Christian Mass of early ages springs the modern Drama, whose primitive form is the *Mystery Play*. This seeks to give, in a religious frame-work, the entire history of man from the Creation till the Judgment Day, as it is presented in historic continuity by the Old and New Testaments. The Lord and the Devil are the two chief characters, who appear in person on the stage, and carry on their conflict. The Devil is comic in these old plays, so are all his demons, cohorts, earthly representatives, such as Herod. To the simple mind of the people, the bad, in attempting to overthrow the good, is foolish, ludicrous, comic. Evil, in its complete circle, is self-destructive; so our ancestors laughed at the Devil, on the stage at least. It often required several days to give an entire Mystery, which is not so much one play, as a series of plays; the Coventry Mystery, for example, is composed of forty-two plays, or, more properly, long dialogues. The dealings of Providence with his children are the great fact which is emphasized; the side of divine order is presented overwhelmingly; in it man is passive, or, at best, a child; and future bliss is made the motive of this world's deed.

The *Morality Play* is the next step in the development of the Drama. Personification is now the means; virtue and vice, moral and mental qualities, even abstract conceptions are endowed with personality and made to act; man himself, in some of these old plays, is personified as Humanum Genus, in his conflict with the World, the Flesh and the Devil. Here we see that the struggle has become a moral one, and is thrown back upon the individual as moved from within. Very great is this step in Dramatic Art as well as in the history of man; psychological interest begins, though extremely simple; characterization begins, though there be but one trait in a whole character; the inner freedom of man has, indeed, dawned. The Mystery Play emphasises the side of Providence, but leaves the Individual as a passive spectator of the fight between the Lord and the Devil. But in the Morality Play the super-human antagonists have come down from their lofty stage and have gone inside the man, and are there waging battle. Still there is a defect in the Morality Play, which soon makes itself felt; it is a bloodless allegory, it takes the moral substance by itself without sensible form; it has no body.

The third step in the development of the Drama is the *Interlude*, a kind of play which flourished in England in the reigns of Henry VII and Henry VIII. In it naturalism appears, a picture of real life is given, in coarse, humerous, drastic outlines. The Drama has now won a body, has become a human, living fact, in all its sensuous fullness. Amusement is the end, not instruction, moral or religious; truth to nature, not an abstraction, is sought for. This is the realistic element of the Drama—the body of it, but not the soul; the ethical element has quite dropped out of sight, and so we find these Interludes sinking easily into coarseness hardly endurable.

But the true Drama must have all three elements; it must reveal the divine way of dealing with the world, as the Mystery Play; it must show the moral germ in the Individual, as the Morality Play; it must be life incorporate, as the Interlude. Now Shakespeare has all three elements, not in their isolation, but so fused together in the heat of his poetic conception, that they make something altogether new. His Drama is not strictly religious, not strictly moral, not strictly sensuous, yet it is all three; it shows the world-order, it portrays personal character in the deepest sense, it deals broadly with living shapes. We see the crude materials of the English Drama unfold separately, then they come together in Shakespeare as their historic culmination. We see, too, that the English people elaborated through centuries the dramatic substance which went to make their great national poet. If we look back still further, we find that his spiritual procession is from the heart of Christianity, in its transition out of Heathendom.

A true criticism of the poet would give validity to all these elements. But the critics have a tendency to divide upon these lines, and to lay stress upon one element. Ulrici sees and unfolds, perhaps better than any other writer, the divine order in Shakespeare. Gervinus, on the contrary, has a special aptitude for bringing out the moral side of these plays. It naturally fell to a Frenchman, M. Taine, to emphasize the sensuousness and realism of the Shakespearian Drama. Undoubtedly all

INTRODUCTION. XIII

these elements are present, and a critical method ought to give all, in due proportion.

There was one other very weighty influence in the development of Shakespeare. Not long before his age the Revival of Letters had taken place, a great spiritual awakening through the study of classical antiquity in its original Greek and Latin sources, as well as in its secondary modern, chiefly Italian, sources. This movement is known as the Renascence; it brought culture, artistic form, as well as a sense of freedom; it gave to classical Mythology and to the heathen Gods a free home in modern literature; it aroused the study and imitation of ancient models, especially of the ancient Drama. In England, in the sixteenth century, this influence was strongly felt, and helped to make the new poet. Shakespeare is the greatest child of the Renascence. Not that he was a man deeply learned in Greek and Latin, but he knew the ancient world from some of its best books, which had been already translated into English, also from erudite men trained at the University, who were his friends and acquaintances. Then he was a genius, one who breathed unconsciously the spiritual atmosphere of his time, and appropriated its principle. His employment of classic allusions, of ancient history and mythology, is not external, but is ingrained—a part of his very being—and has become a vital element of his style as well as of his thought. His relation to antiquity is not that of a professor, but that of a poet, into whose fibre it has grown.

The Greek world of artistic form, accordingly, after passing through many intermediate conditions, at last reaches Shakespeare, and moulds him. The Mystery Play, the Morality Play, the Interlude, were the crude popular materials, which the Renascence seized and shaped in accord with its newly acquired sense of Art; through it the ancient Drama gave form to the modern Drama. Still Shakespeare is no mere imitator of classicalities; he nowhere seeks simply to re-produce a Greek play, though he uses, in several cases, classical subjects. The ancient art-world is the secret, shaping hand in the Shakespearian Drama, but shapes it not in the limits of the ancient pattern. The old artist, though transformed, is still himself in his transformation; the ancient and the modern structures are not the same, though we must see that they have one builder.

Nor should we forget, in this estimate of historic forces, the influence of his own age upon the poet. He could behold in the real world before his own eyes the living embodiment of his Art. The age of Elizabeth was, in many respects, the point at which the opposing forces of centuries met, an arena of collisions; the conflict of Protestantism had not yet ended, that of Puritanism had already begun; both gave rise to fierce soul-struggles, as well as physical contests. There were great tragedies of individuals like that of Mary, Queen of Scots, like that of Essex; there was what might almost be called a tragedy of a nation in the case of Spain, one act of which was the defeat of the Armada by England, in Shakespeare's manhood. Tragic passion the poet could witness in some of his own friends, nay, he could feel the possibility of it in himself. But he, as well as his age, possessed also the principle of reconciliation, which dwells in the heart of Christianity.

Shakespeare's works, taken together, may be looked at as a vast World-Drama, the grand Mystery Play of humanity, showing the free man acting out his freedom in a providential order. As such a play, it has conflict, suffering, tragedy; but it also has the solution of conflict, mediation, harmony. It reveals the darkest depths of guilt, of the soul's estrangement, yet it shows the return and the reconciliation. It would take days to play such a drama, as it did the old Mystery Play; still we ought to see it all at once, if we would comprehend it as a whole—which is the only true comprehension. In these days, the stage can fulfil no such requirement; so we must go to our closet, and there study it out from the poet's printed book.

Shakespeare's life, as seen in his book—and this is the only place to see it—falls into three periods, which gradually pass into one another. Each period shows a phase of his development, and, we may with truth say, of the world's development, for the poet must pass through individually what his race passes through generally; thus he can make his life an image of the universal life. First is the period of young-manhood, the time of exuberance and poetic overflow, when he writes all kinds of dramas—comedies, histories, tragedies—but not yet fully differentiated. The second is his tragic period, when he sees the individual sinking in the conflicts of existence, when he, in consequence, is saddened, and deepened, and intensified into one kind of writing, and produces his four greatest tragedies almost at one time, so that it is impossible to tell, at present, which comes first in order of composition. The third period is that of mediation, when the tragic conflict is still active, but is at last mediated; the individual, though guilty, is not now made to perish, but is restored. These periods, we see, are soul-epochs of the poet cast into the image of Art; but they are none the less soul-epochs of mankind cast into the image of History. This correspondence between the poet's development and that of his race is the final authentic seal of his consecration as poet. His three periods constitute a trilogy, not only of his works, but also of his life—and indeed of the world's life.

In the following exposition, an attempt will be made to be true to the spirit of all these historic elements of the Shakespearian Drama. The ethical order of the world will be specially marked in it—which is the essence of the Mystery Play; we shall point out the moral element of character—which is the part of the Morality Play, but shall touch very lightly upon the sensuous element, which is the part of the Interlude; form and structure we shall emphasize, that the reader may not miss the chief influence of the Renascence

INTRODUCTION. XVII

upon Shakespeare; finally, we shall organize all the plays into one colossal edifice, in which we may behold the life-work of the poet both in its thought and its development.

(Mr. J. Payne Collier, *History of English Dramatic Poetry*, has shown very fully the historic development of the English Drama; Ulrici, *Shakespeare's Dramatische Kunst, Buch I*, has ably shown its inner development. For the origin of the Drama, see Ward, *Hist. Eng. Dram. Literature*, and especially the monumental work of Klein, *Geschichte des Dramas, passim.*)

SECTION III.—THE DRAMATIC: ITS RELATION TO OTHER POETICAL FORMS, AND ITS GENERAL CHARACTER.

The Drama represents man in action. It exhibits him in the infinite web of his complications, with influences passing out from him and coming back to him, and thereby portrays, in the shortest space and in the most striking manner, the relative worth of human deeds. Nor does it rest content with the mere external doings of man; on the contrary, it penetrates his innermost nature, and probes the profoundest depths of his spiritual being. For it unfolds motives, ends, convictions; and, in fact, these internal elements constitute its most important feature. They form the basis of what is called Character, and their true value as well as their logical relation are exhibited in the development and outcome of the dramatic work.

The Drama is the most concrete, and therefore

the highest, of all the forms of Poetry. The Epos is the product of national childhood; it contemplates man in an intellectual infancy which demands the continuous supervision of the gods. It, therefore, lays stress upon the Objective, the Universal; not, however, as mediated through the spirit of man, but as an existence standing outside of him and determining his actions. Hence the tinge of Fate which prevails in all Epic Poetry; for the contradiction between Freedom and Necessity is not yet developed by this early consciousness. Still, self-determination may, and in fact should, peer through these external forms in a naive, unconscious manner; such is the case with Homer, who often seems to make the gods his sport. The Epos, therefore, may be said to be essentially religious, and seeks to unfold, if not to justify, the ways of Providence to man.

The Lyric Poet, on the contrary, portrays his own emotions, desires, reflections—in fine, the entire content of his own subjectivity. Still, there must be felt in his song something of universal significance; it must bring into sympathetic concord the heart of a people, of a whole age. His strain may be one of joy and happiness, or of sadness and despair; it also very often turns to an incessant lamentation about his own injured and unappreciated self, or to a stinging censure of the cold, heartless world. He thus falls out with the existing order of things, becomes negative and skeptical, assails and undermines the ancient faith and simple epical feeling. So old Simonides was accused of impiety. But to mention all the phases of the lyric form of poetry would be here unnecessary, if not impossible; it is as varied and boundless as the nature of man, and extends into all periods of civilization. Its general characteristic, however, is subjective, and it portrays man, not in action, but resting in feeling and reflection.

But in the Drama all this is changed. Man starts up from the repose in which he has been describing and nursing his emotions, and begins to act—that is, he begins to give his subjective nature validity in the external world. His feelings, passions, hopes, ends, are no longer satisfied with quiet, lyrical description, but must take on the form of reality. Nor, again, are these ends which he is trying to realize always merely subjective; on the contrary, they represent objective principles of universal validity, as Right, Family, State. Hence the Dramatic is the concrete unity of the Epic and Lyric; not a mixture of the two, but an entirely new species. The Drama represents an action like the Epos; but it must abandon the principle of external divine interference, and put in its stead the self-conscious, self-acting individual. Hence no demons, angels, or gods are allowed to perform the mediations of the Drama in its highest manifestations; all is human, and expressive of human freedom. For there can be only one reason why the Drama is the highest of all the forms of Art: It most adequately represents self-determination —man as a free, and hence responsible, being. To express the same thought in the more precise, yet more abstruse, terms of philosophy, the Dramatic is the complete unity and double interpenetration, of the Epic and Lyric; on the one hand, it unites the subjective side of the latter with the objective side of the former by making the objective world inherent in the subject, thus filling his emptiness and giving him the truest content; on the other hand, it portrays the subject, giving validity to himself in the objective world through his own activity.

If, therefore, the Epical consciousness is essentially religious, and the Lyrical may become negative, and even skeptical, the Dramatic, on the other hand, is ethical. But this ethical characteristic is made up, not merely of a single principle, but embraces a series of principles which form a regular gradation from the lowest to the highest. Hence it is possible for a lower principle to collide with a higher. It is just this conflict which constitutes the source of all dramatic action. As the science of Ethics, if truly elaborated, would show all these principles, in their proper relation and subordination, from a theoretical point of view, so the Drama in a practical way, by means of human action, exhibits in victory or defeat, success or failure, the true relation and subordination of these same ethical principles. It calls man before its tribunal and unfolds to him the consequences of his deeds, not in an abstract form, but in the form of the deed itself. For this purpose the Drama takes the individual, not in the fixed shapes of Sculpture, or in the colored figurations of Painting, but as he is in reality, in flesh and blood; it must have the living person as the bearer of its principle.

If we consider the Drama in this light, it is not the trivial, sportive toy which furnishes amusement for an idle hour, but it assumes immense proportions. We shall find that it is only another form of proposing the greatest of problems—a new way that people have of looking at the profoundest questions of human existence. For the Drama is certainly based upon the Ethical World; its collisions must rest upon elements inherent in the ethical order of things, and its solutions, if true—which is the same as artistic—must be in accordance with this order. Therefore, to judge of the Drama, we have to know something of the Ethical World—its contradictions and its harmonies, its principles and the manner of their subordination; or, if we do not know these things already, the Drama may be able to give the requisite instruction. And, furthermore, since the Ethical World is the realization of Reason, we are led, through the Drama, to ask ourselves the more important question: What is the absolutely Rational? Not as an idle question of speculation, but as the vital fount of action, as the guiding thread of Life ought we to consider such a theme. The Rational in the Drama and the Rational in Thought and Action cannot well be different; indeed, the one is only the adumbration of the other. So the Drama, in its highest utterances, takes up the problem of Life and solves it in its own peculiar manner.

The clash of appetites and passions; the conflict of rights and duties; the alarming hand of Fate reaching over, grasping after all; and, most prominently, the beneficent form of Freedom standing on a heap of broken chains, are there portrayed, the opposing forces reconciled and reduced to one harmonious, well-ordered system. Thus we may learn a practical, as well as an æsthetic, truth of incalculable value—that the Rational in the Drama is the Rational in Life. By these remarks we hope it may be seen that Dramatic Art is no mere abstraction, distinct from, or opposed to, the real world—no plaything to amuse those refined and elegant natures who long to fly away from this groveling sphere to realms ideal, there to bathe in the sunlight of eternal truth, but it clings to earth, and is the most intensely human of all Art. Nor has the human mind ever failed to appreciate its significance as furnishing a reflex of the highest endeavors and greatest achievements of the race.

There is one man to whom we all instinctively turn with the certainty of finding a rational basis—Shakespeare. Criticism has worn itself almost threadbare upon him, and we often are sated with the interminable talk about him, the most of which is so unsatisfactory; still, we have always to come back to his works as the unfailing source of the highest-intellectual and artistic enjoyment. People feel that his is the greatest name in all literature—perhaps in all history. But this is not enough; we must know what is the special form of his greatness. And so the question arises: Wherein is Shakespeare the greatest of authors? We cannot say in the perfection of form, for herein others, perhaps, surpass him; nor in the mastery of language, for this gets to be a knack which may be learned, and, moreover, means little by itself; nor in the beauty of his images, for they are often confused, incongruous, and far-fetched; not even in characterization; nor in the management of an action, in the strict sense of the term. Great as his excellence in these things, it has been attained, sometimes at least, by far inferior writers. There can be no doubt in the statement that the unique and all-surpassing greatness of Shakespeare lies in his comprehension of the ethical order of the world. Though this side of his genius has been always most inadequately stated, and commonly has been passed over entirely in the essays of his critics, still men have instinctively felt that his works were the truest literary product of modern times, because they were the most perfect and concrete presentation of realized rationality. Men see in him their highest selves, and hence must take him as their greatest exponent. The contrast, in this respect, with even the best creations of nearly all other poets is most striking. We read them; we are charmed with the imagery, the thoughts, the rhythmic flow of the verse. But when we come to the end of one of these works we are confused, lost; we analyze it more closely, and find that the Whole, however beautiful its individual parts, is an ethical chaos. But Shakespeare, in this sphere as elsewhere, is all harmony;

no contradictions cloud his poetical horizon, nor does he ever make the *denouement* a logical annihilation of the entire play.

The supreme question concerning the Shakespearian Drama—or, indeed, concerning any great work in Literature—may be stated in this form: What is the world in which it moves? The poet, along with every rational being, must have, consciously or unconsciously, his ultimate principle, his deepest conviction, concerning the government of this universe. Here is the point in which every inquiry must finally center, and by which the author is to be judged. It is, hence, the very essence of all critical investigation; also of all true poetical activity. As a preparatory survey of the subject, the following three distinctions may be grasped separately at first, then fused together into one complete thought; thus the parts may be seen in the Whole.

First. The Shakespearian Drama is ethical. It represents man as controlled from within, by the forms of his own intelligence; and not from without, by external powers. Human Reason begins to realise itself by subordinating the desires of the flesh and the caprices of the Individual to its Law; it subjects the Bad to the Good, the Negative to the Positive; otherwise, man would become the victim of himself. The nature of "appetite," and the result of its supremacy, are stated by Shakespeare himself with a logical precision:

> Appetite, an universal wolf,
> So doubly seconded with will and power,
> Must make perforce an universal prey,
> And last eat up itself.

With this subordination of appetite begins the Ethical World—a system of principles in which the Individual finds, or ought to find, the reflex of his higher Self, and to which he must subject what is lower. But here arises a new difficulty. These ethical principles are both numerous and of very different kinds; hence they, in their own sphere, may come into collision.

Second. The Shakespearian Drama, therefore, has to portray a world of conflict. This is the element which gives to it interest, life, movement. Two men are animated with opposite principles, and undertake to carry them into execution; each may think that he is right, and, indeed, each may be right; both appeal to their intellectual and physical resources, and draw into the contest others with whom they are connected. The result is, the Ethical World is filled with fierce struggles and dire confusion; it is not the placid ideal realm, where the mind may dwell in repose and feed on spiritual beauty. The emphatic point is that the principles are in conflict; the Individual is only their bearer, their representative. This gives what, in strictness, may be called the Dramatic Collision. It would seem to be one of the chief functions of Shakespearian criticism to unfold these collisions of ethical principles in whatever form they occur in a play; only thus can be reached the innermost germ of a dramatic action.

Third. The Shakespearian Drama has to give the solution; it has to mediate its conflicts, and bring all colliding elements into harmony. Through struggle it passes to repose; to war succeeds peace. This may be the peace of death, as is the case with the tragic character; it may be the peace which comes through repentance; or it may be the peace from an exploded absurdity, as in comedy. But the Shakesperian Solution, in whatever shape it occurs, has one fundamental principle—the return of the deed upon the doer. Man has that which he has done brought home to him in the end; his action, often through the most devious and subtle passages, sweeps back and includes himself. Eternal, divine justice it may be called; indeed, it is found already named, in some of these plays, "justice of God." To the superficial eye its course seems, in some cases, past all finding out; but a knowledge of the Ethical World of Shakespeare, and the gradation of its principles, will reveal the mighty form of an all-controlling Justiciary.

To grasp these three points together in one statement, the Shakespearian Drama unfolds the order of ethical principles as realized in the Individual, and in him moving through conflict to final reconciliation. It, therefore, portrays a movement —a movement through struggle to repose. Such is the first glimpse of the world called into existence by Shakespeare, the vague outlines of which are now to be completed to the fullness of reality. For his work may be well called a world—a world in its vastness, variety, and harmony; an ideal world filled with ideal shapes. which flit amid an ideal scenery. Yet it is also real, a picture of our Earth, an adumbration of human spirit, and hence

INTRODUCTION. XXVII

all men sweetly fraternize with its airy forms.

The development of the subject may now proceed in the following order:

First, we wish to behold the foundation of the poet's dramatic edifice; this is the Ethical World, which must, therefore, be shown in its complete organization, as it appears in his dramas. Second, we are to witness the principles of this Ethical World passing into man and becoming the mainspring of his activity; he then is the Dramatic Individual endowed with Character. Third, we are to see these dramatic individuals grouping themselves in organic relation, and developing according to the inherent necessity of their natures, to a completely rounded action or drama; this will show the Threads and Movements, the elements of Dramatic Structure. Fourth, the single dramas must also be organized into the unity of the poet's lifework; this will exhibit the Classification of the Shakespearian Drama.

SECTION IV.—THE ETHICAL WORLD OF SHAKESPEARE.

The statement has already been made that it is an Ethical World in which the Shakespearian Drama moves. Our object is now to bring into a proper system of gradation its manifold principles; for, when these collide, the higher must not be brought under the lower—that which is most true must be supreme. The law is, everywhere, subordination to the Rational. Even appetite is not bad within its just limits; but, when it conflicts with what is higher, it turns to evil. So, too, an ethical principle, otherwise valid, may become wrong if it stands in the way of another ethical principle better and truer than itself. Such is the Shakespearian conception of this Ethical World; it may be called a graded hierarchy of principles, one over another to the most exalted; each subordinates all which lie beneath, and is subordinated by all which lie above.

Hence, in the Dramatic Collision, it is not necessary that one side be affirmed to be absolutely right, the other absolutely wrong. The thought must be held fast that principles collide—ethical principles. Both sides, therefore, are guilty, yet both sides have a ground of justification; each has to assail what is valid in maintaining what is valid. It is a genuine conflict of duties, perplexing to the soul often, and difficult of decision. The Dramatic Solution, however, must indicate which principle is supreme.

Of this Ethical World there are two grand divisions—the *Institutional* and the *Moral*—each of which is represented in the Shakespearian Drama. Both are forms of rational subordination; the former is objective, existent outside of the Individual, though at the same time the product of his deepest spiritual nature; the latter is subjective, existent within the individual, whereby he is controlled according to his own ideas of right and duty. A verbal distinction should here be carefully observed by the reader. The word *ethical* is not employed synonymously with the word *moral*, though general usage does not distinguish between them. Throughout the present work this distinction, so vital for the correct comprehension of Shakespeare and his Ethical World, will not be neglected, unless by some mistake.

I. THE INSTITUTIONAL ELEMENT.—Institutions seem to be wholly external to man, yet they are really the creation of his Reason. They seem, at times, to be hostile to him also, but they are truly his greatest protection—indeed, the necessary condition of his rational existence. Only through them can he rise above the narrow limits of selfishness into a universal life. Filled with their spirit, he has the Divine within him, and is able to elevate himself to the heroic character. The Individual may be moved by them instinctively or consciously—the first way being the more common, the second being the more perfect; or, he may turn against them, and trample them down with a relentless enmity. Hence arise the collisions of this realm.

In the Shakespearian Drama there are mainly two of these institutional principles—the Family and the State. Both are found in all of the poet's plays, with two or three exceptions, though with different degrees of importance. The Family is usually the more prominent in the legendary pieces; the State in the historical pieces. Each within itself is capable of many phases; any one of these phases may conflict with another. Hence springs the collision, the true fountain of all dramatic activity. A short summary of the different phases employed by Shakespeare may now be given.

1. *The Family.*—This is the institution which rests most deeply in the emotions of man, and hence is the main realm of Poetry. Its various members are united together, as it were, into one person; they are but limbs of a single body which feels for, and with, all of them. Let, therefore, a limb be plucked away, or in any manner deeply affected, the feeling is transmitted through the whole organism of the Family; what one member suffers, the rest suffer along with him. Such is the deep sympathetic unity which lies at the basis of this institution, it has a special name; it is called Love. Now, Love assumes several very distinct forms, according to the different relations possible in the Family, as the Love of Husband and Wife, Brother and Sister, Parent and Children, Lover and Lady-love. Hence arises the Collision in the Family, for its separate forms may conflict with one another; thus its tender emotional character is rent with struggle and contradiction which must deeply affect both sides as bound up together in the same domestic body.

First is the form of Love going before and leading to the Family—the Love of Man and Woman. It is, therefore, based on the difference of sex, which difference, however, is always seeking to be harmonized into unity through feeling. Two persons of opposite sexes are driven, by the strongest impulse of their natures, into the oneness of the

INTRODUCTION. XXXI

Family. Such is the manifestation of the love of Man and Woman, which may be justly called the most universal theme in Literature. But now something comes in between the two individuals; an obstacle interferes with their unity, whereby it may be threatened or even destroyed. Hence arises the Collision of Love, which strikes every note, from the deepest Tragedy to the lightest Comedy. The nature of the obstacle is various; in the Shakespearian Drama it is most commonly the will of the parent. Often, too, the obstacle is not external, but internal, whereof the most frequent instance is unrequited love. The conflict between parents and lovers has manifold shades in Shakespeare. It is tragic in *Romeo and Juliet;* serious, but with happy conclusion, in *Merchant of Venice* (Portia), and in other dramas of like character; comic in *Merry Wives of Windsor* (Anne Page), and elsewhere in the comedies. Unrequited love is tragic in the case of Paris, in *Romeo and Juliet*, but has quite every phase, from earnest elevation to wild burlesque, in *Twelfth Night*. A more detailed treatment of these various forms of the Collision of Love will be given when the special consideration of the separate plays takes place.

Second, from this first relation there follows, naturally, the relation of Husband and Wife. The unity of the Family, which, in the previous form, was merely subjective, is now realized in marriage, and in a common life. But this unity, too, may be assailed from without by the villain, liar, seducer;

or it may be destroyed from within by one or both of the members through uncongeniality, jealousy, infidelity. Thus we behold a new phase of the domestic collision, that of Husband and Wife, which is tragic in *Othello*, mediated by the wife in *All's Well That Ends Well*, comic in *Merry Wives of Windsor* (the jealous husband, Ford); which examples, however, do not, by any means, exhaust the list in the Shakespearian Drama.

Third, from this second relation of the Family springs, in natural sequence, a new one—that of Parent and Child. Already one phase of the collision thence resulting has been noticed—namely, parental authority against the right of love on the part of the child. This is, indeed, Shakespeare's favorite theme, if we may judge from its frequent employment; his solution is universally against the parent—at least in his comedies. But the great Tragedy of Parent and Child is *King Lear*, in which this relation is the sole content of the entire drama.

Fourth, then comes the relation of the children among themselves, that of brothers and sisters, with its manifold complications. Brother against brother, of which there are two cases in *As You Like It;* sister against sister, of which there is a triple case in *King Lear*, are instances, the number of which could easily be increased from the Shakespearian Drama.

Besides these four most direct and intimate relations of the Family, there are many others which are more remote, but which furnish the basis for collisions. Most peculiar is the situation of the illegitimate child, which Shakespeare has strikingly illustrated in three important characters. In such a case the Family becomes contradictory of itself, for the very institution whose function is to rear and protect the offspring of man disowns it, and even casts it out of the social pale. To this more remote relation belong cousins, uncles, aunts, grandparents; let the reader supply the rest to the end of the line of kindred. Finally, consanguinity disappears entirely, though the domestic tie re- remains; this is seen in the step-mother and mother-in-law, with their cognate forms of both sexes—time-honored and much-employed sources of collision in the Family.

There is still another form of love from which the domestic relation is wholly eliminated; both sex and blood sink down into indifferent elements. This Love is Friendship, which, in its turn, may conflict with all the preceding relations of the Family; for it is a unity of individuals in an emotion which disregards consanguinity as well as the difference of sex. In *Two Gentlemen of Verona* Shakespeare has portrayed the collision between Friendship and Love as the primordial impulse of the Family, wherein the latter is shown to be the more powerful and intense emotion.

The reader can now have a conception of the vast materials which domestic life furnishes to the dramatic author. Two or more of these collisions may be introduced into the same play, yet they ought to be nearly related in order to appeal strongly to the sense of artistic unity. Each phase may collide with any other phase; thus the number of combinations becomes almost infinite. Shakespeare has by no means exhausted them, notwithstanding his manifest tendency to avoid repetition, though he does sometimes repeat favorite themes. A further question arises concerning the gradation of these complicated collisions of the Family: Which is the higher element and which the lower? It is in some cases difficult to give a general rule; external circumstances often play into the action and determine the solution. The wife should always place the husband before the parent, but much more questionable is the demand upon her to place the husband before the child; such may or may not be her duty, according to circumstances. The universal principle, however, in this sphere is that what is truest and best for the Family must put down, in the end, every other domestic relation which may stand in the way, and Human Reason alone is to be the judge of last resort.

2. *The State.*—This institution is the great instrumentality for securing justice among men, for bringing home to every person the value of his deed. It thus rises above the limits of the Family. It has to disregard domestic ties in order to attain its object; it cannot avoid punishing the father for his wrong action, though the wife and children must also suffer along with him. Justice is the supreme end, the pillar which supports the world. The Individual has to be rewarded with his own

deed, though many tender relations be painfully torn asunder. That institution which secures justice to man must put aside all others that stand in its way. The State, therefore, in fulfilling the end of its existence, may collide with the entire realm of the Family in any single one, or in all, of its manifestations.

Such is the first collision of the State, the collision which presses itself most directly upon the mind in considering this subject. Moreover, these two institutions have their representatives in the two sexes. The State is essentially the ethical sphere of man; the Family that of woman. This collision offers the greatest variety of dramatic treatment—it may be tragic, mediated, or purely comic; in fact, nearly every play of Shakespeare has something of it, from the slightest external tinge to the substantial germ of the action. In real life, duty to country and duty to family conflict not unfrequently, and the Individual has to solve the difficulty in one way or the other, happily or unhappily.

Second, the State has continually some form of internal collision which is manifested in the phenomenon of political parties. This, within proper limits, produces a healthy activity by preventing stagnation. But it may rise to the proportions of rebellion and revolution; then it is a conflict which demands a speedy solution. Which side should be successsul is to be determined by the truth of its principle; at one time it may be the supporters, and at another time the assailants, of the established State.

Third, the external Collision of the State is war with another State. The ultimate principle here is nationality, which must be vindicated when impeded or assailed. A further development of these Collisions of the State may be deferred for the present; the reader will find a more detailed account of them in the Introduction to the Historical Drama. Shakespeare has devoted to them an entire cyclus of his plays—it is the cyclus of his Histories. In the total Shakespearian Drama, therefore, we behold a Drama of the Family and a Drama of the State; the great division of ethical institutions also divides his works. Here is the primal basis of their classification.

Two other ethical forces, which partake of the nature of institutions to a certain degree, may be mentioned, though they occur less frequently in Shakespeare. The first is Property—perhaps the lowest ethical principle, still an ethical principle. It cannot be violated without wrong, and hence is capable of being made the basis of a dramatic collision. On the other hand, its exclusive pursuit brings its right into conflict with higher rights. It may assail, and even destroy, both the Individual and State, as is seen in the tragedy of *Timon*. Also, in *Merchant of Venice* there is a conflict between the right of Property and the existence of the Individual, which, however, is happily mediated by Portia. But the second ethical force above alluded to is the world-historical Spirit, which is a power above the State, destroying it, or calling it into existence, in accordance with the highest principle of History. Nations rise and fall; there must be something which controls these mighty changes. It is the supreme ethical authority, whose clearest indication is found in the two Roman plays which portray the transition from the Republic to the Empire, but it is really the deep, governing principle of the entire Historical Series.

There is still another organization existent in the world whose dramatic nature, at least, must be explained—the Church. The Church, however, is always a vanishing element in Shakespeare; its content, in so far as it is true and valid, is just the institutional and moral elements which are already potent in their own native forms. It is, hence, superfluous in a certain degree, or tending that way. Still, it is a powerfully organized system, with mighty instrumentalities; it may collide with the State, Family, or any other principle of the Ethical World. Its trained clergymen are continually appearing in a mediatorial, though not necessarily religious, function; its customs, ceremonies, and doctrines are often in the background, though rather as the external setting than as the vital principle of the play. Moreover, the Shakespearian Church, in so far as there is any, is the Catholic Church, which is generally taken, even by Protestants, as the artistic Church. But the Drama is not, and in its highest manifestations cannot be, religious; it is ethical. The conceptive forms of religion which exhibit man as determined externally must here be dropped, or plainly shown as the internal forces of the soul; the demon and the angel must be placed inside of the human breast. The Church, in the Shakespearian Drama, plays alongside of the Ethical World, having essentially the same principles, though in a different form, which form must, however, be employed for certain characters and for certain subordinate purposes.

Sifting out the essential points of what has been said, we find that the gradation of institutions will be in ascending order of importance, as follows: 1, Property; 2, Family; 3, State; 4, World-historical Spirit. It must not be forgotten that they, in and of themselves, are principles, ideas; they can be made a reality only through the medium of the Individual. He must be filled with their spirit; then he is their bearer, their representative. They thus become the deepest ground of character. But the Individual is free-will; he may reject all these institutional principles as guides of action, and follow his own notions of duty. Thus the man of conscience, upright and sincere, may fall into conflict with the whole realm of institutions, from the highest to the lowest. Here we enter a new sphere, the nature of which must be briefly considered—the second grand division of the Ethical World.

II. THE MORAL.—This is still the ethical realm, for there is still subordination to a higher behest, which is now the internal law of duty. Here the Individual has, within himself, the absolute test of conduct; he asserts himself as supreme

INTRODUCTION. XXXIX

over all; he follows his idea of Right, against the realized forms of Right. Subjective conscience thus assails and destroys objective institutions. This is the mightiest contradiction of our own age, everywhere giving rise to the fiercest struggles, whose intensity is but faintly adumbrated in the pages of Shakespeare. Note the difficulty: The Individual, in destroying institutions, destroys the very reality of his substantial, permanent self; still, this self, this subjectivity, is the primitive germ from which are developed and vitalized all institutions, and hence is that which must be protected above everything else.

The purely moral stand-point is not strong in Shakespeare; he is decidedly institutional. He has portrayed no great, heroic, triumphant personage whose career is essentially moral, and who collided with the established system of an epoch and ultimately overthrew it by his thought and example, like Socrates or Christ. Brutus will not answer the requirement at all; both he and his principle failed; the poet, indeed, furtively laughs at his claims. Cæsar, though a world-historical character, has not even a tinge of moral devotion. The sympathies of Shakespeare were decidedly conservative, institutional; indeed, they had to be so to make him a great dramatic poet.

The same fact can be most plainly seen in his treatment of the ordinary moral duties of life. The moment they come into conflict with any institutional demand they are universally set aside. Not that they are wantonly violated; if there is no collision with what the poet deems a higher principle, then they are strictly observed. Veracity is assuredly a requirement of the moral law, yet the falsehoods of Shakespeare's best characters have long astonished, and even scandalized, rigid moralists. Successful deception is one of his chief dramatic instrumentalities, when it can be employed to harmonize domestic or political difficulties. His clergymen, whom one naturally takes to be the very representatives of morality, are guilty of pious frauds in order to weld together the broken bonds of the Family. The mediator cannot be a severe formalist; he must soothe, compromise, yield; strife is not to be triumphant on account of moral scrupulosity. Also, the ground of Shakespeare's indelicate speech lies, not merely in the age, but quite as much in the man; the full flow of a sensuous poetical temperament was not to be curbed by restraints of propriety, or even of morality, when it was so faithful to the higher ethical element. In fact, the poet's institutional sense relaxed—many readers have thought, too much—his moral sense.

A glance may be given to the interminable discussion upon this subject. A confusion of language has been both the cause and the effect of much confusion of thought, and the source of needless disputation. The word *moral* is usually made to do duty, not only for itself, but also for the words *ethical* and *institutional*. Both sides thus seem to prove their points—that Shakespeare is and is not a moral writer. A moral writer, in the restricted meaning of the term, he is not; but a moral writer, in the sense of standing on the basis of institutions, he is. Furthermore, it will be manifest how utterly inadequate for the comprehension of Shakespeare is the criticism which rests wholly in this limited moral view of his works, which moralizes them into pitiful lessons of good behavior. Yet, such criticism not only abounds, but seems to be the prevailing method of considering his Ethical World.

III. THE NEGATIVE PHASE OF THE ETHICAL WORLD.—We are now prepared to pass to a new sphere, which is also adequately represented in the Shakespearian Drama. Hitherto we have considered only the positive side of the Ethical World, and the collisions within it; but it has also a negative side, lying over against it, and hostile to it throughout. The individual representing this negative spirit collides with both the moral and the institutional elements, and for him there can be no ethical justification. Two classes may be noticed, which shade into each other with many varieties: The indifferent bad person, who refuses, or is incapable of, all subordination, and follows appetite; and the active bad person, who seeks to destroy the entire Ethical World in both its forms. The former has its type, and even shape, in Caliban, the natural man, in whom there is the possibility, but not the reality, of a governing ethical principle. The latter finds its best representative in *Richard the Third*, the hero of negation, and hence necessarily tragic. Such is the true villain, the active agent of destruction to which he must, in the end, bring himself also. Yet, for him, too, there is mediation through repentance, as is seen in the case of Leontes, in *Winter's Tale.* Here, in their deepest principle, Shakespeare and Christianity are in accord, though their outward forms be so different. The one restores the villain—the man who has destroyed, as far as his deed goes, the whole Ethical World—bringing him back into harmony with it through contrite works; the other declares forgiveness for the most hardened sinner through repentance.

Such is the Shakespearian hierachy of principles which lie beneath, and control, his Drama. Rational Subordination is its law, beginning with the natural element of man—appetite—and ascending through a scale of ethical powers, each of which commands what is beneath and obeys what is above. The Higher must subordinate the Lower; the final decision is rendered by the universal Reason, which alone can adequately judge of the Rational, the image of itself. This Reason is by no means the mere subjective judgment of the individual, but Reason realized in the world, in the established forms of ethical government. Read the reality; it will tell the story, for it is only an expression of what is universal and rational in mankind.

The moral reader here is inclined to ask: Is not all this an advocacy of doing evil that good may come? The question naively takes for granted that there is no conflict of duties in human activity.

If such were the case, then, indeed, life would be a problem of easy solution. The difficulty lies in the proper gradation; there never was a good which was not purchased by the sacrifice of some inferior good. The evil enters when the greater good is put aside for the lesser; to decide between them, however, is too often the perplexity and the pang of action. Also, this subordination of one principle to another—is it not the old Jesuitical maxim that the end justifies the means? Yes, so it is, with the necessary limitation. Indeed, how are any means to be justified unless through the end? or, rather, how can any means even exist unless through the end? The Shakespearian doctrine may be stated thus: If the end is a higher principle than the only possible means, then the means must be employed, and not to employ it is guilt; but, if the means is itself a higher principle than the end to be attained, then it cannot be rightfully employed. The supposition is that there exists a conflict which cannot be avoided or otherwise mediated.

The following tabular statement may aid the reader in bringing before his mind the general result of the preceding discussion:

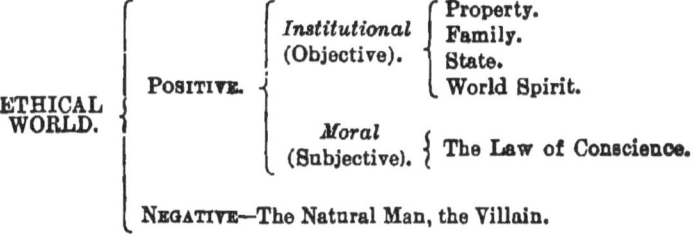

It will, by many, be considered doubtful whether the poet had consciously elaborated an ethical system as above set forth, and had formulated it in the abstract language of philosophy. Such a procedure on his part was not at all necessary for his poetical work; it was sufficient that he grasped, truly and completely, the practical world, and gave a picture of it in its essential features. This involves the ethical foundation which has just been unfolded; the active life of men is full of these collisions, and they form the abiding interest of History. An adequate representation of the world, just as it is, must include these ethical principles, for they make the world through their life-giving energy. Still, there are many indications that the poet had also his abstract statement of these matters; who will doubt his ability to make it? Indeed, philosophers have always admired and quoted his concise and profound utterance of thought. A thinker he was, assuredly, who had brought into intellectual harmony the contradictions of our earthly life. Perhaps the plainest traces of an ethical system are to be found in *Troilus and Cressida,* in which play also he gives a more abstract form to his expression than is usual with him. Still, the exact line between his conscious and unconscious procedure must remain doubtful; who can penetrate into the secret recesses of his subjectivity, and tell us what lies there hidden? What he has revealed, however, we may declare. Look into his book—there is the picture of the Ethical World; whether he was aware of it or not, the fact of its existence remains the same. He, like others before him, may have builded wiser than he knew; but it is both reasonable and modest to suppose that he understood what he was about, and was something more than the little bee, the instinctive architect of Nature.

SECTION V.—ON CHARACTERIZATION.

I. ETHICAL ELEMENT OF CHARACTER.—We can now behold these abstract ideas passing into living reality through Dramatic Characterization, which originates directly from the Ethical World. One or more of its above-mentioned principles must take possession of the Individual, and become the mainspring of all his actions. Such is the deepest ground of character, which can only be adequately comprehended in its relation to the Ethical World. Accordingly, there may be pointed out three classes corresponding to its general divisions: The Institutional person, the Moral person, the Negative person, or villain. It is not necessary to repeat the manifold varieties of these forms—all the subdivisions previously given apply to character; State and Family, in their many combinations—in fine, all ethical powers furnish its impelling forces.

But there must also be more than one such person in a drama; otherwise, there can be no conflict. Two individuals are animated with opposing ethical principles, which both of them are seeking to realize; they grapple and struggle till one subordinates the other, or both perish or are reconciled—such is the Dramatic Colliding Character. In an accurate analysis of it, the first thing is to find its ethical essence, for this is the germ from which it unfolds in every direction. The individual, therefore, must be portrayed as the bearer of some principle whereby he comes into conflict with the bearer of some other principle.

II. PSYCHOLOGICAL ELEMENT OF CHARACTER. —But Character is not merely the embodiment of a general notion; thus, it would remain abstract and lifeless; every character must possess individual traits which it does not have in common with other characters, in which traits, however, the ethical element ought always to be reflected. This is the psychological side, the ground of individuality, and, hence, of variety of characters. This inter-relation of the ethical and psychological phases is one of Shakespeare's great marvels of delineation. The unity—that is, the central principle of the character—is imaged in all the multitudinous traits; the same picture is seen in a thousand different mirrors. This happy transfusion of thought into individuality is what Shakespearian criticism has generally endeavored to express in great fullness.

Here, however, a distinction should be carefully noted. There are many details which are very necessary for the poetical image, but not for the thought; such details may be, and indeed ought to be, omitted in critical treatment. The thought is the main object sought for by criticism, which should not seek to rival the sensuous fullness of the Drama. Shakespearian literature is particularly rich in analysis of character; in this respect the field is overwrought. The attempt is too often made to follow out a character into insignificant relations which do not properly belong to criticism. Then come the endless reflections which proceed from microscopic views; satiety overtakes the reader at every new essay on Shakespeare, and the essential thing often remains unsaid after all. Nothing is more natural than that the same character should affect different persons differently; every man of culture, with a little study, can make, and indeed ought to make, new reflections on the characters of Shakespeare. This class of critical writings may, hence, be expected to continue indefinitely; some person will always be giving a new turn to the kaleidescope and be showing it to the public. But the essential point of a critical comprehension of character is to seize the ethical germ; it is wearisome and profitless to chase down all the psychological details, particularly after they have been shown in their living relation by the poet in his drama.

III. THE UNITY OF SHAKESPEARIAN CHARACTERS.—The delineation of character is usually considered Shakespeare's greatest gift. In the first place, we see, as we study him more and more, that he has met the universal Man and knows him well, that he has reached the common heart of all humanity, that he has pondered the world-character till he understands it. But, in the second place, we see that he has specially observed this world-character passing into its manifold incarnations in the individual; he has beheld the common soul-principle of mankind take on its vesture in Space and Time, and become a living person, who brings into his temporal existence a breath from the eternal sources. The poet beholds both extremes, the oneness of man and the multiplicity of men, in his vision of each human character.

At this point we witness his supremacy. His characters are not simply an embodiment of some abstraction of virtue or vice, though they have, and must have, virtue or vice; nor are they merely the outer active superficiality of a living being, without the inner essence of man, though they have, and must have, life and action. Shakespeare gives to his characters—at least to the greatest of them—a counter-movement in themselves; instead of making them an abstraction solely, he shows them trying to countervail their own abstract principle or trait. Man is limited, but that is not all of him; he is also the limit-transcending animal; he is himself, yet something beyond himself too; he is the finite, but has in him the opposite of the finite, the infinite. Any character which does not take in both these sides is untrue to Human Nature in the complete sense. A delineation which confines itself to this limited trait or tendency, to this virtue or that vice, without showing the soul struggling with these its limits and reaching forth toward the unlimited, gives us, not a whole man, but half an one—that is, no man at all. Characterization must go to the bottom of this double nature of every human soul, else it will show but an embodied abstraction. For therein lurks the truth of all character, the pith of individuality itself: it must resist its own bounds, whatever they be, not only its prescribed vice, but even its prescribed virtue. Thus we behold not love, but a lover; not doubt but a doubter; not tyranny, but a tyrant; the abstraction is individualized. We shall often see Shakespeare throwing his heroes into an antithesis with themselves; their very excellence becomes a limit with which they collide; their heroic quality chafes with its necessary bound, breaks it down, and becomes the opposite of itself. Then the character is tragic, or, if it have the capability to recover from this inner disruption, it is a mediated character.

SECTION VI.—STRUCTURE OF THE SHAKESPEARIAN DRAMA.

It is not enough that single characters be separately analyzed and described, for they, by themselves, are far from making a drama. They must be combined into groups, and these groups must be shown in their development. A Shakespearian character is usually portrayed in its growth; it unfolds gradually its secret possibilities in connection with its surroundings. Also, the interest of a play depends upon the action to a large extent; the element of time cannot be excluded. A critical essay, therefore, should be something more than a character analysis; the synthesis of the Whole must be given at the same time; the organism and its growth are to be grasped together into a unity.

This is the most difficult part of Shakespearian criticism—a part in which there is no exaggeration in saying that it has hitherto wholly failed. Perhaps the demand is unreasonable, or, indeed, impossible. The requirement may be stated in the following form: Wanted, a critical method which will show dramatic structure and dramatic movement along with dramatic character. Can all these elements, which exist in every play, be transferred to an expository essay? The attempt must be made, though it be unsuccessful. The instrumentalities here employed are Threads and Movements.

I. THE DRAMATIC THREAD.—This may vary in its composition from a single person to one or more groups. Readers of Shakespeare have doubtless noticed the group, with its central figure, around which are gathered the subordinate characters. Sometimes these groups run separately through the play; oftener they intertwine with other groups. But the Thread seeks to combine according to the principle at issue. It collides or unites with other Threads according to the exigencies of the action. The Thread, therefore, lays stress upon the thought; it may be the same as the group, or may be different sometimes; whereof the illustrations must be sought further on in the special treatment of the dramas. The object of these Threads is to bring out into bold relief the organization of the play. This should not not be neglected in a critical development, which, therefore, must be made to move upon the Threads as the highways of the dramatic territory. They also contain the collision

INTRODUCTION.

which may thus be unfolded on these lines. The number of Threads differ in the different dramas; their judicious management is one of the vital points of dramatic economy. Too many cause complexity and confusion; too few produce simplicity and bareness. Moreover, they should be interwoven to a certain degree in a drama, though carefully separated in a criticism; the one seeks to weld together the various elements, while the other must find the cleavages, however deftly united.

II. THE DRAMATIC MOVEMENT.—Each Thread moves forward to a culmination, and the totality moves forward to a culmination; then there is a transition to a new thought and a new order of things. All the Threads thus moving together through one phase of the action is called a Movement of the play, wherein there should always be some common principle of agreement or of conflict. Then follows a new phase, which is, or ought to be, logically evolved out of the preceding phase; this, too, is a Movement with its various Threads, each of which must be separately developed. The final Movement is the solution, which brings together all the Threads into harmony.

Long ago it was observed that a dramatic action has a beginning, middle, and end, but these distinctions, which apply to every object in creation, must be deepened into something essential. Moreover, the division into acts and scenes is chiefly made to satisfy the external requirements of the stage, which seldom correspond to the inner development of the collision. The thought must be the controlling principle of the work; and, as criticism proposes to give this thought, it must be governed by the same, and not by the requirements of theatrical representation. Hence nobody should expect that the logical movement will correspond to the division into Acts and Scenes in the modern editions of Shakespeare. Moreover, such a division is often wanting in the old copies, and did not at all originate with the poet.

Manifestly, a critical method which neglects these Movements is imperfect. Only through them can the element of time be endowed with its true significance; and from time springs all development, as well as action. They exhibit the dramatic work in its inner vital activity, without the external expedients for theatrical representation—which is the poetical, but not the critical, form. The attempt is made through them to reach down to the pure movement of the thought without considering so fully the side of its manifestation. Upon this thought the different kinds of Drama are founded; hence these Movements will differ accordingly. It will be sufficient to state here that Tragedy has essentially two Movements—Guilt and Retribution—while there are three in case of the Mediation of the Collision.

Threads and Movements, therefore, constitute the structural elements of the Drama. In an analysis we are first to carefully distinguish the various Threads of each Movement, and follow them through the play. Equally necessary is the synthesis; the principles of the Threads must be generalized into the principle of the Movement, and also the principles of all the Movements must be generalized into that of the play. Thus we get, as it were, into the workshop of the poet; we behold him gradually weaving together the various portions of his complex garment. If dramatic structure is held to be of any moment at all, it should be preserved to criticism. This is accomplished, it may be hoped, to a certain degree, by the employment of Threads and Movements.

There has been essentially but one method of criticising Shakespeare's Dramatic Art since Schlegel, though in other respects the diversity has been great enough. This is, in the first place, to state as the idea of the play some abstract moral or pyschological principle; then to take up the different characters, one after another, according to the caprice of the critic. Shakespearian essays have been mainly a series of descriptions of character, without any inherent connection—a gallery of portraits in accidental arrangement. All architectonic proportion, all development of the Individual, all movement of the Whole—in fine, everything peculiarly dramatic—must thus be left out. A true method would assuredly seek to include just these elements; to preserve the thought, not as a dead result, not as an abstract *caput mortuum*, but in the living process of its artistic realization. Such a method must be found; if Threads and Movements are ineffectual, then search ought to be made for other instrumentalities.

In order to comprehend the Threads and Movements in their manifold relations, the following diagram may be useful to some readers. Its object is to show the general form of Dramatic Structure, though different plays fill it out in a different manner. They may be a combination of parts here given, or a separation, or an entire omission, according to the requirements of the theme. Still, there must be an underlying frame-work which gives consistency and support to a drama, as the skeleton does to the human body.

I. Movement.	II. Movement.	III. Movement.
1. Thread { *a.* Group. *b.* Group. *c.* Group.	1. Thread { *a.* Group. *b.* Group. *c.* Group.	1. Thread { *a.* Group. *b.* Group. *c.* Group.
2. Thread { *a.* Group. *b.* Group. *c.* Group.	2. Thread { *a.* Group. *b.* Group. *c.* Group.	2. Thread { *a.* Group. *b.* Group. *c.* Group.
3. Thread { *a.* Group. *b.* Group. *c.* Group.	3. Thread { *a.* Group. *b.* Group. *c.* Group.	3. Thread { *a.* Group. *b.* Group. *c.* Group.

The Movements divide the total action crosswise, the Threads divide it lengthwise; each Thread in each Movement is to be grasped separately at first, then in all its connections. Let it not be forgotten, however, that these divisions are made by Thought and for Thought, while the poetical work is an organism whose joints are, for the most part, carefully concealed by an overgrowth of living tissue. The following essays have as one of their objects to exhibit prominently the dramatic frame-work; they seek out the structural form, and follow it strictly. Every play

INTRODUCTION. LV

of Shakespeare may be mapped out according to some phase of this diagram; of course the Threads and the Movements may be more or less in number.

It is not pretended that any single play of Shakespeare has the exact completeness of this diagram; it is only a general form. The Movements will be indicated by the Roman numerals (I, II, III); the Threads of the Movements by the Arabic numerals (1, 2, 3); the subdivisions of the Threads by letters (a, b, c). These designations are intended only as an humble aid to the mind; if, for some, they are too formal, let them be passed over without heed.

The same question arises here concerning the poet's method, which arose concerning his Ethical World: Was he conscious of his procedure? The same answer has to be given: There is no absolute proof one way or the other. It is a subjective matter which Shakespeare's testimony alone can settle decisively. But so much may be plausibly asserted: He begins unconsciously and develops into consciousnesss. His earlier method shows a blind, yet mostly true, instinct. His later method indicates that he not only knew of it, but tried to conceal it when getting too manifest. The question, however answered, does not invalidate the fact that there is a method in his dramas.

But it is in this way that the present book intends to enforce, with all its might, the structural principle of Shakespeare's plays. It will not rest content with merely giving the thought or idea of a Drama, though this too be necessary; it will try to follow the thought taking on the dramatic body, wherein that thought first shows itself realized in action. For the Shakespearian idea is not abstract, but organic; that is, there is no idea without structure, and no structure without idea, in the poet's creative procedure. The great merit of the German criticism of Shakespeare is, that it has insisted upon and expounded the thought which everywhere underlies his dramas; still it leaves that thought abstract, it shows no structure, in the main; it gives the idea, but does not make the idea structural. Nor should an exposition indicate this organic element merely from the outside, in a cursory sentence or paragraph; but the exposition itself must be organic, and move on the same structural lines on which the drama is seen to move.

Section VII.—Classification.

We have now seen the construction of the single drama. But Shakespeare has many single dramas of very different kinds; these we must next behold in a system. The old classification into Comedies, Histories and Tragedies is not so bad as some modern critics try to make out; many recent systems are much worse. It, at least, is based upon the inherent nature of the Drama, and not upon the time of origin, which is an accident. It seeks to classify by a principle, and not by a conjectural chronology. This old classification may be retained, and, with some slight modifications, be made to perform fully satisfactory service.

I. Legendary and Historical Drama.—The first improvement naturally sought for in it is a di-

INTRODUCTION. LVII

vision which will correspond to the Histories. Tragedy and Comedy stand in direct relation to each other, though not to History. Hence the word *Legendary* arises in the mind as the true antithesis to the word *Historical.* Such, therefore, will be the first grand division of the Shakespearian Drama; The Legendary and the Historical. Undoubtedly these two forms approach each other in certain cases, and begin to blend; but the distinction is a valid one, being grounded, not upon Time merely, but upon Thought.

The Legendary Drama, in general, employs collisons in the Family, with the State in the background; the Historical Drama employs collisions in the State, with the Family in the background. That is, the one is essentially domestic, the other essentially political. History gives an account of the life of the State, which thus furnishes a material created by itself, to the Historical Drama. The Legend springs up before History—before the State has developed into a self-conscious existence, capable of recording its own purposes and deeds. Hence in it the State is removed for the most part into the dim distance, and forms a kind of unconscious frame-work which holds, and often darkly controls, the collisions of the Family. The Legend continues to be active in historical times, and to assume many different forms, one of which is the Novel; this, too, Shakespeare has employed.

This difference of content necessarily brings about a difference of form. The Legendary Drama has a tendency to complete itself in a single play, for it is not limited to a specific Time—indeed, it has a Time of its own. On the contrary, the Historical Drama is immovably fixed between a Before and an After, both of which loudly demand to be taken into the dramatic account of an epoch. Hence arises the tendency to a consecutive chain of dramas, as the Yorkian and Lancastrian Tetralogies, as the Roman Historical and the English Historical Series. No such tendency can be observed in the legendary plays; each is a Whole in itself, rounded off to completeness in its own Time.

A further essential distinction lies in the manner of termination. Every single historical play has its action cut out of a recorded period, in which one party succeeds and one party fails. The end is, therefore, double—both happy and unhappy—as showing the triumph of the successful, and the defeat of the unsuccessful, party, while the conflict, perhaps under other forms and leaders, is continued. Such a drama, therefore, may be called both tragic and comic; it exhibits a combination of forms in a new form. Still, these distinctions may be impressed upon the whole series, but not upon the plays separately; for instance, the Lancastrian Tetralogy terminates happily, and hence, may be called a comedy in the large sense of the word; while the Yorkian Tetralogy terminates unhappily for the House of York, and, hence, may be called a tragedy.

The Legendary and Historical fade into each other by insensible gradations, and there may be a difference of opinion concerning the boundary-line between them. The subject of *Troilus and Cressida* is fabulous, also that of *Coriolanus*, probably; but the leading theme of both these dramas is political, hence they resemble, fundamentally, an historical play. On the other hand, *Macbeth* is laid on a basis of history; still, its general form, and the manner of treatment, must classify it with the legendary dramas. On the whole, it may be said that Fable, untrammeled by Fact, Time, or Place, offers the freest and most flexible material for dramatic poetry, and that History has to seek a mythical element with which it must temper itself before it can be employed for the highest purposes of Art.

II. CLASSIFICATION OF SHAKESPEARE'S LEGENDARY DRAMAS.—The first division here is into Tragedy and Comedy. Tragedy portrays the collision of opposing ethical ends, which cannot be mediated except through the death of the person or persons who are carrying out these ends. The tragic Individual is so completely absorbed in the realization of his purpose that the loss of his principle carries with it the loss of his life. Comedy, on the other hand, portrays the collision of opposing ethical ends, which can be mediated, and thus the participants do not perish. The Individual in this case must yield, in one way or another, through repentance, or inherent weakness, or the absurdity of his end. The word *Comedy*, it will be observed, is used here to include all dramas which terminate happily—that is, terminate with a reconciliation of the colliding elements, both persons and principles. There is, also, a narrower and more common use of this word, which will hereafter be more precisely designated.

The principle of the division into Tragedy and Comedy is, therefore, Mediation, which a little reflection will show to be one of the deepest elements of human spirit. Can man free himself from guilt, or must he perish? A character which persists in a conflict with a higher principle cannot be mediated, and, accordingly, is swept down by the hand of destiny. But the best thought of the modern world is salvation, which springs from the mediatorial power of spirit. Christianity delights in calling its exemplar of virtue and its type of truth the Mediator; herein it both expresses and inculcates the profoundest doctrine of humanity. In antiquity Fate ruled supreme, and Tragedy was in its highest bloom; but finally man learned how to mediate himself, to master his own conflicts, and thus to attain Freedom. It is no wonder, therefore, that this Mediated Drama or Comedy constitutes the greater portion of the works of Shakespeare, the poet of the modern world. Moreover Shakespeare's life, as we have already seen, was a Mediated Drama, showing in its last phase the reconciliation of the tragic period.

III. SECONDARY CLASSIFICATIONS.—Both Tragedy and Comedy are further divided into the real and ideal. These much-abused terms we shall try to explain, and to employ for a reasonable purpose. When Tragedy does not abandon the sphere of

INTRODUCTION. LXI

reality, in order to express and develop the motives of the Tragic Individual, it may be named real. On the contrary, when Tragedy seeks the realm of the Supernatural, in order to express and develop the motives of the Tragic Individual, it may be called, by way of contrast, ideal. In the former, subjective ends and mental conditions are clothed in their own language, appear in their own natural forms; while in the latter, they assume a supernatural garb, which gives a peculiar character to the entire drama, as in *Macbeth* and *Hamlet*.

In Comedy, which is also named the Special or Mediated Drama, the essential point is the Mediation; this, also, is of two kinds, real and ideal. When the collision is mediated by the instrumentalities of the real world, this species of Drama may be called real. On the contrary, it may be called ideal when the collision is mediated through the introduction of an ideal world. Both indicate reconciliation, though by different means. The latter is, indeed, Shakespeare's most original literary form, and contains some of the highest products of his genius.

It is evident that persons may differ about the fundamental principle of classification, and prefer to classify from some other point of view than the one above given, or not to classify at all. No doubt these dramas are capable of a variety of arrangements. One maxim may be assumed: They should be classified according to their most essential characteristic. The question is: What is that characteristic? Let the reader judge for himself, and, if not satisfied, change the arrangement as his thought dictates. It ought to be stated here that *Pericles, Prince of Tyre,* is not included in the present work, since it is not, in the opinion of the author, a genuine work of Shakespeare.

The method of classifying the dramas of Shakespeare has varied according to the stand-point of the critic. What ought to be taken as the principle of classification? Evidently that distinction which is most vital, which penetrates most deeply into the nature of the Drama. The old division into Tragedies, Comedies, and Histories— a division going back to the life-time of the poet—was based upon the inherent thought of Dramatic Art, however imperfectly these designations were applied in the First Folio. At present, the favorite method is biographical; the system of the poet's works is made to follow the order of their composition. Thus the accident of Time is taken as the ground of classification—the most superficial of all possible methods. The fluctuations of the individual Shakespeare may be faintly traced in this manner, but his thought will remain a mystery. The main point is to comprehend what he did, without laying so much stress on when he did it; at least the fortuitous succession of his works, whose origin often enough must have depended upon matters wholly trivial and external, should not be taken as the highest principle of classification. Shakespeare is the greatest of poets, because his thought is the greatest, most universal, and at the same time the most concrete. To grasp this thought, in all its various forms of expression, should be the supreme object, one may reasonably assert. Besides, it may be doubted whether any chronological order of single plays be determinable, though certain general groups, without definite limits in time, can justly be insisted upon. There are the fewest historical facts upon this subject; the ordinary tables are mostly assumptions, linked together by conjecture—veritable chains of sand. After all, the chronology has to be derived mainly from the Drama, and not the Drama from the chronology.

We have now unfolded and connected together the four main elements of this book as an exposition of Shakespeare. It will seek to declare the ethical order found in each play, the world in which the action moves. It will seek to set forth the characterisation of the individuals, who are the actors in that order. It will seek to show these two ideas—the ethical order and the individual character therein—moving together and putting on the form of a represented action, whereby the structure of the Shakespearian Drama will be manifested. Fourthly and lastly, it will seek to reveal the total edifice of Shakespeare, and the place of each play in that edifice. These four elements belong both to the idea and to the fact; they have been derived speculatively from his dramas, as well as traced historically into his dramas.

A word concerning this Introduction. It, like most Introductions, which give a preliminary survey of the entire subject treated, is the last thing written by the author, and ought to be the last thing, as well as the first thing, read by the reader. It, doubtless, looks to some people as if it contains a pre-conceived method or formula which has not been derived from the poet, and which is to be applied to him from the outside. But, as a matter of fact, it is a deduction from long and careful study of his works, and is intended as a help to the faithful student of Shakespeare. For one who is not a student, who wishes to read and enjoy, but does not care to comprehend the poet, this book, or any other book of the kind, is useless, nay, is a vexation which may arouse his temper. The Introduction is but a map put into the hand of the traveler ere he starts on his journey, from which he is to get what he can before he sets out, but which he will understand better, and fill out with many details after he has returned from his travels.

SHAKESPEARE'S TRAGEDIES.

THE NATURE OF TRAGEDY.

The Tragic in Art, according to the ordinary conception, is that which portrays an unhappy end. This is a necessary element in it; but we must go back and find out the cause of the fatal termination. The death of an innocent person by accident is not tragic in the true sense of the word. A tragedy is not produced merely by an indiscriminate slaughter of the characters at the end of the play. There must be something within the Individual which brings him to destruction; there must be a principle which fills his breast and drives him forward to his fate; his death is to spring from his deed. The elements of Tragedy may be reduced to three: The Tragic Individual, the Tragic Action, the Tragic Solution.

I. THE TRAGIC INDIVIDUAL.—He must be, in the first place, the bearer of some great end, into which he pours his whole being, and which he must carry into execution. These ends are, in general, the principles of the Ethical World, any one of which may take possession of him and make him its instrument. State and Family, in some of their manifold phases, usually constitute the essence of his endeavor, and furnish the deepest ground of his character.) But he may, also, be the moral hero, or even the enemy of the whole Ethical World, the villain. Generally, the Tragic Individual pushes his principle, which may be good and noble in itself, to the point of violating another principle, and by such violation weaves about himself the web of destiny.

In the second place, the Tragic Individual grasps these principles with such a strength and obstinacy that he can be shaken from his hold only by death. Intensity is his great characteristic; his whole being is absorbed in his end, which constitutes the sole impelling source of his action. This unquestioning, often unconscious, devotion to an ethical purpose gives the simplest form of the tragic character. But scruples may arise and cause, for a time, deep struggles and hesitation; thus the character becomes complicated with different, even opposing ends. Still, the result is the same; the Tragic Individual must remain true to the ethical (or unethical, it may be) element of his nature, and he perishes rather than surrender or abandon his principle. Depth and intensity of purpose he has to possess to such a degree that he prefers death to the loss of his end. Hence, for him, there is no reconciliation.

In the third place, he has to maintain his conflict with another principle which is also seeking to give itself validity in the world through an individual. One character cannot make a tragedy; there must be opposition; and this opposition, to be of interest, must be of a permanent, and not of a capricious, nature. Hence it demands, on both sides, eternal principles for the tragic struggle, and not subjective oddities or delusions, which are comic. Then other persons become involved in the conflict—wherewith we have already passed into the next topic.

II. THE TRAGIC ACTION.—Here the elements to be considered are three: First are the *Threads*, which group the characters according to their essential relation, passing through the play lengthwise, so to speak, and making the lines of the action. Second are the *Movements*, of which there are in a tragedy properly two—guilt and retribution, or the sweep into and out of a perverted social order—though there may be more than two in number, and they may have to be named otherwise. A fuller statement of the general nature of dramatic Threads and Movements is found in the Introduction. But the most important element of the Tragic Action is the *Collision*. In its simplest form it exhibits two individuals with opposing ethical ends, which they are seeking to realize; thus both fall into guilt in carrying out the highest principle of their natures. Each is in a sense right, and in a sense wrong—for each is trying to maintain what is right by destroying what is right; both sides may be valid in the Ethical World, yet both sides are in irreconcilable opposition; this gives the tragic contradiction, which is overcome only by the death of one or both contestants.

Such is the external conflict—man against man.

But, at the same time, there may be an internal conflict going on in the breast of the Tragic Individual, who thus is rent asunder by two opposite, yet mighty, forces. He may be aware of the ethical nature of what he has to assail, he may give it full validity in his own conscience, and accordingly, he may know that the fulfillment of his purpose leads to guilt. Hence, while carrying on a fierce struggle with another, he is in a fiercer struggle with himself; for in his own soul the cause of his opponent finds its most powerful supporter. The hostile principle, therefore, has a reflex in his conscience. His arm is paralyzed at the thought for a time; he may even hesitate, like Hamlet, till accident performs the work of retribution. But the true hero must, in the end, strike for his deepest principle; though he may know beforehand that he has to suffer, act he will, and meet, with an heroic heart, the consequences of his deed. In such a crisis alone is manhood tested by an ordeal of fire, and the worth of human actions written in eternal blazonry. Thus the Tragic Collision is doubled, having an internal as well as an external phase. This form of it belongs to modern Tragedy, and particularly to Shakespeare.

III. THE TRAGIC SOLUTION.—The Ethical World is now in a state of conflict and contradiction; its placid harmony has changed to wild discordant turmoil. But so it cannot endure; the struggle must be terminated in one way or another, and peace be made among the warring principles. In Tragedy this can be accomplished only through the death of the Individual who has introduced strife into the Ethical World, and who refuses subordination to the Higher. The Tragic Solution springs from the Trágic Character, which lays the whole might of its being into its purpose. So great is its intensity and persistence that it cannot surrender its end; death alone solves the conflict, by removing the Individual.

The higher principle of the Ethical World must be shown triumphant at last; it must sweep out of existence the man who cannot be reconciled with its supremacy. This is Divine Justice, which sometimes looks so harsh and inexplicable in destroying a beautiful, noble, and even heroic, personage. He may have been guided by the purest motives; he may have maintained a high principle; but he assailed that which was higher, and, hence, must perish. But here this question springs up: How can we know what is the higher and what the lower principle? The ultimate test of all thought and of all action is universality, for this is the essential quality of Reason itself. Reason is the judge of last resort, whose decision is most plainly read in the institutions of man. This, therefore, is the insight: The more universal the deed, the higher it must be placed in the scale of ethical grandeur.

With the death of the Tragic Individual peace returns—a peace bought with blood; but it is the price which often has to be paid for the harmony of the Ethical World. Tragedy, therefore, ends in reconciliation, but a reconciliation through death; a negative, violent end it is, but the most impressive in the whole range of the Drama. Tragedy writes in burning letters the decree of Fate: Man must be able to dwell in accord with the Ethical World or perish. For it, as the mirror of his own Reason, must exist, and exist without contradiction. But the question arises: Is it not possible to mediate the conflict and save the Individual? Yes. At this point, however, we have passed out of the realm of Tragedy into the Mediated Drama.

Under the head of tragedies proper, which does not include the histories, we place six dramas of Shakespeare. Each of these dramas belongs to the tragic period of the poet's life-trilogy, with the exception of *Romeo and Juliet*, which is the forerunner and prophet of that period. The time cannot be precisely marked, but it embraces five or six years, between 1601-2 and 1607-8. We may consider, without going far astray, that the culmination of the poet's tragic period was in his fortieth year.

So much is pretty well ascertained by external and internal evidence. But when we undertake to find the separate dates of these plays, and their chronological relation to one another, we at once pass into darkness. The completed *Hamlet* was printed in the Second Quarto, in the year 1604; *Othello*, according to accepted evidence, is now assigned to the same year; *Macbeth* and *Lear* belong to the same year quite as much as to any year before or after. Thus these four greatest plays of Shakespeare all seem to hover about the year 1604, which was the poet's fortieth year, and, as already stated, the period of his tragic culmination. They were certainly not all composed at that time, though they may have been finished then; in fact, they go back years, and the roots of *Hamlet* and *Lear* can be traced in the poet's early period, though the fruit did not ripen till his middle-age.

These four tragedies are essentially one in time and one in spirit; they may be considered as one work, as a closely connected poem, the great Tragic Epos of Human Nature. From this fact we may derive the method of studying them; they are not to be forced into some supposed chronological sequence, from which we may imagine the growth of the author, but they are to be studied in their thought and structure, which reveal the poetic unity. The relation of the poet's development to his written product we wish to discover when we can; but, in the present case, we must find it not in his separate dramas, but in the total period, and in the total work of that period.

We now see Shakespeare revealing passion in its full intensity; but he also shows, on the other hand, the tragedy of passion. For all passion is tragic, in so far as it has a tendency merely to indulge itself in its own right. Thus it falls into conflict with the Ethical World; it defies restraint within and without. The Shakespearian word for this restraint which the individual must put upon passion is patience; tragedy becomes a grand conflict between passion and patience, whose completest expression is found in *King Lear*. The poet has laid into that word, *patience,* a wealth of meaning, which the richest experience of life alone brings. Undoubtedly there may be a passion, which, within its true limits, is not only good but heroic; but we behold the ever-present tragic germ in it, as it flings itself, with all the might of individuality, into this one good, instead of adjusting itself harmoniously to the whole cycle of the good. Thus the noble character in its very excellence commits a deed of violation, and throws into confusion and conflict the supreme order, which we have called the Ethical World.

Here, then, we come upon the test which we are seeking. The essential element of the Tragic must be traced back to some collision between the principles of the Ethical World. The classification of tragedies should, accordingly, follow the degree and order of these conflicting principles. Thus tragedies are brought into the unity and harmony of thought, being arranged according to their deepest characteristic—the point at which they are one and from which they differentiate. The first on the list is *Timon of Athens*, which constitutes a class by itself, having the essence of its collision in Property, perhaps the lowest ethical principle. Both the individual and society are shown in a tragic relation to Property.

Then comes the second group, embracing

Tragedies of the Family in its various relations. Three great works are here brought together; the first is *Romeo and Juliet*, the Tragedy of the Lovers; the second is *Othello*, the Tragedy of Husband and Wife; the third is *King Lear*, the Tragedy of Parents and Children. We might now expect the State as the next higher ethical principle, to furnish the basis for some tragic conflicts. Such is the case, but they are set in the framework of History, and, hence, must be relegated to the Historical Drama. In this same tragic period of life the poet wrote his Roman Histories, which are also tragedies.

In the four plays already mentioned the collisions are purely ethical, and they are portrayed after the manner of real life. The characters are moved by no fantastic shapes, by no strange appearances; the natural form of motives, ends, subjective states is strictly maintained. But now a new group of tragedies follow in which supernatural shapes are introduced to determine the Tragic Individual; he is seemingly swayed by external powers over which he has no control. But these external powers, closely scrutinized, show themselves to be the same ethical forces which we see at work in the other tragedies. The form of them is new; being transmitted through a peculiar mental medium, they are changed into mythical shapes, which exist both in the World and in the Individual.

This is the third group, in which two of Shakespeare's tragedies are placed: *Macbeth* and

Hamlet. In the former, the Weird Sisters are the supernatural power which starts the action a-going, and drives it on to the end. In the latter the supernatural power is the Ghost, which also starts the action a-going, and whose impelling force reaches to the end of the drama. The conflicts of Family and State are seen in both these tragedies; but into the natural world of real shapes is woven a supernatural world of mysterious shapes.

TIMON OF ATHENS.

There is no historical evidence for determining the exact year when this play was written. It was first printed in the Folio of 1623, and no contemporaneous allusions give any help toward settling the date. But in a general way it may be said to belong to the middle period of Shakespeare's poetic activity, which we have called his tragic period, being that of his four great tragedies. The order of time in which it stands to these four tragedies, is not now ascertainable, though it was doubtless written after *Romeo and Juliet*. It cannot well be placed in the poet's last period, as some writers have conjectured, inasmuch as that is the period of *Winter's Tale, Cymbeline,* and *Tempest,* when Shakespeare, full of the richest experience which the years bring, had a tendency to mediate the dark, tragic conflicts of life, and to bring back the erring spirit to an outer and inner harmony. This play, however, has less reconciliation of the much-tried man with the world than any other work of the poet.

Though upon a classical subject, the play is not classical, not even historical, in spite of the historic names of its two leading characters. It suggests momentarily the most glorious era of

Athens, the era of Socrates, whose name is recalled by that of Alcibiades, and of Aristophanes, who in his extant comedies makes allusion to the actual Timon. But, mingled with Greek names, are found mostly Roman names, and the whole play has rather a Greco-Roman than a Greek atmosphere. Plutarch furnishes suggestions concerning Timon, but the story, in its main features, has been derived from a dialogue of Lucian, which tells of Timon's wasteful liberality, the ingratitude of his friends, his flight from society, and his final misanthropy, together with other minor incidents found in Shakespeare's play. Whether the poet drew directly from these classical sources is a matter of dispute; the story had been told before his time in an English book, called *Paynter's Palace of Pleasure*, which he knew; there was also an old drama (possibly more than one) on this subject. Thus we may affirm Timon to be a dramatic inheritance of the ages, from Aristophanes to Shakespeare.

The character is common to all times and places; it shows a man who through his own excess falls into adversity from prosperity, experiences ingratitude, lays the blame on civilization, and flees to the woods. But in the present case there is afterwards no return to society, such as Shakespeare portrays in some of his comedies; the character of Timon is such that he draws no blessing from his trial; he seems the more hardened in hate by his discipline; the flight into Nature brings to him no healing mediation, but becomes the last flight into the realm beyond.

The character runs on a line with the poet's great tragic characters, showing a deed, a disposition or a passion, which being pushed beyond its true limit, lands in the opposite of itself. Timon is liberal without bounds, and so passes to being illiberal without bounds; generosity becomes its own tragedy, the unbalanced passion hastes to be antipathetic to itself. When the citizens show their ingratitude, it throws him into ingratitude; he was unable to remain generous in spirit, when his property was gone. As he finds no rational principle in property, so he finds none in himself; as he loses his wealth, so he loses his humanity. His open-handedness we find to be a selfish indulgence of a passion, which, when the means of gratification is gone, turns to the bitterest hate; his generosity is not centered at the heart; even philanthropy, if self-seeking, gets to be self-contradictory, and becomes its own opposite, namely, misanthropy. This transition in a human soul is what the poet has sought to portray in the character of Timon.

The play is, however, one of the less celebrated and less attractive among Shakespeare's works. The theme itself is not the most enticing, and its treatment must be pronounced to be in many respects unsatisfactory. The inequality of the execution will be acknowledged by every careful reader. Some parts are wrought out with great skill and completeness; others are hastily and rudely sketched, while certain necessary links seem to be omitted altogether. The versification is often a mystery, and the prose frequently appears to be written with exceeding carelessness. But the main characteristic of the play is the dark coloring in which it portrays social life. Its speech is steeped in bitterness; it contains the most vindictive utterances against mankind to be found in Shakespeare. A noble, generous character is victimized to the last degree, and driven forward to suicide. Unselfishness apparently becomes tragic in a selfish world. Still, the other side is not neglected; this very unselfishness is seen to be at bottom selfish. Timon is guilty, and has to take the consequence of his deed. He turns misanthrope, full of vehement sarcasm and red-hot imprecation. The latter part of the play, in particular, is a bath of gall.

To account for these peculiarities conjecture has been very busy, if not very satisfactory. But it is a wearisome and profitless task to chase down probabilities; let us at once pass to the more useful task of comprehending the drama. This is, as previously stated, defective in execution, but its conception is in every way Shakespearian. To unfold this conception in its completeness is our present object. The relation of the individual and of society to property and the conflicts which arise therefrom constitute the fundamental theme of the play. For property is also an ethical principle—not the highest by any means, perhaps the lowest, still an ethical principle—to violate which within its sphere is guilt, and not to subordinate which outside of its sphere is also guilt. A person, therefore, who disregards it utterly, and a person who esteems it as the highest end, may, both of them, become involved in a tragic destiny. These two forms occur in the present drama, whose general movement shows the course of the property-despising man, through prodigality to misanthropy and death; and of the property-loving society, through avarice to the loss of national independence.

Perhaps this idea of property may give some difficulty, and ought to be scanned a little further. Property is the beginning of an ethical order of things, and its necessary condition. In property, man first beholds and respects the right of his fellow-man, and has in turn his own right respected. Without property, person, in primitive times at least, had no true reality—was a slave, or a being without rights. It is the progress of the world's history which has secured right to person independent of property. But a man who ignores or denies the right of property, in a civilized society, must become unethical, and hostile to all institutions, if he carries out his doctrine to its consequences. Hence the Communist starts with assailing this primary principle, and ends with the destruction of all social order. But the other side, also, ought always to be taken into account. Property, though itself an ethical principle, may come into collision with other and higher ethical principles. The unbridled pursuit of gain leads to the most fearful corruption, and can result in the destruction of the virtue, of the greatness, and, indeed, of the existence of a nation. The unlimited right of property, too, may beget and protect the direst wrong, oppression, and even slavery. It is just this conflict in the Ethical World which the poet, true to his conception of Art, has made the basis of his drama.

Let us now consider, in a brief statement, the structure of the work. There are two Movements in the play, as we usually find in Shakespeare's tragedies—two grand sweeps of the Ethical World of the poet into and out of a corrupted condition. The First Movement extends to the time when both Timon and Alcibiades, who have not their end in gain, take their departure from Athens on account of the above-mentioned conflict; a money-getting society drives them away. The Second Movement depicts the conduct of these two persons in exile. Timon becomes a misanthrope, turns not only against his own city, but curses all mankind as a property-acquiring race, and is involved in his own curse, finally perishing, it would seem, by suicide. Alcibiades, the soldier and man of action, returns with an army, humiliates and punishes his country for its wrongs. Thereby is indicated that the nation, having banished its best general, can no longer defend itself, but is sapped within by its exclusive devotion to property. In this subjection would naturally begin its discipline and purification, but the poet in the present instance does not show his disordered Ethical World restored, as he has done in some other tragedies—in which fact we may mark an imperfection, comparing this drama with his better procedure. The First Movement embraces the first three Acts, the Second Movement the last two Acts; wherein we observe another rule of structure, to which the poet, for the most part adheres.

The Threads around which the action centers are two, that of Timon and that of Alcibiades. Both these persons are in a conflict with the society in which they live, as respects property; that society is devoted primarily to the acquisition of wealth, yet with a decided relish for the gratification of the senses. These two men are alike in not seeking gain, though otherwise different enough. Upon these structural lines we may now see the drama unfold.

I.

1. The first of these Threads, that of Timon, is by far the more important and prominent. It exhibits in its development the most wonderful contrast, for it portrays the transition from a boundless benevolence to the deepest hatred of man, and from a life of luxury to a life of abject, but self-imposed, wretchedness. Its two factors are Timon and the society around him. This society is first drawn in the most lively colors; its various classes are all represented in the picture, with the same fundamental trait of character. The artists are here in the persons of the Painter and Poet, both of whom are ready to lay their offerings at the feet of Timon—for a consideration.

Art is thus in pursuit of gain, and seeks it at the hands of patronage. But the Poet gives some honest counsel along with his flattery. He sings of the fickleness of Fortune, and warns Timon that all those who now seem to be friends will drop off at the first blow of adversity. His little poem, therefore, is a kind of programme, and foreshadows the course of the play. The commercial world has also its representatives present in the Merchant and Jeweler, the latter of whom, especially, has a sharp eye for business. He knows how to put his wares where they will bring several times their value. Presents of greyhounds, of milk-white steeds, pour in from thrifty lords who expect and receive a triple return for their gifts. Finally, Senators, the representatives of the State—and, hence, the most important personages of the time—lend their presence to this carnival of parasites. They also appear as the chief usurers and extortioners of an extortionate nation. The fundamental consciousness of all these people is the same—love of gain, pursuit of property, regardless of honesty or honor. Even the old Athenian seems to be a type of the ordinary citizen:

> — I am a man
> That from my first have been inclined to thrift.

He barters away the hand of his daughter to a servant of Timon for a sum of money which is given by the master.

Next to the desire of wealth comes the love of

sensuous enjoyment, which is also furnished to these people by Timon. A number of idle lords and sycophants surround him for no other purpose than to share his bounty. Dinners are dispensed with unsparing liberality; masques, dances, music, make his house one continued scene of enchanting pleasures. "The five beet senses acknowledge thee their patron," says the disguised Cupid. It is a life immersed in the senses, without conscience or honor, and is the usual accompaniment of material pursuits. But Timon is soon to be disagreebly shaken out of his dream. Sunk in enjoyment, he has permitted his property, vast as it was, to melt into nothing, and with it he, too, must vanish from the scene.

But this society, so selfish and sensual, has naturally produced its opposite. Here is the example, Apemantus, the cynic. This character really belongs to history—to the days of the ancient Greek and Roman world, in its decline and corruption. We now behold an individual who, instead of gratifying the senses, abuses them, and thrusts from him all the reasonable comforts of life. To the flatterer succeeds the scoffer; to abject servility succeeds intentional discourtesy. The love of property has no place in his breast; on the contrary, he has become the hater of men, from their pursuit of gain. He is just the person to expose the rotten condition of society, because he contemns it so deeply. His main function in the play is, therefore, to reflect the age in its negative phases. He holds up to Timon, for whom alone he seems to have some affection, the consequences of prodigality; he speaks openly and bitterly, exposing the flattery and treachery of the whole crowd of followers. But not alone to Timon, but also to all persons with whom he comes in contact, he tells with stinging satire what they are; he is the mirror which reflects the inner character of each individual of the company. Thus, amid all this hollow formality, the real spirit is shown; a man may utter his polite phrases, but Apemantus is there in his presence to cast his true image. Moreover, Apemantus is now the picture of that which Timon is destined to become, namely, the misanthrope. Still another trait must be added, which, however, appears with distinctness only in the latter part of the drama. It is the vein of affectation which lies deep in the character of Apemantus. His cynicism is largely the result of vanity, and not of conviction. Insincerity must thus attach to him in a certain degree, and he is a true member of this false and dissembling Athenian world.

Such is the society. Now we are prepared to consider the character of Timon, who is, for a time, its central figure. His fundamental trait is the lack of all notion of property. With this one element are connected his other qualities, good and bad. Generosity, strong affection, honesty, are some of his virtues; prodigality, love of flattery and pleasure, borrowing money, and running in debt are the most of his weakness. His principle is that his friends should share his wealth equally with himself; he tells them that they are more welcome to his fortune than he is himself. A sort of communism is thus broached by him, and in his exceeding generosity he quite abjures the idea of property. To retain is not his nature; "there's none can truly say he gives if he receives." This principle is manifestly one-sided, and can only bring its followers to ruin. What is given out must come back in one way or another, else the source ceases to flow. But Timon will only give, and so hands over his entire fortune to the enjoyment of his friends. He becomes the victim of sharpers, who, with pretended affection, send him their presents knowing that they will receive something far more valuable in return. His property is, therefore, essentially abandoned; it may be compared to a dead organism which every creeping thing is busily consuming and carrying away.

Timon excites our admiration by his lofty enthusiasm, and by his noble striving after an ideal life in which all things are common and all men are brothers. But such a principle is an absurdity, an impossibility, for it rests upon a one-sided view of human nature. Man must be individual to be man; he cannot be absorbed into a universal humanity. Society also is based on the fact that each member of it seeks to own—that is, to acquire and to retain. One contributes his labor in order to get in return, and to keep as much as is reasonable. The consciousness of Timon is contrary to the organization of society, which cannot rest on spending alone, but also on obtaining. As everybody else is seeking to acquire and retain, Timon must soon be deprived of his property. It is at this point that we can see the ethical guilt of Timon; his principle and his conduct are logically destructive to society.

But there is one class which remains honest and faithful in this corrupt community—the servants of Timon. His own household shares in his true nature. Flavius, his steward, has also warned him of the consequences of his conduct, has done everything to stem the tide of extravagance, and is, in fact, the most rational character in the drama. It is a contrast between the high and the low; integrity and honor have taken refuge in the humblest class of people. Thus there still remains a sound part of society, though the top is rotten; there is still a source from which a new life is possible. But it is only one bright and small ray in a very dark picture.

The incidents may now be noticed in rapid succession. The money has run out; no more can be borrowed. The faithful steward is in the greatest embarrassment. The usurers have become alarmed for the safety of their loans; a crowd of importunate servants throng Timon's doors to collect their masters' debts. He now wakes up to the bitter situation; he has no land, no money, no credit, yet has incurred many obligations. But he is certain of his friends—they will be ready to advance him whatever sums he may need. Still, he learns on the spot of the refusal of the Senators to aid him, but he thinks that their blood is caked and cold with age; he will now apply to his warm-blooded and younger friends. Thus Timon has been compelled to abandon his principle of not receiving. He has hitherto disregarded property; now property makes itself felt. His ideal communistic dreams have vanished in his pressing emergency.

But what will be the result of this application for money? Requests to grant a loan are sent around to his friends. One tries to bribe the servant to report not having seen him; another has just lent out all his funds. Sempronius has a double reason for refusal: He won't furnish anything because he is applied to first; then he won't furnish anything because he is applied to last. Amid these various pretexts the truth also leaks out—"this is no time to lend money, especially upon bare friendship, without security." Such do Timon's friends turn out in the hour of need. Nothing else could have been expected from the beginning, for their highest end is, and has been, property; friendship was only a means. He imagined that others will be to him as he was to them. But the rest of society is seeking ownership; hence he is rejected on all sides, even by those who are under the greatest obligations to him. The result is, Timon spends all his money and is left helpless. He began with a large fortune, which he did not acquire; hence he does not know the significance of property. It is also a curious but natural trait that all these friends claim to have warned Timon against his reckless prodigality. The comforting "I told you so" is the sole coin sent back to their needy benefactor.

The crowd of creditors becomes larger and noisier; Timon's door is besieged by them as by enemies. The very men who are most clamorous for their money are those who have enjoyed his bounty and shared his hospitality. They now demand pay for the gifts which they have in their own possession, and present the bill for the dinners which they have themselves eaten. The bitter conviction comes upon Timon that his whole life has been based upon a deception. Friends are not friends; all is false and hollow. Still, he by no means believes his principle to be incorrect—it is only too good for mankind; hence he will not abandon his principle, but will abandon mankind. He has learned the fact that the pursuit of the individual in a social system must be, to a large extent, to gain and to own; property is the foundation. Timon, therefore, flees from society and goes to the forest. He will not dwell with his species in an organization so hostile to his conviction; he will henceforth live alone, and, because men are just the opposite to himself, he will become the man-hater; for it is man who has organized the system of property, and exists through its mediation. Such is the ground for the grand and striking transition of the drama, which portrays a human being passing from the warmest feelings of benevolence to the most intense hatred of his fellow-creatures. Once more he will invite his former friends to a feast. They come with fawning apologies and gluttonous anticipation; he is wholly confirmed in his bitter judgment. The dishes are uncovered—they are full of warm water. It is Timon's sole retaliation for their deception. In burning words he tells them their true character, and, involving in one common curse his guests, his country, and all humanity, he departs for the woods.

On looking back at the conduct of Timon, and of the society around him, it will be manifest that both have committed wrong in respect to property. Timon has disregarded it wholly as an ethical principle; the logical consequence of his actions would be social disruption. It is true that no law can prevent a man from squandering his substance, no more than it can prevent him from committing suicide; yet both acts are violations of right in its true sense. That Timon's wrong is mainly committed against himself cannot change its nature. But he also borrows and spends what belongs to others; hence his offense extends beyond himself. And, on the other hand, it will be equally manifest that the society in which Timon lives is violating all ethical principle in its exclusive pursuit of wealth. It seems to acknowledge no other end of existence but to make money; through fraud and treachery it seeks to obtain what really belongs to another. Thus, besides its meanness and moral corruption, it also violates the right of property, though in just the opposite manner to that of Timon.

When Timon does not receive in return what he has given, he passes over from benevolence to malevolence. He becomes wholly uncharitable, and shows that he never had genuine charity, which is self-centered, and is not determined by the gratitude or ingratitude of the recipient. Timon revenges like Lear; he cannot endure the ungrateful deed, cannot take into himself the wrong of others without requiting it, and so he ends by doing as bad a thing as they. But true charity will suffer even the violation of charity without becoming uncharitable; it cannot be driven by any outside circumstances into the opposite of itself. Not so Timon; he makes the grand change, passing from gushing tenderness to savage sarcasm; the humanitarian sentimentalist turns the misanthropic satirist. It is a mistake to call the whole play a satire; the point is to see sentiment curdling into satire.

2. The second thread of the First Movement is to be next considered, namely, that of Alcibiades. It also portrays the collision with this wealth-acquiring society, but in a new phase. Alcibiades is the man of action, and, hence, very different from Timon, who is essentially a theoretical enthusiast— though Timon is also represented as having been in the service of the State for a time. Such is the contrast between the two men; yet both are alike in their disregard of gain. Alcibiades we first meet at the house of Timon. He is a soldier, not rich, but he has certain decided notions of honor. Next he is seen before the Senate pleading for the life of a friend who has been condemned to death for killing an enemy. He urges

the honorable nature of the conflict; his friend's and his own services to the country. The Senate, however, will not listen to such a plea, but adheres to the strictness of the law—for which conduct they cannot be blamed. But, on account of a hasty word, they are led to banish Alcibiades, the only man among them whose object was, not wealth, but the protection of the State. His sense of honor and his end in life the usurious Senate cannot appreciate. Reproaching them with their avarice, he departs from Athens vowing vengeance against the city. From the defender of his country he has become its enemy— a change quite parallel to that of Timon. Thus the one-sided pursuit of property has ended in the destruction of its sole bulwark; the brave soldier is gone who

> — Kept back their foes
> While they have told their money, and let out
> Their coin upon large interest.

Still, we can by no means justify Alcibiades. His conduct is unethical, and if this play were completely Shakespearian, he, too, would receive the consequences of his deed. He should not ask, as a personal favor, that the law be set aside; nor should he, when his request is not granted, become the enemy of his country, even though he be banished. There is a touch of Coriolanus in him, yet without the latter's penalty. He, too, is without charity in the highest sense, as he has not endurance of evil, but wreaks revenge not only against fellow-man but against country.

Such seems to be the signification of this thread

in its relation to the rest of the play, though the connection must be confessed to be very loose, and by no means fully developed. The result of the entire First Movement is now before us. The Athenian world, by making property the highest end of existence, has driven off Timon and Alcibiades; it has destroyed spiritual improvement from within and national protection from without; it has reduced the enthusiastic lover of mankind to misanthropy and despair; it has turned its greatest general into the most deadly enemy.

II.

1. We are now prepared to begin with the Second Movement—the conduct and fate of these two men in exile. Here, too, the thread of Timon is the more prominent. He curses society, institutions, mankind; he prays that all the destructive elements of the world may be let loose upon the race. Not only does he flee from the face of humanity, but he tries to get rid of every social custom. Like Lear, he even casts away his clothing, as the last remnant which distinguishes him from the beast of the field. It is the complete abandonment of his species, and return to animality; he disdains himself on account of his human shape; he will not eat human food, but dig in the earth for roots to sustain life. But what is here? As he turns up the ground he finds a heap of gold. This is what he 'had fled; for it is the image and representative of all property. The old cause of his misfortune and transformation cannot be left

behind; it extends its influence even to the woods. But now he will keep it, and make a new use of it; he will employ it as a destructive weapon against humanity.

Not only property, but also society, will appear at the new abode of Timon in the forest; the world will be brought into the presence of the misanthrope, judged, and damned. In order, however, to effect its destruction, its own negative elements are introduced and sent on their pitiless errand. First come Alcibiades and the two prostitutes; the one is the assailant of the State and the ethical institutions of man, the others are the destroying angels of the physical being of man and of the Family. These two agencies, if let loose upon society without restraint, seem quite sufficient to sweep it from the face of the earth. Timon at first curses them because they belong to the human race; though Alcibiades is his friend, friendship now only arouses in him the most bitter and vehement sarcasms. But, when he learns that their expedition is directed against his native city, he wishes them complete success in their destructive career, and contributes a portion of his gold for the accomplishment of their purpose. Bandits come to rob him; he thanks them for their profession because it is the enemy of property; he gives them gold also, and sends them to Athens to assail the wealth whose principle has been his own ruin.

Other figures who belong to the old company appear, of which the most interesting is Apemantus; he seeks out Timon in the forest. Here a new trait of his distinctly appears. He is jealous of Timon's misanthropy; he wishes to monopolize for himself the hate against mankind, and the fame thereof. We are now certain that the cynicism of Apemantus is at bottom an affectation, and not a conviction; it is a capricious whim, or, at most, a theoretical hobby. He can have no valid ground for it; he has not felt the loss of fortune or the treachery of friends, for he never had either fortune or friends. But Timon's conduct rests upon his deepest conviction and his actual experience; his sincerity will carry him to the logical consequence of his principles, though the result be death. Apemantus, were he consistent and honest, would long since have fled to the woods, and not have continued to lurk around the abodes of the great. It is the difference between the sincere and affected misanthrope. Timon, therefore, will have nothing to do with him, and drives him back, we may suppose, to society.

The Poet and Painter again come before us, though now portrayed in grosser colors than before. The Poet, at least, could have been charged only with flattery in his previous utterances; now he is also guilty of wanton falsehood. The servants, however, still remain true to the memory of Timon. Flavius, the good steward, hunts him up in his solitude, in order to take care of him. Thus Timon is brought to acknowledge that there is one honest man—one of the human race whom he cannot hate. Still, he will not tolerate any upright shape. Flavius, too, is driven off under the threat of curses. Finally, the Senators of his native city are brought to his cave. They make the humblest apologies and offer the greatest rewards; they are even ready to grant him absolute power if he will return and drive back Alcibiades. No, he will not stir; on the contrary, he gives the State over to destruction. It ought to be observed that Timon is here represented as a soldier able to cope with the experienced Alcibiades; a new trait, which does not well consist with his previous character.

Society has now passed in review before Timon as misanthrope; it is only fit to perish. He has reached the true conclusion of his doctrine: Whoever desires to rid himself of affliction, let him hang himself to a tree; the human species is a nuisance—it ought to have sense enough to abolish itself. The ultimate application of his principle to himself he does not disguise; if mankind ought to perish, he must be included. Timon is honest and consistent; hence he kills himself. Such is the logical outcome of Pessimism—it must destroy its supporter. Were Apemantus sincere in his expressed beliefs, he ought to meet with the same fate. The tragic destiny of Timon, therefore, springs directly from his conviction; we find its germ in the very beginning of his career, in his views concerning property and society. In other plays Shakespeare has introduced a flight to the woods as the means of mediating the conflict and restoring the individual to society. But for Timon there can be no restoration; he has utterly lost his reconciling principle.

In the character of Timon we must see the contradiction, and its solution; he may be called generous, noble, worthy, yet he is the opposite also. His conduct springs from an impulse, uncontrolled by reason; he gives without self-control, as Romeo loves without self-control, and both are tragic. Timon is benevolent, yet has not true benevolence, which gives for its own sake and out of its own fulness, without the expectation of a return. His bounty gathers the parasite and flatterer, not the grateful soul which has been relieved in need; it seems, in fact, not to reach the sufferer, but spends itself upon the unworthy. Timon is at first the sentimentalist, who indulges in fine words about generosity and humanity; he is sincere, or believes himself sincere; but, as usual in Shakespeare, we behold this man tried in the furnace, to find out whether his be a true self-centered virtue or not.

2. The second of the two exiles, Alcibiades, has already been noticed in his interview with Timon. He marches against Athens, the city sues for peace, but its humiliation is accomplished. It is punished for its wrongs; the exclusive devotion to property has brought about national subjugation. Thus it is manifest that this second thread was introduced as the poetical means to visit retribution upon society for its offenses. Alcibiades reserves the enemies of Timon and of himself for death; the rest of the citizens are allowed to survive the loss of independence. Both Timon and

Society have now paid the penalty for their ethical violation, though the wrong of Alcibiades against the State is left without explanation or punishment. This Second Thread, throughout the entire drama, is in a very incomplete condition, but its general purpose is manifest from the conclusion.

In fact the play, as a whole, leaves the impression of a sketch completely filled out in some portions, in other portions possessing the barest outlines of the characters and action. Motives are inserted which are not afterwards used, some are omitted which ought to have been mentioned; both redundancy and deficiency are easy to be pointed out. Several unexpected differences between the First and Second Movements occur in the characterization; these have been noticed in the case of the Poet, of Apemantus, and of Timon also. The work, therefore, seems to lack the final revision which gives to every element its proper relief, and organizes the whole into a consistent unity. The reason of this incompleteness has often been conjectured, but never can be known. Still, the conception of the play is eminently worthy of the great Dramatist, but it remains a grand fragment of his genius, which, had it been completed, might have taken an equal rank alongside of *Lear*, whose coloring and treatment it often resembles. But, in its present condition, there is much passion in it but no patience, much vengeance but no endurance. Timon never says, as Lear does, "I can be patient"; even in his prayer he grows satirical toward the Gods.

Finally, a few of the conjectures may be mentioned which have sought to account for the peculiarities of the play. Some critics have supposed that it was originally one of the poet's most perfect works, but was ruined by the various mutilations of the actors, or, possibly, of the printers, or of the copyists. Another supposition is that it was based upon an older drama by a different author, which was partially remodeled by Shakespeare; still others say that it was first written by Shakespeare in part, and then completed by an inferior hand. Again, an opinion has been advanced that the poet lost, to a large extent, his Art in one period of his career, and that *Timon* is a work of that period. It has also been held to be an imperfect second edition of a youthful product of Shakespeare. All these conjectures are confessedly without any historical basis, and merely seek to imagine some external ground for the incomplete character of the drama; as far as its comprehension is concerned they furnish little or no aid, and, hence, must be passed by in the present treatment without further discussion. There is, however, a very popular theory which attempts to account for the selection of this subject by the poet. It is supposed that Shakespeare, from some unknown cause, became disgusted with society and men, and gave expression to his misanthropic feelings in the present work, and, to a less degree, in some other works. But nothing can be more unwarrantable than to infer that the expressions of any of his characters are the real opinions of the man Shakespeare. He undoubtedly comprehended Timon, but it is hard to believe that he was Timon, even for a short period. In fact, the tragic fate of the latter rather goes to show that the poet wished to give a warning against the danger of misanthropy, instead of being a misanthrope himself. The universality of his genius precludes the possibility of limiting him to any one character; he had Timon in him, but he never was Timon.

ROMEO AND JULIET.

This play shows in many ways that it belongs to the youthful productions of Shakespeare. Its theme is the passion of youth; it has the wild freedom and intensity of youth. There is a lack of that severity of treatment which belongs to the later works of the Poet. There are important parts which are dismissed with an undue brevity and bareness of statement, and then again there are other parts developed at length which appear quite unnecessary to the action; there is often a sensuous fullness of delineation, and often an abstract meagerness; there are found the finest and purest bursts of poetry intermingled with frigid conceits and far-fetched antitheses. Everywhere in the drama can be noticed an inequality—an inequality in thought, in language, in the structure of the plot. Still, beneath all this play of caprice and irregularity there is felt to be a deep, pervading harmony throughout the entire work. The inequality seems to be the inequality of the subject—the inequality of youth, with its fitful, tempestuous passion. It has been well named the tragedy of love—love in all its conflicts, love in all its extravagance and volcanic tossings, love despised, and love triumphant. It portrays this passion boiling over with a fervor which sweeps down all traditional barriers—even the most deadly enmity—and which advances firmly to a struggle with death itself. The theme is, therefore, love unconquerable by fate, whereof the individual is the merest instrument, ready to be sacrificed without the least hesitation. Such is the feeling that warms this poem in every part—youthful love in the most glowing intensity; for it is just the intensity which characterizes the love of Romeo and Juliet above all other loves, and which prefers death to permanent separation.

At this point, then, lies the tragedy. Love, the emotion of the Family, in its excess destroys the Family; though it be the origin and bond of the domestic institution, it now assails and annihilates that institution. Love, in its very devotion, becomes narrow, even selfish, because it gives itself up to pure self-indulgence; it sacrifices its rational to its emotional element, and perishes along with the individual. The gratification of passion, even the passion of love, has in it the tragic germ, and may destroy itself along with the man who yields to it, like any other passionate excess. Romeo's love is high, noble, pure; it has no ulterior motive of gain, rank, or lust; still it is a story of uncontrolled self-indulgence. Love is his strength, and his weakness; in one sense he is heroic, marching boldly to death; in another sense he is unmanly, yielding to an emotion without any self-restraint.

Romeo thus is caught between the upper and

the nether millstone of his passion, and is ground to death. Shakespeare often flings, as it were, his characters into the vortex of a self-destructive antithesis, which always lurks in the great deed and in the great passion; so, heroic natures, in their very mightiness, dash against their own fate and are tragic. Timon, in the excess of his humanitarianism, becomes the misanthrope; Macbeth, heroically putting down treason, turns traitor himself; Lear, in giving away authority, deems he still retains it and exercises it; Hamlet will neither follow his revenge on account of conscience, nor follow his conscience on account of revenge. So these lovers, Romeo and Juliet, through love, really destroy love and themselves, for this life at least, and the poet has not united them beyond, though the reader may, if he chooses.

That Shakespeare was conscious of this principle, even in its abstract form, is shown by what he puts into the mouth of the Friar:

> For nought so vile that on the Earth doth live,
> But to the Earth some special good doth give;
> Nor aught so good but strained from that fair use,
> Revolts from true birth, stumbling on abuse.
> Virtue itself turns vice, being misapplied,
> And vice sometimes' by action dignified.

Evil has in it the possibility of good, may be the means thereof, and the Friar will employ evil as the means of good, wherein he will himself commit an excess, and furnish an example to point his own moral. On the other hand, good, being strained, becomes evil. Here we see that the poet has been thinking deeply upon the ethical element in character as the basis of his tragedy; he states the counter-play of both evil and good into their opposites. Some may think that he was too young when this drama was written to have such thoughts; but really it betrays the youthful and immature artist to reveal his abstract principle of procedure.

In later works he will hide it better, that is, will drape it in his poetic garb; still he will always tell his secret to one who listens carefully. But in that Italian world of passion, these two antithetic tendencies of good and evil were the great, ever-present fact which the Friar must have had before him.

The play moves in an Italian environment, the hot climate and the hot blood are specially noted; it has an impulsive, intense tinge, which passes into all affairs of life, but particularly into love. Then amid these elemental natures without self-control, stand the two controllers, both absolute, the Prince and the Priest, seeking to allay or suppress the seething emotions. The pilgrim still goes to Verona, not so much for its monuments and history, as to catch from nature a breath of that passionate atmosphere which he has brought with him in imagination from this poem; but really Verona, lying at the foot of the snowy Alps, seems a little too far north, and he wonders anew if Shakespeare ever visited Italy. Still there is a breeze from beyond the mountains blowing through the play, as there might be in the Veronese territory. Benvolio we think of as a cold-blooded Northerner trying to pacify the Italian volcano by rational considerations. The nurse is surely an Englishwoman, and when we come to think of it, the drama itself is written in English at first hand, is not a mere translation or even transfusion of an Italian play. But what is most significant, the outcome, in spite of the Italian sources, is Anglo-Saxon to the core, for that outcome proclaims, in words of blood, that the man without inner control has no outer control but Fate; so the Prince and the Priest, absolute controllers of body and soul, do not control after all. Therein is implied that an institutional world which rests upon man's freedom, is the only means of governing man, and of keeping off from him the hand of Fate reaching out of the dark invisible spaces.

If we should connect the meaning of this drama with the life of the poet, we would say, that it is his youth's solution of emotion. This absorption of one's self in feeling, this yielding even to the sweetness of love, means tragedy, even when the love is pure; it drives the man against the restraint of institutions, if he has no self-restraint to start with. Emotion breaks forth into passion, which is destiny; thus it is written here. Shakespeare had in his heart this volcano of feeling, but he had also in his head the tragedy thereof; intense passion he shows, but shows it dashing itself to pieces against the walls of the Universe. In this Italian atmosphere, then, we feel the Teutonic current; and, in spite of its warm Southern tone, and color, and sympathy, the play reveals itself written by a Northerner and resting at last upon Northern consciousness.

The story, of which *Romeo and Juliet* is but one form, is of popular growth and can be traced back to antiquity; it touches the essence as well as the limit of love, love in life and in death. The idea of two lovers, whose union is so strong, that they perish at some obstacle which they cannot or think they cannot overcome, is something which the people have, in all ages, made into a legend, showing both the ideal and the tragedy of love. In the Greek world it is found in the tale of Hero and Leander; Roman Ovid has given it in his Pyramus and Thisbe; it passes into medieval Greek romance in Xenophon's *Ephesiaca;* then it specially flourishes in late medieval Italian romance, from which it passes to France, Spain, England, and reaches its final transfiguration in the play of Shakespeare. Before the latter's time a narrative poem, a novel, and a drama had appeared in England upon the subject of *Romeo and Juliet*, of which three works the two former have been preserved. Shakespeare drew his materials chiefly from the narrative poem, called *Romeus and Juliet*, by Arthur Brooke, which appeared in 1562, that is two years before the poet's birth. Since Shakespeare's time, the subject has been wrought into every literary form, from tragedy to travesty.

It will be seen that the poet takes his theme out of the heart of the ages; the people, the race must make his legend. This is what is given to him to transmute; he can no more create it than he can create his own language, though language, too, he transmutes. Even his characters must be drawn from reality, yet transformed in the process into an image of what is true in the spiritual world. Shakespeare found nearly all his incidents and personages in Brooke's poem; this crude material he transfigures, wherein lies just his originality. In fact, the function of the poet is not to create matter in any shape, but to spiritualize it. *NB*

Of the history of the present drama, in its origin and composition, a few outlines can be given. It first appeared in print in 1597, in what is called the first Quarto; but for the beginning of the poet's work upon this subject we must go back several years, six or seven probably. The second edition appeared in 1599, and is usually called the second Quarto; upon its title page it is said to be "newly corrected, augmented and amended," three designations which seem to contrast it with the first Quarto, inasmuch as the latter is in every way inferior to the second Quarto. According to Mommsen's count (Daniel makes the number a little greater) the first Quarto has 2220 lines, the second 773 lines more; that is, the augmentation is more than one-third. It is hardly worth while to repeat the conjectures that have been made to account for the differences between the two Quartos. So much may be reasonably affirmed: the earliest composition of this drama dates back to 1590, about; the poet had it completed substantially in 1599. We may infer, therefore, that the play of *Romeo and Juliet* grew in the author's mind, and was not finished in one sudden outburst of genius. In this play, too, we must conceive of Shakespeare as the careful, thinking artist, as the one who combines the profoundest reflection with the greatest spontaneity. The second Quarto, if compared with the first Quarto, will often be found to show a greater poetic exaltation in its language, as well as a deepening of the characters. One other inference may be drawn at this point: the poet had become aware of his reading public, as well as of the listening one; then, as now, some of his greatest admirers never set foot inside of a play-house; so he "corrected, augmented, and amended" the first Quarto certainly, and probably his manuscript play, and gave it into the hands of a responsible bookman, Cuthbert Burby, (otherwise spelt Burbage) whose name appears on the title-page, and who, according to Collier, (Hist. III. 285) was a brother of Richard Burbage, Shakespeare's fellow-actor, partner and friend. We shall see that Shakespeare, in a similar manner, not only revised and augmented, but re-cast his *Hamlet* for the second Quarto of that play. The popularity of *Romeo and Juliet* with the reading public is shown by the fact that a third and a fourth Quarto, and possibly more, were printed during the poet's life-time. It is gratifying to think that the poet beheld, before his death, the advance guard of the great army of readers for his book, who are now altogether the most numerous, as well as the most ardent, upholders of his poetic sovereignty.

Much has been written on the poetic atmosphere which surrounds this drama. Certainly it is a marvel of warmth and color, and it always suggests that hidden relation between the theme and external nature, which is the soul of true poetry. Schlegel and Coleridge have compared the poem to a warm Southern spring with its fragrance and flowers and transitoriness. More accurately others have suggested the fervid Italian mid-summer, (Lady Capulet says it lacks but "fourteen and odd days" of Lammas-tide, which is the first of August) when "the day is hot" and "the mad blood is stirring." The summer warmth, sultry and charged with storms, is, indeed, an element of the poem's atmosphere.

But if we would seek the setting of nature in which the whole action is placed, we must imagine a picture whose background is that of night, while into this night is breaking a light in some form, the outer light of sun and stars, as well as the inner light of the poet's fancy, which seizes upon the shining heavenly bodies, and brings them into relation with the grand theme—Love. Let us briefly trace this interplay between darkness and daylight in the horizon of the poem. First, Romeo makes a companion of night, during the period of his unrequited love; but when morning appears:

> Away from *light* steals home my heavy son,
> And private in his chamber pens himself,
> Shuts up his windows, locks fair *daylight* out,
> And makes himself an artificial *night*.

This is the beginning of his love, and the beginning of his tragedy: he flees from light and gives himself up to his emotions, to the night-side of his nature. But when he sees Juliet, the flash breaks through darkness, in imagery as well as in reality:

> O, she doth teach the torches to burn *bright!*
> Her beauty hangs upon the cheek of *night*
> Like a rich jewel in an Ethiop's ear.

Again, in his soliloquy (Act. II. Sc. 2) though it be night, we have a grand sun-burst:

> But soft! what *light* through yonder window breaks?
> It is the East, and Juliet is the *sun*.

The rest of the scene is, indeed, a new-born day for Romeo, though it be after sunset. Even the stars, "two of the fairest stars in all the heaven," are taken and transfigured in this wonderful nocturne:

> Her eyes in heaven
> Would through the airy region stream so *bright*
> That birds would sing and think it were not *night*.

A very picture of the entire cosmos now, in the soul of the lover, when he finds his love requited. Juliet, too, is moved in the same way, and the words of her corresponding soliloquy (Act. III. sc. 2.) are transmuted into a similar imagery. But now it is day-time; so she wishes "the fiery-footed steeds" of Phoebus to gallop to their lodging, "and bring in cloudy night immediately." Then follows her sweet fantasia on Night, as the dark background on which she make, the light of love to rise:

> Come, Night, come, Romeo, come, thou day in night!
> For thou wilt lie upon the wings of night
> Whiter than new snow on a raven's back.

This is the parallel to Romeo's making Juliet the sun, as it rises in the east; the two lovers have become one, and are speaking the same speech. Juliet also transforms her lover's body into stars, as he had done with her eyes, and makes him outshine the sun. Next, in the parting scene, their feelings play between night and dawn, in alternate strains, with the intervening chant of the lark and the nightingale. Even at the tomb we hear Romeo speaking of the light which breaks from the darkness of the grave:

> Here lies Juliet, and her beauty makes
> This vault a feasting presence full of light.

The Friar, in his soliloquy, has the same picture in a matutinal sky-view, as "the grey-eyed morn smiles on the frowning night":

> And flecked darkness like a drunkard reels
> From forth day's path and Titan's fiery wheels.

It is no wonder that the Prince, in the last words of play, says:—

> The sun for sorrow will not show his head—

Which is the final look we take at this Italian landscape, painted in Nature's own *chiaroscuro*.

The whole drama thus seems to be moving in what may be named cosmical imagery, in the eternal presence of heaven's luminaries breaking through darkness. Over this finite world hovers an infinite; light cannot go out in night, love cannot be conquered even by death. The deep, far-reaching symbolism in this environment of the celestial orbs we all feel; they send their sheen from beyond—from beyond the earth, from beyond the grave. Up into such a lighted heaven the night of this poem looks; it seems but the physical dome there hung with lamps, yet they illuminate the dark tragedy below. Shakespeare may have had no intention of using light and darkness in this way; but the poet lives in a deep, unconscious intimacy with that totality called nature, which his soul weds, and then transfigures, without violence, into an image of itself, so that the natural world becomes the pure transparent reflection of the spiritual world.

It will now be our object to point out the harmonious structure which underlies the drama and gives it a general consistency of thought, but above all, imparts to it that profound concord so readily felt but not always so easily explained. Whether the poet had in mind, when he wrote the play, just the method here unfolded, or was wholly unconscious in his procedure, is a question which cannot now be discussed; but, whatever answer be given, it cannot affect the validity or the necessity of the explanation. Shakespeare is, at least, a phenomenon whose law is the subject of rational investigation, just as the phenomena of Nature must be explained and reduced to laws, whether Nature be conscious of her own laws or not.

If we study the organism of the play, we find in it two essential Movements—two grand sweeps of the Ethical World, upon which the poet is wont to base ultimately the tragic action. The First Movement culminates in the union of Romeo and Juliet, and portrays the events and obstacles antecedent to that union; it shows the transition from the unrequited to the requited love of the hero, ending in marriage. But their union has produced a still deeper social disunion; the domestic concord of the pair has called up a more universal domestic discord. This Movement embraces the first two Acts. The Second Movement, including the other three Acts, will show the Ethical World purifying itself of the inner discord, by eliminating the lovers and reconciling the parents. Romeo does the deed of violence, the lovers are separated and finally perish at the tomb of the Capulets. Their death mediates the hatred of their houses, harmony is restored to the troubled Veronese world, both in State and Family. Thus the entire action is a sweep into and out of a disordered social condition, compressed into a two hours' spectacle.

Such are the general Movements of the entire work; but through the whole action there run a certain number of Threads, which must be carefully distinguished. One of these Threads is the Prince with his attendants, representing the State, which stands above all the conflicting elements and enforces their obedience to its commands. Its efforts are directed to keeping peace between the two hostile families, to securing, by its power, an external harmony and order; still, the enmity is so intense that upon slight provocation, it boils over, and bears down all authority. This Thread is the least prominent one in the play; the Prince appears but three times, and each time to quell a disturbance. It will not, for this reason, be separately developed, but will be indicated in connection with the other two Threads, with which it is closely united. The first Thread, therefore, is the two houses, the Montagues and Capulets, with their respective adherents, both of which have one common trait—mutual hatred. The hostility between them is so deep-seated that it not only assails the higher authority of the State, as above mentioned, but also the Family, in such a manner that through this hate the Family turns against itself and assails its own existence, and, indeed, finally destroys itself in its children. Thus there is portrayed a double collision—the Family against itself and against the State. This Thread is the disturbing principle of the play; it disturbs both public order and domestic peace. The second Thread, however, is the most important one of the play—is, in fact, the play itself. It turns, not upon family hatred, but upon the opposite passion —love—which constitutes the basis of the Family. Its bearers are Romeo and Juliet, a Montague and a Capulet, whose union thus falls athwart the enmity of their houses, and is sought in vain to be reconciled with the same by Friar Laurence, the great mediator of the drama. Both, too, are brought into conflict with the suitor Paris, who is favored by the parents. Love thus is the source of manifold collisions, which the poet has taken the pains to portray fully. First comes the unrequited love of Romeo, in which the conflict is wholly subjective, in which the individual is struggling with his own passion. Then follows his requited love, which, however, has to endure a double collision from an external source— with the will of the parents of Juliet on the one hand, and with the suit of his rival, Paris, on the other. With this naked statement of the elements of the play, which is intended only as a sort of analytical table of contents to aid the reader in grasping the whole, we shall now proceed to a concrete development of the thought of the drama.

I.

The first Movement begins with a tumult between the Montagues and Capulets, and its suppression by the State. The very first scene thus depicts the extent and the intensity of the hatred between the two houses; it reaches down to their servants, who are ready for a fight whenever they meet, and involves the relatives of both families, together with their respective adherents in the city. Order is trampled under foot, a violent struggle ensues in the streets, till the Prince, as the head of the State, has to appear for the purpose of vindicating authority and restoring peace. We are also told that these brawls have repeatedly taken place. Thus it is shown that the conflict between the hostile families is so violent and widespread that it assails the State and threatens the existence of public security. Such is the social background upon which the chief action of the play is to be portrayed. We see a hot emotional people, full of feuds and hate; here is passion which overbears all law. So it is with Romeo internally; as in the community reason cannot control feeling, so he has no rational self-control.

1. This world of strife and contradiction is, accordingly, an outer image of Romeo, who now appears in it, manifesting the full intensity of his love. He shuns society, seeks the covert of the wood, avoids daylight, desires not even to be seen. His passion is so strong that he cannot master himself; he sighs and weeps; he goes out of the way of everybody, in order not to expose his state of mind and to give full vent to his fancy and emotions. His absorption is complete; he is so swallowed up in one individual of the opposite sex that he cuts himself off from all other relations of life—from father, mother, relatives, and friends. Thus the intensity of his love is the key-note of his character, and it is this intensity which will bring forth all the tragic consequences of the drama.

But his love is unrequited; he loves, and is not loved in return. Here we reach the cause of his strange demeanor and the source of all his affliction. There has arisen a struggle within his own bosom which he cannot allay. He gives expression to his conflicting emotions in language so strongly antithetic and contradictory that it often seems unnatural and frigid, yet it is only a highly-wrought picture of his own internal condition. His pleasure is to indulge in love-talk, and in the feeling which it depicts. No manful self-mastery is here, but a species of self-gratification. His utterances are the very embodiment of contradiction:

> Feather of lead, bright smoke, cold fire, sick health!

Such extravagance belongs to youth and love, though it perhaps begins to get outside of the domain of the Beautiful. Romeo's mind is in a state of contradiction; his language is in the same state. He feels at times that his condition and his words are humorous, and may excite a laugh; still the matter is no comedy to him. He has lost his self's center:

> This is not Romeo, he's some other where.

The sympathetic Benvolio tries to soothe him, and advises him to change, to examine other beauties. But the passionate lover scouts the suggestion; he cannot be taught to forget. We should take note of this declaration, for it is sometimes asserted by critics that his first love was not genuine. The collision, so far, is purely subjective—in the breast of the individual; but, to produce a dramatic action, there must be a struggle with an external power, which the poet now prepares to introduce.

Hence we must pass to the love which is requited, and which brings him into collision with the hostile family. Romeo, in company with his friends, among whom is the gay scoffer, Mercutio, goes to a masquerade at the dwelling of Capulet, the mortal enemy of his house, evidently for the purpose of beholding the fair Rosaline. While there, he sees Juliet, and at once transfers to her all his passion. Indeed, its intensity is so great that he for the moment questions his former affection. This passage has been often construed as if Shakespeare meant to assert that Romeo's first love was only a fanciful delusion. How utterly aimless, how ridiculous, must this whole first Act then become! For we would seek in vain to find its object. The poet, if such were his meaning, would be simply denying his own work. These words of Romeo, are but the exaggerated expression of his present impulse. He passes to Juliet and talks with her; the language between them, though full of dark and far-fetched metaphor, is plain enough when supplemented with the look and the kiss. If he could not endure the previous struggle, what must become of him now? Juliet is also caught; her fervor seems equally great. Both have loved at first sight. Through all this volcanic might of passion the tragic end is peering, for separation now means death.

Thus Romeo *has* changed, notwithstanding his protestations to Benvolio. This transition is the central point of the whole first Movement of the play, and, indeed, gives the true motive for the tragic termination of the action. But it has been so generally misunderstood, according to our judgment of the drama, that the grounds for it require a full statement. It is declared that this sudden change from one individual to another is unnatural, and is, moreover, a great blemish in the work. The apparent lack of fidelity is said to give offense to our ethical feelings, and to destroy our respect for the hero. Also, Romeo seems now the most inconstant of lovers, but afterwards is faithful to death—which fact looks like an inconsistency in the character, and an unsolved contradiction in the play. The defenders of the poet have injured him more deeply than his assailants; they have defended his work by destroying it. The first love of Romeo, so fully detailed by the author, is pronounced to be no love—a mere caprice. But a careful view of the circumstances will show that this change is not only psychologically justifiable, but is the only adequate motive for the death of the lovers — that is, for the tragedy itself.

Romeo is consumed with the most ardent passion; its intensity is its great characteristic. He has given himself away, has made a complete sacrifice of his individuality, but there is no return for his devotion. This is the motive upon which the poet has laid the chief stress; the first love of Romeo was not reciprocated. The necessity of a corresponding passion is felt by everybody, though its logical basis is not usually thought of. Love is the surrender of the individual to one of the opposite sex, through the feelings. Each must find his or her emotional existence in the loved person; each must be only through the other. This mutual sacrifice of self on the part of both constitutes the unity and harmony of love. For, when individuality thus offers itself upon the altar of affection, that same individuality, to be consistent with its own principle, must demand a like sacrifice from the second person; otherwise, it is in utter contradiction with itself. A new individual must enter the bosom and take the place of that self which has been immolated.

But let one side be wanting, the reciprocity is destroyed; there is the sacrifice without the compensation. The lover loses, for a time at least, his own individuality, as far as his emotion is concerned, without gaining another. Hence he is harrassed with an internal struggle, more or less severe according to the intensity of the passion. As to the quantity of the literature of the world which is based upon unrequited love, the reader can form his own estimate; but it may be said to be the first, most natural, and most prevalent of all the collisions which spring from the tender passion. In such a struggle a restoration may be, and usually is, brought about by the healing influence of time. But the sacrifice may be so complete, and the passion so intense, that recovery is extremely difficult by this means—nay, impossible. Then there is only one other way—change the object; find some new individual who will make the sacrifice. It is a matter of not uncommon experience that rejected lovers resort to these sudden transfers of affection; not from spite, however, as is often supposed, but from a real necessity. This sudden change of Romeo has the authority both of Shakespeare and of the legend from which he drew his materials; thus it is stamped, as completely as may be, with seal of Human Nature, by people and poet.

Such is the conflict in Romeo's bosom, and such is its solution. The fervor of his love does not permit him to recover himself; he, indeed, must change in order to get repose and harmonize the struggle. It is, therefore, not fickleness, but rather the permanence and strength of his passion, which causes its transference from Rosaline to Juliet. This change is grounded in the fact that his love is unrequited, and yet so intense that it must have an object—a corresponding sacrifice. He cannot retrace his steps. He is just seeking that which comes across his way in the form of Juliet, for Rosaline cannot now have any reality for him. The relief is instantaneous—he recovers himself at a bound. The merry mocker, Mercutio, cannot now drive him off by bitter jests, but is beaten at his own game, and compelled to exclaim: "Now art thou sociable; now art thou Romeo!" etc.

For Juliet, the motives are quite different; she has no case of unrequited affection on her hands. Hence the question may be asked, why then does she, too, so easily fall in love? Juliet is in the full bloom of youth—ready for the sacrifice, yet without its experience. Now, Romeo approaches her in the hot glow of his love, and, with his sly words and eyes darting flames from beneath his mask, he infuses into her soul all the strength of his passion. Nor is this anything unusual or unnatural, for man and woman belong together, and must come together unless there is a good reason for their remaining asunder. No such reason exists in the case of Juliet; she is taken by the first manifestation of love. Romeo gives a hint: "They (my lips) pray; grant thou, lest faith turn to despair;" she requites; a kiss seals their union. Thus her love is motived by that of Romeo, and the intensity and completeness of his sacrifice call for and demand an equal intensity and completeness in her devotion. Her possible tragic destiny also peers through at this point; the fate of her lover must be hers.

The intensity now reached by Romeo and Juliet is kept up by both throughout the play, and constitutes its great distinguishing feature; for the love of man and woman has here attained such a potence that neither can exist without the other. In the vast majority of mankind it never reaches quite so high a degree; it stops this side of death. And, indeed, it should never reach quite so high a degree, for thus it turns to guilt and prepares the tragic fate. Romeo and Juliet are devoted to one another as individuals, and not so much to the Family as an institution. Their love thus turns to an ethical violation, since it renders domestic life impossible if the one chance be lost. The rational object of marriage is for man to exist in the Family, which, if it cannot be reached through one person, must be sought through another. The Institution is higher than the Individual; but, in the present drama, the love of an individual assails the Family on its universal side; thus there must result a tragic termination. For, truly considered, love, which is the emotional ground of the Family, is here destroying the Family itself. Love thus annihilates its own object, puts an end to itself; so do Romeo and Juliet, its bearers.

The first Act concludes with the excitation of their mutual love. The next step is the mutual acknowledgment, so that their union rises out of mere emotion into conscious purpose. This declaration to each other gives the famous balcony scene, one of those everlasting reprints of the human heart. The theme is the sacrifice of the sexual individual, which results in the formation of a higher unity, the Family. Previously this unity was only felt; now both declare it to be their most exalted principle forever. The activities of the mind, particularly the imagination which makes symbols, and the understanding which grasps relations are intensified into a whirlwind of energy by their passion. In the scenes of their meeting, all external nature around them is seized upon and made the bearer of their emotions; sun, moon, stars, birds, the lark and nightingale, are turned into the ministers of their love. The play of mental activity is as great as that of passion, and relieves the directness and blunt expression of mere sentiment. The conceits, however, and the images are not always in good taste, though they are, in general, psychologically true; the charterization cannot do without them, for they exhibit the strength of the emotion of the lovers. Their intense feeling seeks the world to find means for utterance; their minds hunt up the most recondite relations between objects; all externality seems there only to express love. The hatred of their families is burnt up in a consuming fire; both are ready to disown their own names if these furnish any obstacle to their union. Still, they feel that a new and terrible conflict has arisen which they now have to face—a conflict with the ancient prejudice and hostility of their families.

But their union is not yet complete; it must be carried out to its full realization in marriage. This the deep and earnest nature of Juliet has already demanded:

> If that thy bent of love be honorable,
> Thy purpose marriage, send me word to-morrow
> ——But if thou mean'st not well
> I do beseech thee——
> To cease thy suit and leave me, to my grief.

It is no holiday flirtation, but her ethical feeling is even stronger than her love, since, rather than violate it, she is ready to undergo the pain of separation. She distrusts too, her strong emotion; it is too rash, too sudden; she wants time to give it permanence. This ethical element in the character of Juliet is generally not attended to. She is considered, on the one hand, as a simple, unreflecting girl; on the other hand, she is sometimes represented with a dash of coquetry. Both these views are mistaken. She here first insists upon due deliberation, and then seeks the true ethical union found only in marriage. For in marriage the Family is first realized, since to the emotional or subjective element of love there is thus added the objective or rational element of an institution. This consummation could be reached, according to the belief of the time, only through religion, which gave the divine sanction to the union already formed in the emotions. Thus the Family was called into existence, as it were, by the fiat of God; it was a new and holy creation in the world, which was under His special blessing and protection. The ceremony is, therefore, performed by a priest of the church. Their unity is now a reality.

We already see that Juliet, though set on fire by Romeo's love is really a stronger, more self-centered character than he. She has to bid him go in season; she thinks for him as well as for herself. She never is sunk in the oblivion of passion, like Romeo; she still can reflect, and control herself. Hereafter this side of her nature will be surprisingly unfolded.

The marriage of the lovers introduces us to the grand mediator of the play, Friar Laurence. We are ushered into his presence in the quiet of early morn. The holy man of contemplation is shown in all the surroundings; the very atmosphere breathes serenity and repose. His reflection leads him to consider the contradictions of nature and of mind; he notes that excess calls forth strife; virtue itself, being strained, turns to its opposite. Here is given the germ of his character. He recognizes the source of all conflict, and seeks the means of its reconciliation. He employs the religious form of expressing this contradiction—grace on the one hand, rude will on the other. Still, his more natural way of thinking is rather that of the moral philosopher than of the religious teacher. He has himself subordinated all the passions of the soul; his order indicates his exclusion from secular struggles; he stands in striking contrast to the passion-tossed world around him. In Southern climates, where the blood is hot, it is the main duty of the confessor to assuage the harrassing emotions of the individual who cannot control them himself, and, hence, must have them controlled from without. The Friar is the mediator of the whole community. The very intensity of their passions demands one who is without passion to direct, advise, and soothe. Romeo, we see, has been a frequent visitor; the Friar was his confidant when no one else was, and has already often calmed his excited feelings concerning Rosaline. Such is the beautiful character of the Friar, standing in the midst of this tempest of passion, controlling, directing, pacifying it; for both love and hate seem equally ungovernable ebullitions of the without his reconciling presence; he is represented as a profound student of the natural properties of objects; he has his chosen herbs and drugs in wonderful power upon the senses.

mental principle is the shunning of all extremes; and just here lies the basis of his deceptions, of the pious frauds which he practices. A rigid moralist he is not, and cannot be in consistency with his principle:

Virtue itself turns to vice, being misapplied.

As mediator, he has to smooth over difficulties and harmonize collisions; he cannot be hampered by moral punctilios at every step. He brushes them away; but still he seeks to be true to the highest end, and subordinate to it every minor scruple. It is to be noticed that all of Shakespeare's mediatorial characters have quite the same traits; they falsify and deceive, without the least hesitancy, in order to accomplish their important mediations. The Friar unites Romeo and Juliet in marriage, for this is the only solution; separation means death; religion adds its sanction to love, to the right of subjectivity, even against the consent of the parents; and the new family unites within itself the heirs of both the Capulets and the Montagues, whose ancient hatred must henceforth vanish in their descendants. Such a consummation is assuredly a great religious object.

Yet, just at this point, the Friar is caught in the grand his own principle. He carries his shunning are ushered into that he commits an excess, and in morn. The holy matrimony he destroys harmony. in all the surroundings; d it turns to vice. In breathes serenity and repose. himself open to the him to consider the contradicti will rush in and destroy his plan. Like Romeo, the Friar also has a passion—a love of subtle management, and this will prove fatal to his mediation, and almost fatal to him. He is rather a prudential philosopher than a strict religionist; it is to be noticed that he offers to Romeo, in time of trial, not the comfort of religion, but "adversity's sweet milk, philosophy." He, the thinker, knows of the danger of extremes, yet falls into an extreme, through his very cunning. The reconciliation is wrenched out of his hand by Destiny, who always finds it very hard to deal with truth, but very easy to deal with deception.

2. It is now time to go back and bring up to this point the counter-movement to the marriage, resulting from the wooing of Paris. He is the competitor of Romeo for the hand of Juliet; but he rests his suit, not on the love of the daughter, but on the consent of the parent, and herein proceeds according to the received social formality. Just the opposite is Romeo, who entirely disregards formality, but acts from love. Hence arises the conflict. Both parents of Juliet favor Paris, but the father at first declares distinctly that the consent of the daughter must be obtained; afterwards he abandons this principle, and tries to force the marriage with Paris—an act which helps to bring on all the tragic consequences of the drama. The strength of each suitor was shown at the masquerade. Love proved to be more powerful than form; Paris had his chosen one carried off from under his very eyes.

This excellent young man, upon whom certainly the poet nowhere casts any reproach, has been often misjudged by critics. He is not a villain, not a fortune-hunter, unworthy of Juliet; the only drawback is, he does not possess her heart. On the contrary, he is a truly ethical character. His conduct and final death at the tomb of Juliet show that he was influenced by love. He was not, therefore, seeking a marriage from interest. The pith of his contrast with Romeo is that, although he is a worthy man, he has not, and cannot have, Juliet's affection, which fact, however, is nowhere made known to him in the play. His love is unrequited, like the first love of Romeo; hence it cannot form a rational basis for marriage. Such is the collision of the right of choice against the will of the parent. Paris is a true tragic character, who has an end justifiable in itself, which, however, collides with a higher justifiable end, and he perishes in the conflict; for the intensity of Romeo is such that he slays the man who stands in the way of his union, as well as slays himself when union is impossible.

II.

Such is, in the main, the First Movement of the play culminating in the marriage of the lovers. But this marriage rests upon a volcano muttering underneath—the hate of the two houses. Will it break forth? The test is at once to be applied to Romeo; if he can contain himself, he may be saved, but he will have to manifest a quality which he has not hitherto shown. Here the Second Movement begins, which portrays the outburst sweeping on to separation and death of the lovers, to final reconciliation of the hostile families. The two previous Threads are continued.

1. Tybalt, the hottest head in the play—we wonder not that he dies so soon, but that he has lived so long, in that turbulent society—seems to have regarded the presence of a Montague at the masquerade as an audacious affront to his house. He seeks a quarrel with Romeo; but, for the latter, all enmity against the Capulets has vanished in his union with Juliet. Romeo quietly endures the insult of Tybalt, hate seems to be conquered by love, and we think that the young man is beyond the stroke of his destiny. But his friend, Mercutio, an outsider belonging to neither of the families, takes up the quarrel and is slain for his interference. The passionate reaction now comes over Romeo, hate shows itself stronger than love, and he slays Tybalt. So Romeo has not stood the test, which was to endure the family hate; just as little was he able to endure the first test, which was love unrequited. He is still Romeo, ruled by his passion, if not of love, then of hate. The Italian vendetta, which it was his problem to master, has mastered him; he knows the result of "this day's black fate," and cries out: "O, I am Fortune's fool". Again the enmity of the two families has disturbed public order; the State appears, in the person of the Prince, and decrees the immediate banishment of Romeo, who has so deeply

violated the principle of authority.

This Mercutio, who has become the instrument of the banishment of his friend, and fallen a sacrifice to his own interference, is a character in every way noteworthy. He is the light-hearted mocker who has not earnestness sufficient for a real passion or a deep conviction; he is the product of this Italian life in which excess of sentiment calls up the scoffer of sentiment; like Romeo, he gives himself up to his bent, which is raillery uncontrolled. His chief mental trait is humor, coupled with a light, airy fancy. The poet has portrayed him in a series of situations, all quite different, yet all manifesting the same fundamental characteristic. First is his somewhat lengthy description of Queen Mab and her functions, wherein he makes fun of the fairy mythology, and wherein, at the same time, he manifests the most beautiful fancy. Here he makes the ideal world his sport, yet in a most ideal manner. Humor and fancy were never so harmoniously blended. Next he takes up the real world around him and treats it in a similar manner; he mocks in the most lively way the formality and affectation of the time—in particular, the formal training and fencing of Tybalt. But, above all, he is the mocker of love, and its manifestations in Romeo are the subject of infinite merriment. Such is the contrast: for the one, love has a tragic depth; for the other, a comic lightness. His fancy also finds expression in puns and conceits; he always sees the ridiculous side. He rallies Romeo, for instance, by not very delicate innuendoes, when the old nurse appears bearing a message from Juliet. Thus the world dissolves in his humor—he assails everything with it; all his surroundings furnish only food for his sport. But there is nothing cynical or bitter in his character; it is a laugh—light, airy, mercurial, like his name. What causes such a man to fight? His volatile nature is brought into trying circumstances that require, at least, strong self-command, which he does not possess; it must fly off, for it has no controlling center within itself. He thinks that Romeo has been insulted, and has basely submitted; puff! he is up and off. This, added to an evident dislike of Tybalt, seems to be the motive of the fight. Though the relative of the Prince, he is the friend of Romeo, and takes sides with the house of Montague. As an offset to him, Paris, another relative of the Prince, allies himself to the Capulets, and perishes. The last words of Mercutio are full of repentance, though he cannot refrain from the jest and pun with his dying breath. The logical justification of his fate is not very apparent, but it probably lies in the fact that he, though an outsider, is the first man to stir up afresh the enmity of the two houses after it had been healed, or ultimately must have been healed, by the marriage of their two representatives, as well as by the conciliatory conduct of Romeo. The hate breaks forth anew—Mercutio is the first victim; it is his own act which calls forth his death. His mistake he sees, and his final curse is upon "your houses."

Banishment is decreed; the unity of love must be violently torn asunder. The conduct and feelings of the lovers, which are now manifested, are in the most perfect consonance with their principle. Both think of death; loss of existence is preferable to the loss of union, so great is its intensity. They are brought forward in different scenes, but their pathos is quite the same. The tragic motive is again manifest—permanent separation means destruction. In the breast of Juliet, however, there is a double conflict—her dearest relative has been slain by her husband, and now that husband must leave her. Not dissimilar is the situation of Ophelia, whose lover has slain her father. Juliet, in the beginning, thinks of the death of her cousin, Tybalt. Her family thus comes up first in her mind, and she curses Romeo. But soon the deeper principle manifests itself; that which rends her heart is the separation, and she says directly that she would rather endure the destruction of her whole family—Tybalt, father, and mother—than the banishment of her husband. Just as great is the desperation of Romeo. Again he must betake himself to the Friar, who will comfort him with "adversity's sweet milk, philosophy," and will soothe his agitated soul—the true function of the religious mediator. The good monk adopts the only solution possible—the separation must not be permanent. Romeo can only be buoyed up with hope of a speedy return. This hope is furnished to him by the Friar. He is now prepared to endure the parting from Juliet, which accordingly takes place, and the separation is accomplished.

2. Let us now go back again and consider that part of the action which collides with this union, namely, the suit of Paris, supported by the consent of the parents. In the absence of Romeo, this part becomes the sole element of the drama, and Juliet has to support the struggle alone. Her fidelity is to be tried to the utmost. Afflictions will be laid upon her, increasing in intensity, till death; but she will never, for a moment, flinch in her devotion. The father, who previously asserted for his daughter the right of love, in true accord with the Shakespearian view, now changes his basis, and commands Juliet to marry Paris. This change lies in his impulsive, volatile nature, as far as the poet has given to it any motive. He suddenly makes a "desperate tender" of his daughter's love without having consulted her choice. It is one of the turning-points of the drama, this abrupt reversal of his former opinion. Juliet is continually weeping. Her father thinks her mourning is for her relative, Tybalt, while it is really on account of the absence of Romeo. She thus seems to have a share in her own misfortune, by not informing her parent of her love; but, then, any declaration of the sort would have been equally fatal. It is the tragic dilemma—either way leads to death. Paris is pressing his suit; both the father and the mother of Juliet favor him; she resists. The result is that she is berated by her parents, and threatened with expulsion from home and with disinheritance.

Here is the next affliction after the banishment of Romeo. The conflict between the right of love and the will of the parent is manifested in all its intensity, but she cannot yield. She resorts for comfort to the nurse, who knows of her love, and from whom she expects sympathy; but this last source, too, is cut off. The old woman advises her to submit, and cites every consideration but the right one, namely, love—which is the sole possible motive with Juliet. Thereupon she is done with the nurse; their friendly relation henceforth ceases, and the nurse disappears from every essential mediation of the play.

The nurse has been hitherto one of the important instrumentalities of the drama; her function is partly mediatorial, though in a far less degree than that of the Friar. Her portrait is taken from nature direct; nothing can be more real and life-like. She almost supplies, in care and affection, the place of a mother; she is the friend and confidant of Juliet, while Lady Capulet appears in the distance, a stranger to the nursery, and the supporter of the marriage with Paris. The maternal feeling of Lady Capulet does not seem very strong. She leaves the impresion of a cold, heartless woman. The nurse, on the contrary, supports, for a time at least, the love of Juliet against her family. She is, however, of low birth, vulgar in language, and coarse in character; and, ultimately, she is open to the sway of interest. The ideal devotion of Juliet she can in no sense appreciate—it lies far beyond her horizon—and so she advises its abandonment. The realistic fullness and limited range of her characterization give the clearest picture in the play; her garrulity, her habit of citing old memories in which she dwells, her sudden changes of thought, her trickery and teasing, are all united into the most vivid individuality.

This household of the Capulets is indeed a strange soil for such a flower as Juliet. She may be said to have two mothers, a patrician and a plebeian, both of whom have imparted to the young girl their ideas of love and lovers, and so nourished in her the passion, for which her natural aptitude was already sufficiently great. The nurse breaks out into coarse allusions, while Lady Capulet speaks to her daughter in a strain of refined innuendo:

> This precious book of love, this unbound lover,
> To beautify him, only wants a cover * * *
> That book in many's eyes doth share the glory,
> That in gold clasps locks in the golden story—

especially in Lady Capulet's eyes. Both mothers, however, are alike in the main point, they are swayed by material interests in matters of the heart; so Juliet has really no mother, the strong devotion she shows, is her own, though kindled by Romeo.

As soon as the nurse gives this advice to abandon Romeo her mediatorial function ceases; the case is out of her reach. The Friar alone can understand and solve the difficulty. Accordingly Juliet betakes herself to his cell. At once she finds both sympathy and aid, for it is the character of the Friar to give complete validity to love. He is ready with a plan—she must drink off a liquor which produces the semblance of death, and be buried in the vault of her family, whither he and Romeo will come to her rescue. This means appears far-fetched and without adequate motive. Why could she have not gone directly to his cell and secreted herself, or have slipped off and hurried to Romeo at Mantua? Yet the design of the poet is manifest. Since he is portraying love in its highest intensity, he makes it endure every gradation of trial, and finally death itself. The most terrible thing to the human imagination is, probably, the idea of being buried alive, and shut up in a vault with dead bodies. But she, a tender girl, resolves to undergo what would make the heart of the most courageous man blench. It is the affliction next to death, yet love gives her the daring to endure. Read her soliloquy as she drinks off the contents of the vial. There she recounts the possibilities; imagination starts up the direst phantasms; madness stares her in the face; still, she will drink. This occurrence, therefore, is in perfect harmony with the spirit of the play. Before death, Juliet is brought to the tomb alive. It is one of the series of trials, increasing in pain and horror, in whose fire her love must be tested.

But just here incidents are portrayed for which it is extremely difficult to find any adequate justification. What necessity of exhibiting the sorrow of the parents over their child, whom they suppose to be dead—all of which must be a false pathos to the audience? The only excuse is, their grief is not very deep, and the cries of formal lamentation are made to sound hollow. Friar Laurence again appears in his true role of mediator and consoler, but his dissimulation now seriously impairs his high ethical character. Both the weeping of the parents and the deception of the Friar could have been here omitted without injury to the action, and to the decided advantage of thought and logical consistency. In fact, the entire drama has a certain natural fullness which makes it often vivid, but obscures its unity as a Whole. It lacks the more rigid adherence to a central thought found in the later works of the poet.

The conflict of Juliet with the will of her parents is thus met by the plan of the Friar, who protects her against her family as he protected Romeo against the authority of the State. Nothing now seems in the way of the speedy reunion of the separated lovers. Romeo is still in exile, filled with longings and anticipations of the time when he will be restored to his Juliet. His thoughts by day and his dreams by night have no other employment. Suddenly the terrible news arrives —Juliet is dead. His love is at once all ablaze; he will still be united with her, though in death. He resolves to set out immediately for home. But herein he disobeys the Friar, and acts without the latter's knowledge. Thus the Friar's plan is interfered with and destroyed. Romeo proceeds upon mistaken information, and the good monk fails in his scheme of reconcilement. The lover hastens to the tomb, there to lie in death with Juliet, but he meets Paris. The latter attempts to interfere with his resolution, and to stand in the way of his union with Juliet. Paris is slain, for such is the intensity of this love that it destroys every obstacle in its way, and destroys itself when it cannot be realized, for Romeo kills himself, in preference to living without this union. Juliet wakes, sees her lover at her side, dead; she also cannot live apart from their union in the family. They are thus alike in devotion, but it is manifest that Juliet is the truer and loftier character. Her sacrifice belongs to her sex—is its profoundest ethical principle. But Romeo does not rise above this same character. He is too much like a woman; as the Friar says; his pathos is too feminine. On this account Romeo can never be as great a favorite as Juliet; he falls below the true type of manhood.

Thus Romeo breaks down in his third great probation, as he did in the other two. He is the same in all, without self-control; he could not endure the unrequited love, could not endure the trial of family hate, could not endure for a moment the test of Juliet's death. Each time he calls down upon himself the blow of Fate increasing in might to the last, because he will not be a freeman; he indulges his emotion, which finds vent in fancy, and then his fancy runs uncontrolled to imagery. He is determined by judgement neither in his actions, nor in his metaphors. Still we must appreciate Romeo, he has an heroic side of character, he is a lover unto death; granted his weakness, he has in that weakness enough strength to be tragic.

In this respect Juliet is different, she is more self-centered, has reflection, and the power of self-suppression. She meets her trial, in the suit of Paris, with self-control, and with an artifice which we wonder at, not altogether admiringly. But in the presence of Romeo, she is transformed by his passion, even her speech and imagery become like his, and run a race with his extravagance. Her deepest trait is still devotion to her love, for the sake of which she employs deception, and thus exposes herself to stroke of Fate along with the Friar. Compared to her, Romeo is single-souled; she has doubleness, nay, duplicity; she can assume a character and play it, and what is more wonderful, meet her tragic situation with ambiguities of speech which become almost comic. Note the part she plays to her parents and to Paris, telling the truth in words, but in fact falsifying, or perchance dramatizing a disguise. Yet she is deeply in earnest, has the noblest end in view; but for this end she employs deception, in which Fate catches her; still when caught, she defies Fate, and triumphantly dies.

Again authority has been assailed; blood has been spilled in another fray. The Prince, as the representative of the State appears the third and last time. There is, however, no one to punish. The play must explain itself. The Friar, together with the page of Paris and the servant of Romeo, unfold the causes of the untoward calamity. This is not an unnecessary appendage, for Shakespeare always makes, in the end, the play clear to its own actors; thus only is it complete in itself. The Friar, after telling all his plans of mediation, offers to die; but, of course, that man cannot perish who chiefly sought to ward off the tragic consequences of the fatal love.

Thus we see that the logical result of this feud has been the annihilation of the Family. Each house willed the destruction of the other, and therein the destruction of itself. For their conduct must return upon themselves, and the drama only portrays the manner of that return. Both families lose their children, their heirs, and, in their loss, must pass away forever. The Prince, too, suffers along with them, for "winking at the discords," and he declares in the plainest terms, the great law of retribution by which all are punished.

We have now reached the termination of the purely tragic movement of the play, namely, the union of the lovers in death. Their last and greatest trial has been passed; both have remained true to love. Their tie was so strong, their oneness so complete, that they could not really exist as separate individuals. The grand object of the play has been frequently stated: it is to portray a love so intense that separation must cause death. But such a result is contrary to the common experience of mankind, and hence the poet seeks every possible means for manifesting the *intensity* of the passion. That it lay in the character of Romeo never to recover his individuality, after it was once surrendered to his affection, is shown in the First Movement of the play; the taking away of the loved object is literally the taking away of himself, so complete is his sacrifice. Juliet's passion is motived, both in kind and in degree, by that of Romeo; her devotion must be as great as his. The Second Movement of the tragedy portrays the separation of the pair—at first supposed to be only temporary; but the moment Romeo, and afterwards Juliet, become possessed of the notion that the separation will be eternal, self-destruction is the logical necessity of their characters. It is indeed the tragedy of love. This coloring of intensity it keeps throughout, amid all its vagaries and excrescences. This is, in fact, the deep underlying unity of the work, whose power every one must feel. The guilt of the unhappy pair must be placed here, also, if we can predicate guilt of them, and certainly we must do so if we are able to justify the tragedy. The emotional nature of man must be controlled and subordinated to the rational principle, and, under no circumstances, can it have the right to utterly absorb and destroy individual existence.

At this point an opposite movement sets in for a short time—the reconciliation of the two hostile houses. The Prince insists upon it; the public order of the city has been violated; he has lost two kinsmen in the feud; he, too, has been punished in his family. But, more emphatically the poet insists upon it; he would have us see that such a visitation is not without its purpose in the plan of the world; it clears up, purifies, harmonizes. Shakespeare's tragic view is a glance into the providential order, and is a revelation thereof to men, showing the movement of a society into and out of a disrupted ethical condition. Tragedy with him means not death merely, but is a sacrifice; Shakespeare's tragedy is at bottom mediatorial, and reaches into the divine scheme of the world. The lovers, Romeo and Juliet, die, but their death has in it for the living a redemption.

Still, the individual perishes. But hereafter Shakespeare will save the individual too, by producing a new kind of drama, a mediated drama, which is neither pure tragedy nor pure comedy. In the present play the parents repent, which is soul-saving, but their repentance has not relieved them from the consequences of their guilt; they have lost their children, their families cannot be rescued. But in a new class of dramas, the last and ripest fruit of the genius of Shakespeare, *Winter's Tale, Cymbeline, Tempest*, repentance will mediate and restore the individual, that is, will save him from the tragic consequences of his deeds. In the end of *Romeo and Juliet*, the early product of the poet's tragic muse, there is a faint glimpse of that mediation which is to become, not an external appendage to his play, but the very soul, as well as the turning point of his dramatic Art. Whereof it is interesting to note here a prophecy.

OTHELLO.

Very little is known of the history of this play during the life-time of the poet, and the single important fact about it is clouded with a question of authenticity. As far as we now can tell, it was first printed after his death, both in Quarto and Folio. External evidence seems to show that the play was in existence in the year 1604, which is at present quite generally taken as the date of its completion. Internal evidence confirms this date. *Othello*, accordingly, belongs to the same period in which we have placed the poet's other great tragedies—his second or tragic period. Formerly it was thought to be among his latest works, but it does not harmonize well with the tendency of his last period, which looks toward mediation of the tragic conflict. Spirit, style and date make it an inseparable member of the grand quadruple tragedy, which seems to turn around the year 1604 as its center in time.

- The impression left by this play is generally said to be that of sadness and despair. Life seems given over to the sport of external influences, and man is swept to destruction whether his conduct be good or bad. Villainy and cunning, it is thought, are portrayed as too successful and powerful, while innocence is exhibited as too weak and unfortunate.

There is often expressed a deep dissatisfaction at the result; virtue is not rewarded, or is even punished, and retribution does not manifest itself in its native might. Perhaps such will always be the first and most immediate impression upon the auditor or reader. But this melancholy view of the work springs from a hasty judgment—from taking into account only a portion of the various elements of the play. On the one hand, Othello and Desdemona are not innocent, but are guilty of a violation of ethical principles, which calls forth their punishment. And, on the other hand, Iago is not the incarnation of villainy for its own sake, but he has some very strong and very natural grounds for his conduct, which, however, do not justify his action, though they explain his character. In this play, as in all others of Shakespeare, a careful analysis is necessary in order to bring all the motives to the surface, and to comprehend adequately their meaning and purpose. They must be marshaled before the mind in their relation and in their completeness. If only a part of what is told us by the poet remains in the memory, the judgment is not likely to be correct. Accordingly we may expect that diligent study and comparison will bring to light some less manifest elements which must have an essential influence in determining the character of the whole drama.

It is well known that there is always ready to be made, against this kind of criticism, the charge of seeking and finding what the poet never intended. Such a charge may be just sometimes, but it usually means that the objector did not think of the various points in question when he read the play. Hence he infers that Shakespeare could not have thought of them. There is often an ill-concealed egotism lying at the basis of such statements, for the benefit of which one reflection ought always to be made. It took Shakespeare weeks, perhaps years, to plan and write *Othello*. If so much time was required for his mind, in order to make the drama, how much time will you (the objector), with your mind, need in order to comprehend it? To enter into his conception thoroughly, to see his work arising from all sides and coming together into a complete and harmonious whole, will demand more than a three hours' reading or representation.

In the character of Othello we note that antithetic movement, which is found in so many of Shakespeare's tragic heroes, and, we may add, in Human Nature. A soul without jealousy is thrown into a course which converts it to a type of jealousy itself; a spirit noble, gentle, forbearing, becomes most vindictive and bloody; the civilized man relapses to savagery. This change comes through the deed, the deed of guilt, which is man's scourging destiny, and turns him to the opposite of himself, turns him to his own triumphant enemy, who slays him. As a counterpart to the man, we see, in this tragedy, the woman, who shows in her sphere the same tragic antithesis of character, true unto death to her husband, yet untrue to truth; faithful to family, yet unfaithful to the moral order of the world; sweet, noble, innocent, yet guilty, for it is her guilt which weaves the tragic net of destiny in which she is caught.

If we grasp the entire sweep of the action, we observe that it first moves towards union of the lovers, out of a conflict with parent; but this union, outwardly attained, rests inwardly upon a deeper disunion, which, in a suitable environment, unfolds rapidly, and hurries the pair forward to the ultimate separation in death. As is usual in Shakespeare's tragedies, a dissonance, a deep incompatibility is introduced into the Ethical World, which has to be purified of it by eliminating the individuals who caused it.

There are three essential divisions or Movements of the entire action. The first is the external conflict in the Family. The right of the daughter to choose a Moor for her husband is asserted against the will of the parent. Both sides appeal to the State, which decides in favor of the marriage, and Othello carries off his bride in triumph. The guilt of Desdemona is here indicated. The second Movement shows the internal conflict in the Family between husband and wife. The married pair, though successful in their external struggle with the father, are now rent asunder; for between such characters no secure and permanent ethical union is possible. Jealousy must arise. Iago seized only what was already prepared, and used it for his own purposes. The guilt of Othello and his Ancient is here shown. The third Movement is the retribution, which brings home to every person the consequences of his deeds. Tragedies usually have only two parts —guilt and retribution. But there may be an introduction, as is seen in the first Movement of the present play; or there may be an appendage to the tragic action, as is the case with *Romeo and Juliet.*

I.

The presupposition of the drama is the love, elopement, and marriage of Othello and Desdemona, who constitute the single central thread of the first Movement, and with whose union three leading persons come into conflict. The lovers are thus already joined in marriage, against which the hostile elements begin to array themselves. First comes the rejected, yet determined suitor, Roderigo, who has been ignominiously dismissed by the father, and apparently disregarded by the daughter. Still, he persists; the great end of his existence is to secure her hand, for which purpose he is willing to spend large sums of money. This weakness makes him a fit subject for the practices of Iago, who buoys him up with hope and draws at will from his purse. But, when the marriage is sanctioned by the State, and is beyond reversal, what will poor Roderigo do? Since the object of his life is to attain Desdemona, he is easily led into the thought of attaining her in unholy fashion, when she can no longer be his lawful wife. He is first foolish in pursuing such an object; then he becomes immoral, and assails the Family. Roderigo is the white suitor of Desdemona, and stands in striking contrast to the black suitor, Othello. She prefers the hero of a different race to the imbecile of her own nation. But his chief function is to be the ready instrument of Iago, who uses him like the merest tool, and destroys him when he no longer subserves any purpose.

The second enemy is Iago, whose hate is not so much directed against the marriage as against Othello in person. Hence he plays a very subordinate part in the First Movement of the drama, but is reserved for the second collision. To unfold and arrange in proper order and prominence the different motives which actuate him is one of the chief duties of a criticism on this work. In his conversation with Roderigo he assigns as the cause of his hate that he has been degraded in rank, through having a less experienced and less meritorious officer promoted over his head by Othello. Hereafter he is going to look out for himself, since nobody else will pay any attention to his claims. He proposes to employ any means in his power to accomplish his end; everything high and holy—honesty, fidelty, morality—is to be trampled under foot if standing in his way. The service of the individual, therefore, he declares to be his ultimate principle. But, to attain his purpose with success, there must be a disguise. "I am not what I am," is his curt and striking statement. His instrumentality is to be dissimulation.

Iago asserts, in the strongest manner, the supremacy of reason; men can make out of their body and their appetite what they will. Still, his reason extends not beyond subjective cunning; he ignores the validity of all ethical principles. Virtue is a pretense, love is merely lust, reputation is a delusion. The question naturally arises, why has his intelligence become so debauched? The ground thereof lies in his own experience, as will be pointed out hereafter. But, here, also there is a large element of pretense, since he knows the exact nature of his conduct. Mark, too, that for his hatred of Othello he has not assigned to Roderigo the true motive; he is already dissembling in accordance with his principle. His talk is intended for Roderigo alone, whom he wishes to keep as an instrument, and to whom he is compelled, therefore, to give some motive for his conduct and some clew to his future action. For Roderigo, fool as he is, must have a plausible explanation of the strange fact that the Ancient of Othello works against his master, before any money will be forthcoming.

But the true motive for Iago's hate is given in his first, and also in his succeeding soliloquies, but nowhere in his conversation with others, since he would not be likely to announce his own shame, or herald his self-degrading suspicions. He considers that Othello has destroyed the chastity of his wife. Public rumor has n̶a̶d̶e̶ the scandal abroad. He is made the obje̶c̶t̶ ̶o̶f̶ ̶i̶t̶; he feels that he has suffered the deepe̶s̶t̶ ̶i̶n̶j̶u̶r̶y̶ which man is capable of giving or recei̶v̶i̶n̶g̶. This is the thought which gnaws the heart of Iago, and spurs him to revenge;

> — The thought thereof
> Doth, like a poisonous mineral, gnaw my inwards,
> And nothing can or shall content my soul
> Till I be evened with him.

Such was his own declaration to himself, whom he certainly had no motive for deceiving. Nor is it consistent with his shrewd understanding to assume that his belief rests on self-deception—that he really did not know what he was about. Iago has declared his actual conviction—a conviction which is confirmed by events which afterwards transpire. It is often taken for granted that his suspicions are wholly groundless—in fact, that he does not believe them himself. The question of Othello's guilt with Emilia belongs to the second division of the play, where it will be hereafter considered. But that Iago is sincere in his belief cannot be consistently questioned. The single motive usually assumed for his conduct is what he states to Roderigo about the lack of promotion. Such a view, however, is psychologically false; Iago is not the man to tell the truth to another and lie to himself. Moreover, why is the form of the soliloquy employed, unless to express the real internal ground of his action, which could not be imparted to others? Coleridge calls Iago's soliloquizing "the motive-hunting of a motiveless malignity;" in spite of the authority of the great critic, we must think that his sentence has obtained its currency more to be due from its epigrammatic point than from its accuracy.

With the interpretation above given, there is

a motive quite adequate for the subsequent vindictive conduct of Iago; otherwise, he is an unnatural character—a monstrosity. His slight in regard to promotion would doubtless excite his enmity, but not an enmity sufficient to involve Desdemona in destruction, or even Othello. To inflict worse than death upon a man because he did not advance a subordinate when he could have done so, is altogether disproportionate to the offense; but to cause his wife to perish also is merely horrible. Thus Iago is a monster, a wild beast, and needs no motive at all—not even neglect of promotion—to bring on a rabid fit of cruelty. But what then becomes of the artistic merit and beauty of this drama? Moreover, Shakespeare's rule is to motive all his most important characters; such a being as the villain pure and simple is not to be found in any of his works. The second motive is, therefore, the true one, and at the same time is adequate. The family of Iago has been ruined by Othello; now, Iago, in his turn, will ruin the family of the destroyer of his domestic life. Hence Desdemona is included in his retaliation. He thus requites the Moor with like for like. His conduct is logical, and his revenge only equals the offense. But there is absolutely no proportion between motive and deed, if he involved Othello's family in destruction merely because the latter would not promote him. Such seems to be the proper relation of the two grand motives mentioned by the poet; the first one is intended only for Roderigo, while the second is the true and single motive for the subsequent actions of Iago.

The third opponent of the marriage is the father, Brabantio. Here we have the essential part of the First Movement—the conflict of the Family carried up into the State. The opposition of Brabantio gives the collision which Shakespeare always takes particular delight in portraying—the collision between the right of choice on the part of the daughter and the will of the parent. It is often supposed that the tragic destiny of Desdemona is motived by her disobedience; but such a view will not bear investigation. Shakespeare everywhere justifies the right of choice when it is the sole issue, and therein he is true to the modern consciousness. It belongs to the woman to say who shall be her husband, for she, and not her father, has to form with him the unity of emotion which lies at the basis of the Family. But, even if we grant that there is some guilt in such conduct, it certainly cannot be tragic guilt, which involves the destruction of the individual. The ethical code of Shakespeare is plainly against this interpretation, for he always mediates such a conflict by the triumph of the daughter, as we see in the instances of Hermia, Portia, Jessica, Anne Page, Miranda, etc. The case of Romeo and Juliet cannot be taken to support the contrary view, for it, too, offers a peculiar ground of tragic destiny. Assuredly, Juliet's fate does not spring from her opposition to a marriage dictated by her father.

Another motive must, hence, be sought, which the poet has not failed to indicate. It lies in the fact that between husband and wife existed the difference of race. An ethical union is impossible under such circumstances; the chasm is too wide —at least in the present condition of mankind. The Family, like all institutions, is grounded in prescription; this prescription has placed upon marriage certain limitations which cannot be violated without giving the deepest offense to the ethical feelings. The principle of prescription belongs to every age and nation, in different degrees, and is shared by all the truly moral people; those who violate it are regarded as outcasts. A difference of rank often destroys the possibility of an ethical union, though the parties are of the same race and of the same country. In Europe, to-day, the marriage of a lord and servant girl collides with the moral consciousness of the whole public. The rational basis for such a strong sentiment is not wanting; it is that, where so great a difference exists, the unity demanded by the Family is impossible. Both parties know that they have violated one ethical element of marriage; hence comes the dark suspicion that another ethical element of marriage may be as readily disregarded, namely, chastity. It is clear that the jealousy which fires Othello will hardly fail to arise from such a union, and turn it into a source of bitterness and death.

As Desdemona has contracted a marriage which is impossible for the Family, it culminates in destroying the woman who enters into its baleful embrace. The true tragic element of her character we are now prepared to appreciate. On the one side, she is the most chaste and innocent of women; her love and devotion are absolute. So faithful to her relation does she seem, that many people can see no justification for her fate. But let us now turn to the other side. While in the highest degree true to one ethical principle, she utterly disregards another. The entire realm of prescription which rests upon distinction of race she casts to the winds, and marries an African. In the most beautiful manner she is true to the Family, but is untrue to that upon which the Family reposes. For the sake of marriage she violates the condition of marriage. Her tragic pathos, therefore, lies in the fact that she espouses the one whom she loves, which is her right, and yet thereby involves herself in guilt. The collision with her parent is allowable, but not with her race: that is, the one is not tragic, the other is. If Othello were not a Moor, there would be no motive for the fate of Desdemona; and, conversely, if she commits no offense in her marriage, it is hard to see why the poet should give himself the unnecessary trouble of making Othello a Moor. The only answer which can be given, under such a supposition, is that he followed blindly the sources of his plot, at the sacrifice of both decency and thought.

But even his plot, in the original Italian novel, very strongly insists upon the distinction of race, and repeatedly urges the collision which is likely to spring from it. Desdemona herself speaks of it, and fears that from her the lesson may be drawn "not to companion one's self with a man whom

Nature, Heaven, and manner of life disjoins from us," (*di ne se accompagnare con uomo cui la Natura, et il Cielo et il modo della vita disgiunge da noi.*) She also speaks of the conflict with her father, and fears that she may be "an example to young ladies not to marry against the will of their parents," (*di non maritarse contra il voler de suoi.*) Of the deceptions and fibs of Desdemona the old novelist has little or nothing, this element is added to her character by Shakespeare, who, in this way too, shows her spinning the thread of her own fate.

A correct appreciation of this subject is not without difficulties in our time; any view is likely to be assailed with the charge of prejudice. But there seems to be no doubt that Shakespeare makes race an ethical element of marriage, as important as chastity. Nor does he differ much from the great majority of mankind at present. That philanthropist is yet to be found who would be willing to see his daughter marry an African, however intense might be their love. His repugnance does not necessarily proceed from prejudice, but from the conviction that such a union is unethical; the lives of the pair, even if they lasted, would be a continuous tragedy. The prospect of his posterity would also be apt to call forth language and emotions quite similar to those of Brabantio.

A question has been raised concerning the degree of Othello's Africanism, about which extreme opinions have been held in both directions. But he was not a Hottentot on the one hand, nor was he a Caucasian on the other; he was, however, born in Africa, and his physiognomy is thoroughly African. The point which the poet emphasizes so often and so strongly is the difference of race between him and Desdemona. He is her equal in rank, for he comes of royal lineage; he is the peer of her family in honor and fame, for he is the most distinguished man in Venice. The sole difference which is selected as the ground of the collision is the difference of race. This fact is sufficient for all dramatic purposes; to ascertain the exact shade of his skin may be left to those who have leisure to play with probabilities.

Desdemona, therefore, asserts the right of choosing her husband against the will of her father, which collision, as above said, is continually recurring in Shakespeare, and which he always solves by giving full validity to love, though in opposition to parental authority. But, in the present instance, he has surrounded the choice of the young girl with a peculiar obstacle, and introduced an element found nowhere else in his dramas. The love of Desdemona is made to leap over quite all the social limitations known to man; she bids defiance, not only to the behests of Family, but also to the feelings of nationality and to the instincts of race. She is a practical cosmopolitan.

Her father Brabantio, is decidedly of the opposite character. He is not wholly illiberal in his external conduct; nevertheless, he bears the stamp of a hide-bound patrician, devoted more to his class than to his country. He would hardly be called national in his feelings; the cosmopolitan love of his daughter, therefore, excites in his bosom the liveliest emotions. It is, indeed, so incomprehensible to him that he can only account for it by the employment of some supernatural means on the part of the Moor. His limits are essentially those of his own order. But he cannot avoid taking his share of the blame; it is his own conduct which has led to the unfortunate result. Othello has been a frequent guest at his house, and thus he has himself furnished the opportunity of the courtship. For Othello had rendered the most important services to the State. On account of these services he was tolerated, indeed, welcomed to the home of the Venetian aristocrat. But never for a moment did the latter think of removing the social ban. The limits of race Othello has thus broken down on one side—he has obtained honor and high command in the State. Here he cannot be barred out, for he is the chief instrument of its existence. It might be thought that these civil distinctions are higher than any other. This may be so; still, they cannot overcome social distinctions—or prejudices—if such it were better to call them. The contrast is drawn in the most striking manner by the poet. Brabantio admires him, treats him with the kindness of a friend, regards him as a benefactor, often invites him to his own house, and seems to accord to him complete social equality. Yet when it comes to have Othello as a son-in-law, his nature revolts. For him the limit of race is impassible;

he would prefer the booby Roderigo, because he is a Venetian, to the hero Othello, because he is a Moor. Brabantio can only curse fatherhood when he contemplates his descendants of a different race.

But this narrow, Venetian view of things is an absurdity, and cannot be permanent. The State which defends itself by the aid of a distinct and despised race must expect to bestow honors upon those to whom it owes its own existence. That race cannot long be excluded from social equality under such circumstances, for the State is the higher, and will give the greater validity to the instruments of its own perpetuity. It must happen that these social distinctions will be ignored or subordinated, in the end, by the State. Consequently, we see in this play that the Duke, the head of authority, can only confirm the union of Othello and Desdemona. Such is the strife here portrayed between social prejudice and acquired honors by an individual of a despised race. It is manifest that the Venetians must themselves defend their State if they wish to preserve intact their Society. The latter is subordinate to the former.

Desdemona, accordingly, refuses to make these distinctions of her father and countrymen. She is an artless girl, unacquainted with the world, and seems to have been brought up in pretty strict seclusion by her father. Still she is not without artifice, for all this while she is deceiving the parental eye; it is her very nature to put on a mask, and innocence itself in her seems to prevaricate. She sees the Hero—the all-sufficient man; this is enough to captivate her heart. She hears his adventures—how he has met the greatest obstacles of the world and conquered them all. He appears to be the master over accident. It is his bravery against external danger which is portrayed; no feats of mind, or skill, or cunning are recorded. His composition has in it more of the Achilles than of the Ulysses. On this weaker side, namely, the intellectual, he will hereafter be assailed, be overcome, and perish. He is essentially the Hero, of surpassing courage and self-possession. Desdemona has, on the other hand, the characteristic element of the true woman—a loving trust. She must have a support to lean upon, a heart to confide in; the stronger they are, the more intense is her devotion. All the qualities most attractive to such a nature she sees before her. She has not imbibed the social prejudices of the time, or, perhaps, despises them; she sees Othello's "visage in his mind;" she ignores his color and race, and breaks through the barrier. Othello, too, is caught for the corresponding reason. The trust and devotion of the woman call forth love; the leaning for support arouses the most intense pleasure in giving support. The causes of their love are reciprocal:

> She loved me for the dangers I had passed,
> And I loved her that she did pity them.

The Heroic in the man calls forth the devotion of the woman, and the devotion and sympathy of the woman can only beget their like in the man. Such are the motives which the poet has elaborated in order adequately to account for this extraordinary union. The father is repaid for his social equality, which, at bottom, was a mere pretense; he is now to behold it in reality, for his own family is to be transferred to a totally different race.

Such is the collision in the Family. We are now prepared to see the same conflict pushed forward into the State. Brabantio has roused the neighborhood, and is in hot pursuit of the lovers. He finds the Moor, arrests him as a criminal, and cites him before the highest tribunal of justice. But mark! even before the arrival of Brabantio, a messenger of the government has come in great haste for Othello. The Duke is in pressing need of his services. The country is in danger; the Turk is threatening Cyprus. The two conflicting elements are thus brought together side by side. Othello obeys the double summons—on the one hand as a criminal, and on the other hand as the defender of the country. Then follows the trial. It is the same tribunal which has to try him as a malefactor and to appoint him to command against the foe. Brabantio, in his accusation, can only account for such an unnatural love by the employment of witchcraft or of some potent drug. Such is his charge. The reproach of race is always on his lips: to him it is inconceivable that his daughter should fall in love with a black monster whom she feared to look upon. How his fellow-patricians were affected by his situation may be judged from the language of the Duke, before he knows who the offender is:

> Whoe'er he be that in this foul proceeding
> Hath thus beguiled your daughter of herself,
> And you of her, the bloody book of law
> You shall yourself read in the bitter letter
> After its own sense; yea, though our proper son
> Stood in your action.

But, though the Duke might condemn his own son, he could not condemn Othello. The decision is a very unwilling one, but how can it be helped? The choice must be made—the safety of the Nation or the punishment of the offender. The appeal of Brabantio is, doubtless, most powerful. His "brothers of the State cannot but feel this wrong as their own," and, if such actions be permitted, who will be their children—the future rulers of Venice? But there can be only one result of such a trial; the State is deciding whether it shall exist, or a subordinate principle shall be asserted. The parent gives up all hope when his charge of witchcraft is disproved; he has already cursed fatherhood, in which alone such a collision is possible, and now, with a heavy heart and an ominous warning to the lovers, he asks that the Senate turn to other affairs. Othello departs, with his prize, for the wars; in his struggle with both Family and State he has been triumphant.

Such is the conclusion of the First Movement of the action, in which is portrayed the external conflict in its twofold phase. The various hostile elements have assailed the union of Othello and Desdemona from the outside, and have failed.

This First Movement almost constitutes a drama by itself, with its collisions and happy termination. Were Othello a Venetian, it would be difficult to tell why the play should not end here. But in the difference of race has been planted the germ of the internal disruption of the pair. The man has also been introduced to us whose hatred will nurse this germ into a speedy and colossal growth. So this little introductory comedy, ending in the union and triumph of the lovers, really rests upon a deeper tragedy, which is now to unfold.

II.

The Second Movement of the play exhibits the internal conflict of the Family—a conflict which brings to ruin all who participate in its guilt. The scene is now transferred from Venice to Cyprus, where Othello has supreme authority. The struggle, therefore, will not be disturbed by any external power, but will be allowed to unfold itelf in its natural and complete development. The couple, too, are here removed from the social prejudice and dislike which would assail them at home. By this transition, therefore, they become the head of the society around them; free scope is given to them to make the most of their union. Relieved of every possibility of immediate external interference on the part of authority, Othello and Desdemona must now fall back upon their internal bond of marriage.

But a disruption will take place, of which the dark plotter is Iago, who now becomes the central figure, and whose actions are the single thread of this Second Movement. His object is to sunder and destroy the pair; for this purpose he holds his three instruments, Roderigo, Cassio, and Emilia, as it were, in one hand, and Othello and wife in the other hand. The motive for his conduct has already been stated to lie in the deep injury which he believes that he has suffered from the Moor. His method is to excite in Othello the most intense jealousy, to produce which he employs various means that will be considered in their proper order. Now, it is a leading peculiarity of Othello that his character is fundamentally free from jealousy; he is of a noble, open, magnanimous disposition. The problem, then, is to explain how an unsuspicious person becomes filled with the most deadly suspicion. The character of the Moor is a contradiction—and, hence, an impossibility—without some adequate ground for the great change which it undergoes. If he were naturally jealous, there would be needed no motive for his conduct; but the difficult point lies in the fact that he is naturally without jealousy. His characterization, as well as that of Iago, has been pronounced unnatural; and so it is, unless some adequate impelling principle can be given to account for this total inversion of his nature. We shall attempt to explain the cause of his change, and to portray his gradual transition from the first surmise to the final deed of blood.

The several parties have arrived in the island. Othello still remains behind, detained by a storm which has separated him from his wife—an ominous prelude of the succeeding play. While they are waiting for his ship, a conversation arises which exhibits a new phase of Iago's character—his disbelief in the honor of woman. It must be regarded as the result of his own experience. Married life has for him brought forth only its bitterest fruits. He treats his wife with the greatest asperity and contempt, which she, with slight protest, for the present endures. But at the whole sex he aims his sarcasms; his doctrine is that woman is naturally lustful and faithless, and, moreover, fitted only for the lowest functions—

To suckle fools and chronicle small beer.

That the husband's opinion of Emilia is true is very plainly indicated in the last scene of the Fourth Act, where she openly admits that chastity is not the principle of her life. Othello is also well acquainted with her character. He knows of her falsehood and infidelity; he will not believe any of her statements, and loads her with the most opprobrious epithets.

We are now brought face to face with a question which is by no means pleasant to consider, but which has to be discussed if we wish to comprehend the poet's work. Must we regard the Moor as guilty of what Iago suspects him? There is nothing in the play which shows that Othello was innocent of the charge, but there is much which shows that he was not innocent. The very fact that this suspicion is cast upon him almost at the beginning, and is nowhere removed, seems sufficient to raise the presumption of guilt. It hangs over him like a cloud which will not pass away. Then Emilia's character, instead of precluding, strengthens the supposition of criminal intercourse, and the notion is still further upheld by the knowledge of her habits which Othello betrays. But the veil is never wholly removed. Why does not the poet openly state the offense, so as to leave no doubt? It is evident that he does not wish to soil the union with Desdemona by dwelling on Othello's incontinence, nor does he desire to throw into the background the difference of race as the leading motive of the play. Still, he would not have us forget the dark surmise; there it remains suspended over the Moor to the last. Iago, to be sure, is a liar; but his lies are meant for others, and not for himself. Besides, Iago is not more certain at first than we, his readers and hearers, are; but the complete success of his plan, which is based on the Moor's guilt, confirms, both for him and for us, the truth of the suspicion.

So much is indicated in the course of the play; but, if the deeper motives of the various characters are carefully examined, this conclusion would seem to become irresistible. Iago is manifestly assailed with the same burning jealousy which afterwards wrought such terrific effects in Othello. Now, what will be the manner of his revenge? The most logical and adequate would be, "wife for wife;" hence his first thought is to debauch Desdemona. But nothing more is heard of this plan, for it could not possibly be successful. Then comes his most shrewd and peculiar method of avenging his wrong. If he cannot dishonor Othello in reality, he can do it in appearance, with almost the same results. His purpose is to make Othello believe that Desdemona is untrue. This will be a revenge sufficient for his end. It will destroy Othello's happiness and peace of mind just as well as the truth; it will bring upon Othello that which he has brought upon Iago.

Another phase of the question now comes up for solution. How was it possible to excite such a passion in a character like that of Othello? The free, open, unsuspecting nature of the Moor is noted by Iago himself; his noble and heroic disposition would appear least likely to be subject to jealousy. Yet this is the very form of revenge chosen by Iago with surpassing skill. This is, therefore, just the weak side of Othello's character. Why? The solution of the problem lies in the fact above mentioned—that Iago's suspicion concerning Emilia is true. Othello has been guilty of adultery; he is, therefore, aware that the infidelity of wives is a fact. Here lies the germ of his belief in the faithlessness of Desdemona. His own act thus comes home to him and renders him accursed; his faith in justice can only make him more ready to think that he will be punished through his wife, since that is the mode which his own guilt suggests. Such is the initial point of the fearful jealousy of the Moor, which Iago knows exactly how to reach, since it is a matter lying wholly within his own experience; and he knows also that Othello, on account of previous criminality, must be as capable of this passion as himself. Both the revenge of Iago and the jealousy of Othello, therefore, can be adequately motived only by the guilty conduct of the Moor towards the Ancient's wife.

Moreover, there is no other ground for the relation of marriage between Iago and Emilia except as a basis for these two main motives of drama. Thus, too, we see one of the fundamental rules of Shakespeare vindicated—that man cannot escape his own deed; hence Othello is the author of his own fate, since by his guilt he has called up the avenger who will destroy him and his family, while, without the view above developed, he must appear as an innocent sufferer deceived by a malicious villain. It will, therefore, be seen that two things of the greatest importance have their sole explanation in this view, namely, the manner of Iago's revenge, and his knowledge of the assailable point in Othello's character. Here also we find the solution of the Moor's contradictory nature. He is, in general, unsuspecting; but, on account of his guilt, he is capable of one suspicion, namely, that wives may be faithless. The poet has thus added to the distinction of race—for which the Moor could not be blamed—a second motive, the criminal deed, of which he must take the responsibility. The military life of Othello will furnish the third principle—that of honor, which will impel him to destroy the wife whom he thinks to have violated it in its deepest and most tender part.

The plan of Iago, and the grounds upon which it reposes, have now been unfolded. The next task before us is to scan with care the instruments which he employs to effect his purpose. The first one is Roderigo, who stands in a wholly external relation to the main action, and is always introduced from the outside for some violent purpose. He is twice turned against Cassio, and is continually directed by the hand of Iago. His unholy pursuit has brought him to Cyprus, where he is still fed with hope, and relieved of his money by the artful Ancient. But he becomes very impatient; he is always angry at his first appearance in the scene, yet a few words from Iago fill him again with great expectations. It is curious what a predominating influence Iago's superior intelligence has over him. When alone, he knows that he is robbed and deceived; he even resolves to go home after giving Iago a good tongue-lashing. But he always yields, even against his own judgment; he cannot resist the plausibility and flattery of the Ancient, and he twice exposes, and finally loses, his life in his foolish and unrighteous enterprise.

The second, and by all means the most important, instrument in the hands of Iago is the Lieutenant, Cassio. The man is in every way adapted for exciting Othello's jealousy. He is on intimate terms with Desdemona; he is fair in external appearance, gifted with the graces of deportment, and his youthful face stands in marked contrast to the older look of Othello. Modern parlance would call him a ladies' man. But the decisive fact in his portraiture is that he is an open, notorious libertine. Iago himself has reason to suspect him, too, of undue intimacy with Emilia. This suspicion—in itself by no means so improbable, on account of her character—is, however, not confirmed in other parts of the play. But, to remove all doubt concerning Cassio's moral weakness, the poet has introduced a special person, the courtesan, Bianca. There is no other ground why such an offensive relation should be dragged into the drama. Cassio has been long acquainted with Othello, who, therefore, must have known his private habits. Cassio, it is manifest, is in every way a fit subject for suspicion, on account of his character, his external appearance, and his relation to Desdemona.

Already Iago has observed a familiarity—a little indiscreet, yet entirely innocent—between the Lieutenant and Desdemona. But Iago can do nothing unless he can bring about a total separation between Cassio and Othello, so that they will not communicate together. This, then, he proceeds to accomplish, thus destroying all opportunities for explanation, and giving occasion for the intercession of Desdemona. The dark plan of Iago is wonderfully carried out; he holds and directs Cassio with one hand and Othello with the other, yet neither knows what is controlling him. The drunken brawl causes the Lieutenant to be dismissed. Roderigo here is made the external means. Dissimulation could not be more complete. Iago has three disguises; he makes three men, Roderigo, Cassio, and Othello, believe that he is working in their interest, yet is at the same time ruining them all. He hopes also to get Cassio's place, though the main motive is to wreak revenge upon Othello, of which Cassio is a convenient instrument. Ambition is not his deepest impelling power, but revenge.

At this point we behold the supreme phase of Iago's characterization: It is his confession that he is a villain. The form of the soliloquy again appears, in which he expresses his deepest convictions. He knows that he is involving the innocent and the guilty in one common destruction; he acknowledges that he is a devil clothed in his blackest sins—that is, Iago is entirely conscious of the nature of his deed, and does not try to conceal it from himself. He at first indulges in an ironical defense of the advice which he gives to Cassio for recovering the Moor's favor; in appearance it is the best possible counsel, but it is counteracted and turned into the most deadly poison by his own dark insinuations to Othello. Such a defense, however, is the divinity of Hell, from whose sophisms his mind, at least, is free. It is thus his great boast that his intelligence is not caught in the meshes of deceptive casuistry. He does not seriously try to defend his action; still, he will have his revenge. Iago is the self-conscious villain. He knows that he is overthrowing the moral world, as far as his conduct goes; yet it must perish, since it stands in his way. There is no excusing of himself, no palliation of the deed.

> When devils will their blackest sins put on,
> They do suggest at first with heavenly shows,
> As I do now.

How complete the consciousness, and how audacious the statement, of his own character! It has been said that Iago deceives himself with his display of motives; that he persuaded himself to believe a falsehood, in his accusation of Othello. This soliloquy ought to banish forever such an opinion. No man ever knew his own mind better than Iago. Here it is seen that he clearly comprehends and acknowledges the nature of his deed. He is aware that every man is a villain who does what he is doing. However deserved may be his revenge upon Othello, he can have no justification for ruining Cassio and Desdemona, and resorting to the means which he now employs.

The third instrument of Iago is Emilia, his wife, who is the devoted attendant of Desdemona, and is employed by the latter in her communication with the cashiered Lieutenant. Iago thus has a means of obtaining information concerning their plans. Desdemona is now set to interceding for Cassio; she is urged on by both Emilia and Cassio, who are in their turn directed by Iago. This part of the plan easily succeeds.

Such are the instruments; but Iago himself has to manage the far more difficult case of Othello in his relation to his wife, Desdemona. This brings us now to the main development of the drama, and, perhaps, the most complete psychological portraiture in Shakespeare. Iago begins the manipulation of Othello's mind through a series of influences adapted exactly to the shifting phases of the Moor's disposition, and increasing in intensity to the end. Given a noble, unsuspecting character, the design is to portray those causes which not only turn it into the opposite of itself, but make it destroy its most beloved object. The primal basis to work upon lies in Othello's own consciousness of guilt. The first point is to touch faintly his suspicion, which is accomplished most easily, for he readily imagines what he himself has done to others may happen in his own case. We see how the slightest hint from Iago casts a shadow over his whole being.

> *Iago.*—Ha! I like not that.
> *Othello.*—What dost thou say?
> *Iago.*—Nothing my lord, or if—I know not what.
> *Othello.*—Was not that Cassio parted from my wife? etc.

A word from Desdemona is sufficient, however, to allay his mistrust, but another word from Iago is sufficient to arouse it anew in all its intensity. Can any one doubt that this hasty suspicion, on the part of an unsuspecting character, can have any other ground than the consciousness of the same kind of guilt which he is so ready to suspect in another? Iago's artifices are unquestionably skillful, but he found a most fruitful and well-prepared soil; and, besides, his very skillfulness rests upon his comprehending and utilizing so thoroughly the psychological effects of Othello's crime. It is impossible to think that an honest and innocent man could have been so easily led astray.

Othello's suspicion is now fully aroused, but with it the difficulty of Iago's task is proportionately greater. How will the latter prevent that suspicion from becoming universal—from being directed against himself as well as against Cassio and Desdemona? His first plan, therefore, must be to confirm his own honesty in the mind of Othello with the same care and skill that he infuses distrust against the other two. He has to fill the Moor with suspicion, and, at the same time, to avoid the suspicion of doing that very thing.

It is this double, and apparently contradictory, ability that gives such a lofty idea of Iago's intellectual power. But how does he proceed to accomplish his purpose? At first, by the apparent unwillingness with which he tells his dark surmises, and by the pretended dislike with which he assails the reputation of people. In these cases he seems to manifest the most tender regard for the rights and character of others; indeed, he repeatedly confesses his own tendency to suspect wrongfully. Such a man appears to be absolutely just—more just, indeed, to others than to himself. But all these things might be the tricks of a false, disloyal knave, as Othello well knows and says. Now comes Iago's master-stroke, by which he completely spans the Moor's mind, and turns it in whatever direction he pleases—"Othello, beware of jealousy;" and then he proceeds to give a description of its baleful nature. What, now, is the attitude of the Moor? This is the very passion with which he knows himself to be affected. Never more can he harbor a doubt of Iago's honesty; for has not the latter warned him of his danger? Iago thus tears out and brings to the Moor's own look his deepest consciousness—his greatest peril. He knows the truth of the admonition. Iago now can proceed with more certainty and directness; he cannot be suspected of exciting jealousy, for this is the very thing against which he has given so potent a warning. Thus Othello is thrown on his own defense— is compelled to dissemble his true feelings; thus he declares that he is not jealous, when he really is. He is forced into the necessity of disguise—exchanges positions with Iago; yet the latter well knows, indeed says, that jealousy cannot be eradicated when once excited, but ever creates itself anew—feeds on its own meat. Such is the twofold purpose of Iago, as manifested in this dialogue—to inspire Othello with suspicion, and yet to shun suspicion himself.

Othello is caught; the reason is manifest. A universally suspicious nature could not have been thus entrapped; it must have suspected the purpose of Iago also, with all his adroitness. Othello is, however, naturally unsuspecting. But guilt has furnished the most fruitful soil for one kind of suspicion; that soil Iago cultivates. Hence the Moor is afraid of only one thing—the infidelity of his wife; the tricks of Iago lie outside of the horizon of his suspicion. On the other hand, a completely innocent nature could not have been thus entrapped; the psychological basis would be wholly wanting. Here is seen the reason for the marked outlines of Othello's character. He is not naturally suspicious, otherwise he must have suspected the purpose of Iago; nor is he guiltless, for, if he were, his jealousy could not have been reached by any such artifice.

Nothing can be more impressive and instructive than the contemplation of this mental development. It is most clearly shown that man's deed becomes forever a part of his being—that he can never free himself from its effects upon his own disposition. The deed does not fly away into the past and lose itself in vacuity after it is done, but sinks into the deepest consciousness of the doer, and gives coloring to his future conduct. The negative wicked act must cast its dark shadow upon the soul, and thus change the character of the individual, whereby he is prepared for punishment. In the case of Othello we shudder at the manner in which guilt finds the most subtle avenues for returning upon the doer. The deed may be secret to the gaze of the world, but it sinks deep into the mind; this is altered, and retribution will follow. Such a portraiture is worth, to a rational being, all the insipid moralizing of ages.

Iago can now be more bold; Othello cannot suspect him. Hitherto he has directed his hints and surmises against Cassio; but now he begins to assail Desdemona with the most artful innuendoes. She is from Venice, where it is the custom to be untrue. She deceived her father; you know she pretended in his presence to tremble at your looks when she loved you most—a statement which has increased force from the parting admonition of Brabantio: "Moor, she has deceived her father, and may thee." As preparatory to the final and culminating charge, Iago renews his warning against jealousy. But this third point the Moor anticipates, so well prepared has he been, and thus shows that it was always in his mind. It is the distinction of race. Hardly is it hinted by him, when Iago catches up the unfinished thought and dwells upon it with terrific emphasis. How unnatural, horrible, the union between man and woman of different complexion and clime! and hence how much more ready will she be to break it, after becoming disgusted! We see with what effect this reproach takes hold of Othello in his succeeding soliloquy. It recalls all the bitterness of many years, the taunts of Brabantio, finally the collision resting upon this very basis, which collision he has just passed through. Desdemona broke over all social distinctions of nation and race; here is the retribution—jealousy. The greater her sacrifice the more unnatural does it seem, and the more suspected she becomes. Moreover, we catch a glimpse of that to which this jealousy will lead —destruction for himself and for the loved one rather than be dishonored in his domestic life. The passion of jealousy rests upon the monogamic nature of marriage; when that relation is disturbed, jealousy will, and ought to, arise in all its intensity. Another element is added in the case of

Othello, springing from his military career—honor. He cannot endure shame and reproach—he who has never had any taint cast upon his courage or reputation.

The passion has overwhelmed him; he cannot do or think of anything else; his occupation is gone. So Iago knows; not all the drowsy medicines of the world will restore to him peace of mind. Iago, indeed, has obtained his knowledge from experience; in fact, his own present activity has the same root. For a moment Othello reacts, suspects, notices that no positive proofs have been produced, but only surmises. He turns upon Iago and grasps him by the throat; yet, how can he continue his suspicion; how can he blame Iago? Did not the latter warn him of these very consequences? One word from his Ancient, therefore, makes him release his hold. Othello must believe that Iago has been honest with him. Once more Iago speaks of his jealousy; it is a thought that cuts the Moor through and through, whose truth he can not deny.

Othello will have more direct proofs than surmise; Iago is ready with them. He then narrates the dream of Cassio, which Othello, of course, has no means of verifying. But the charge is direct, plain, and based upon an occurrence. Next comes the apparently complete demonstration—the handkerchief. Here is a fact which Othello does verify sufficiently to discover that Desdemona has not the article sought for in her possession. Still, whether Cassio has received it or not he cannot verify as long as they are asunder. Finally, the trick wherein Othello overhears the conversation about Bianca, and thinks it is about Desdemona, seems to him to be an acknowledgment of guilt from the mouth of Cassio himself. It ought to be added that, before this, Iago has made the direct charge that Cassio has revealed to him Desdemona's infidelity. Othello is so overcome that he falls into a swoon, and then afterward, through the words of the Lieutenant, he seems to get a complete confirmation of Iago's statement. Othello is now resolved; the swoon indicates the changed man; he has gone through his demonic baptism; his mad suspicion has been wrought up to the point where no explanations can mitigate its ferocity. He investigates, but his resolution is already taken. No declaration of Emilia, whose character he cannot trust, and no denials of Desdemona, who is the person suspected, can shake his belief. The passion has taken too deep a hold; he will not, and can not, withdraw himself from its grasp. The plan of Iago has reached its climax. He began with faint surmise, he proceeded to direct assertions, and lastly he gives what seems to be a demonstration to the senses.

Two persons, Emilia and Cassio, have now revealed themselves fully, and we are enabled to ascertain their function in the play. In regard to Emilia, she makes no pretense to virtue as her principle in life; indeed, she quite acknowledges her own infidelity. We have already seen with what contempt she was treated by her husband; in her character and declarations is found a complete justification of his suspicion, though she naturally denies to him the truth of the charge. Previously she was submissive, but now she requites his disrespect in full measure; she also intimates that he is untrue to the marriage relation. This ill-starred couple, therefore, have already passed through the experience of Othello and Desdemona, and both show that they are well acquainted with all the manifestations of jealousy.

But her most peculiar trait is her insight into the whole spiritual net-work of Iago's plans; she thus is an explanation of her husband to a certain extent. In the first place, she at once comprehends the exact nature of Othello's passion; she declares that her inference is from the similar behavior of Iago. Secondly, she sees that some person has excited the Moor's jealousy; it could not have arisen of itself in his bosom. Thirdly, she is certain that Iago is this person, though she does not say so openly, and she gives him several secret thrusts. The motives which impelled Iago, and the grounds upon which he based his success, appear to be distinctly apprehended by this strange, shrewd woman, whose redeeming traits are her devotion to Desdemona, and her courageous defense of innocence.

Cassio has always fared well, receiving the greatest praise from even ministerial critics, notwithstanding his scandalous relation to Bianca. It is hard to tell why he has been so lauded, unless the reason be found in the temperance speech which he makes after being cashiered for getting

drunk. Soberness is apt to bring such repentance,
along with resolutions to reform. He also laments
the loss of reputation, by which he clearly does
not mean reputation for morality and decency, but
the empty bauble of military glory. It is true that
he is a favorite of the simple-hearted Desdemona,
but, on account of his character, he is employed as
the instrument of her destruction.

III.

The Third Movement of the play, the Retribution
follows. The tragic preparation of the previous
portions is carried to the consummation. First,
Roderigo is led to assail Cassio, but is slain by
Iago. It is his just desert, for he has willed, and
tried to accomplish both adultery and murder.
Desdemona is killed by the Moor; jealousy has
done its worst—has slain its most beloved object.
The ground for her fate has been already stated.
She violated the conditions of the Family in marrying
a husband of a different race. Othello himself
feels that she has shocked the strongest
instincts of nature by her conduct; hence he can
easily be brought to believe her untrue. That is,
jealousy is sure to arise under such circumstances.
It cannot be her disregard of the parental will
which brings on her tragic fate. The second and
subordinate motive of Othello's jealousy, namely,
his previous incontinence, can, of course, have
nothing to do with the guilt of Desdemona. That
has its baleful effect upon his character, as has
already been shown; it brings upon him a fearful

retribution, and determines the method of Iago's revenge. Still, a man may be fired with jealousy and yet may not be ready to destroy its object. A third element, therefore, is added to Othello's character—honor. It is intimately connected with his military life. The soldier always prefers death to what he deems dishonor; he would rather destroy the dearest object in existence, and be destroyed himself, than be stained with disgrace. Hence, when Othello is convinced of Desdemona's guilt he must proceed to kill her.

Desdemona's last word is an unveracity—who wishes to call it the harsher name? Yet it is told in love, in deep devotion to her husband, who then and there shows the influence of her prevarications upon himself: "She's like a liar gone to burning hell." Such is her reward for her sacrifice of truth to affection; her deceptions have undermined her husband's faith in her, quite as much as the insinuations of Iago; knowing that she falsifies, he cannot believe her when she tells the truth. To her love she immolates veracity--that is, her husband's faith in her; one virtue in excess blots out the other, as is so often seen in Shakespeare. To Iago's warp she furnishes the woof; without her aid his schemes would be nothing. Desdemona's tragic career is made up of three elements; first, the conflict with the parental will; second, the race-conflict; third, her foible of character, which meets these conflicts, not with the firmness of truth, but with an amiable yielding to falsehood.

Iago at last is unmasked. The whole breadth of

his wicked plan is exposed, mainly by his wife Emilia. It has been before noted how completely she fathomed the design of her husband; she is, indeed, the reflection of his spiritual nature. Now she glances through the entire scheme of villainy. Iago knows her sharp insight; he tries to stop her speech, but, when he cannot, stabs her. The truth flashes upon the mind of Othello. He is ready to practice upon himself that severe justice which he imagined that he was employing against others. Honor, too, will no longer permit him to live. As he once slew a Turk who traduced the State, so now he will slay himself who has acted so as to deserve the same fate. There seems some design of the poet in one incident: Othello attempts, but is not permitted, to slay Iago. The latter has really suffered a greater injury from the Moor than he has inflicted; he cannot, therefore, receive his punishment from the hands of Othello.

This tragedy deals essentially with one relation of the Family—that of husband and wife—though the father of Desdemona appears for a short time. There are three pairs, whose function is to represent in regular gradation negative phases of marriage. First come Othello and Desdemona, a unity resting on love and fidelity, but which is, nevertheless, contrary to a necessary condition of the Family. Hence their tie is disrupted, and both perish. The second couple is Iago and Emilia, who are married, but have no emotional basis for their union; both are certainly wanting in love, and both are probably wanting in fidelity.

They, too, are destroyed. The third pair is Cassio and Bianca, who are unmarried, but still represent the purely sensual relation of the sexes in its hostility to the possible existence of the Family. They both are preserved; the poet would seem to indicate that they had committed no tragic violation of an institution which they had never entered. Then there are various cross-relations of these individuals, which give other negative phases of married life, as that of Othello and Emilia. The peculiar attitude of Roderigo towards Desdemona must also be classed as one of these manifestations. In general, the conjugal bond of the Family has here its various collisions portrayed, and this drama may, therefore, be named the Tragedy of Husband and Wife.

This play has suffered, perhaps more than any other work of Shakespeare, from the amiable sentimentality of expositors who have wrenched and tortured it, till they behold in it two angelic beings caught unawares and hurled into the infernal pit by a black demon in human form. But in their attempt to save Othello and Desdemona, they destroy Shakespeare; they tumble into chaos the ethical order of the poet, which is the best part, nay, the very soul, of him. Satan is not the ruler of this world, nor does Shakespeare picture it thus; and, surely, to damn Providence is not the way to save man. In this play, too, we are to see the moral cosmos, and the poet as its stern but loyal revealer.

Moreover we are to let the light from other

plays shine upon this one, which we shall find to be no exception, but in harmony with Shakespeare's poetic law. He serves up to man man's deed, which is destiny instinct with freedom and responsibility; we are to see that such is what he does in *Othello*. We disjoint the entire Shakespearian edifice, if we make the innocent perish simply through their innocence. In the physical world accident may destroy from the outside, but not in the ethical or providential world, which it is the function of tragedy to represent. There the action is always returnable, and adjudges the penalty. Iago is inside Othello as well as outside; if he were merely outside, he could do little harm. The play shows two Iagos; the one is external, but is conspiring with an internal Iago in Othello, and rousing in the latter his own jealousy and deviltry. The outer demon calls to the inner, and wonderful is the response.

Doubtless the best way of finding out what the poet intended is to compare his sources, when we can get at them, with his completed work. Now, we know the quarter whence *Othello* is derived; it is taken from an Italian novel, by Giraldi Cinthio, which was printed in 1565. Whether Shakespeare took the story directly from the original, or obtained it in some other way, cannot at present be ascertained; but it is very clear that the play is based upon Cinthio's novel. The incidents and the order of them are quite the same in both; the localities, and the change from Venice to Cyprus are the same in both; the chief personages and

* You mean, short story! --- novella

their general relations are the same in both. Still the poet has made some alterations. The novel of Cinthio gives to Iago and Emilia a child three years old, which Shakespeare for the best of reasons takes away from that ill-assorted pair. Cassio has, apparently, a wife in the novel (*donna in casa*), who is not, and ought not to be, found in the play, in consistency with his function. And just here is the source of that desperate line, which speaks of Cassio as "a fellow almost damned in a fair wife." This slipped into the play just at the beginning from the novel, and was not afterwards corrected. Possibly Shakespeare at first intended to employ Cassio's wife, but dropped her, as Iago's wife, Emilia, represented sufficiently all that he wanted.

We now begin to catch a glimpse of the poet in his study, as he starts to arrange his material. We look further, and find that he has kept the incidents of the novel, but added or changed the motives; that he retains the figures in the main, but deepens them into characters. This is the Shakespearian alchemy; the story, the plot, the personages are seized from the outside as the poet's own by divine right; but behold! that outer world of incident is transmuted into the inner world of spirit, and the castle of Fate in which man seems to be imprisoned by the Gods is shown to be a structure built of his own deed.

The poet, accordingly, furnishes to the novel what we may call motivation, which makes his drama. This he must do with intention, as it implies a conscious changing of one thing for another, or an addition of something which did not before exist. In the novel, for instance, Iago is not moved by jealousy of Othello, as he is in the drama, but by an unlawful love for Desdemona, which, when unsuccessful, turns to hate. Accordingly, the initial point of his character is wholly changed, and just herein we must mark the distinctive Shakespearian conception which transforms the entire treatment of the story. Iago's hate in the novel is directed against Desdemona, not against Othello primarily, as in the drama. The poet himself puts this change into the mouth of Iago:

> Now I do love her too,
> Not out of absolute lust * * * *
> But partly led to diet my revenge
> For that I do suspect the lusty Moor—

Here the change from "absolute lust," which is the motive of the novel, to jealousy, which is the motive of the drama, is indicated. Iago is really the jealous man at the start, who simply transplants himself into the fertile field of Othello's soul. To this primal conception of Iago all the characters now adjust themselves. Emilia, the wife, is changed much from her part in the novel, in which she is not suspected by the husband or by the reader, and gives no cause for suspicion, through conduct or speech, being a fair and honest young woman, (*bella et honesta giovane,*) and a mother too. Othello's jealousy, in the novel, springs up from a mere innuendo of Iago as in the drama; but the suggestion of the guilty deed lying back of the jealousy and motiving it, belongs to Shakespeare alone, who must, therefore, have introduced it with design as a motive. Cassio's relation to Bianca, once faintly hinted in the novel, is woven into the texture of the whole play, and is made one of the forces of the dramatic action. With the motive of Iago in the novel, that of unlawful love for Desdemona, the poet fits up a new but subordinate character, Roderigo. Moreover, the conflict of Desdemona with her family in the novel is disposed of in a few sentences, but the play gives the entire First Act to it alone. Here again we may note Shakespeare's delight in portraying this collision between the right of the parent and the choice of the daughter.

If we now weigh what the poet has added to the novel, we find that it is not in the line of incident—even the affair of the handkerchief is in the old story—but in line of motives. These have been elaborated in the preceding essay. Not only do we find them in the drama, but we find the poet consciously putting them there from a novel which does not contain them; for once we have been able to catch Proteus in his transformation.

In such manner we see the poet transmute a slender Italian tale into a colossal image of his world-order, and make out of it a book which lasts forever. At the same time he has placed into this world-order the free-acting, accountable man, and has shown him therein as the architect of his own destiny. But in the old book of Cinthio, accident rules chiefly, man is unfree and a victim; the devil runs loose for the purpose of seizing his guiltless prey. A view of Providence may be found in the Italian romancer, but it is a dissolving view, vanishing into dark vacuity. Still, there are modern eyes that see in the masterpiece of Shakespeare hardly more of the divine order than is to be seen in the work of Cinthio; a lapse which seems almost like that of original sin. At such a view of the play, it is no wonder that a tender-hearted commentator should cry out in agony: "I wish this tragedy had never been written."

KING LEAR.

This drama, during the life-time of its author, has a very short history. Two Quartos (and possibly more) were issued in the year 1608, from which fact we may infer that the play was popular with Shakespeare's reading public, already large, and evidently keeping pace with his play-going public. But it must have been written several years before 1608; it, too, had to have, apparently, some time for growing into popular favor. It was acted in the year 1606, as is inferred from an entry in the Stationers' Registers, at which time we must consider it to have been in a state of substantial completion. Allusions to events of the year 1605 are supposed to be contained in it, with much probability; but, for this reason, its composition need not be limited to that year or to any given year, or even to a half-dozen years. The subject must have been working a long time in the poet's mind; he had seen it on the stage, had read it in poem and chronicle. We may be sure that Shakespeare's *King Lear* did not suddenly spring from his brain in perfect shape; he composed it gradually from the green-room, with his eye turned outwardly upon the public, doubtless, but what is most important, with his eye turned inwardly upon the demands of his theme. Somewhere between the years 1603-6, in the height of his tragic period, it must have attained its present supreme form, since, on the whole, it is Shakespeare's most perfect, if not his greatest, tragedy.

The story or mythus he found ready-made, as usual; it had been elaborated by his own people and handed down in many popular shapes. The chief incidents are given to the poet, who, in this case as elsewhere, adds the motives; the fortuitous occurrence, in his hands, becomes the human deed, and the outer figure of man is filled with the inner soul. In the legend, Lear divides the realm among his three daughters, but there is no meaning in it specially, till Shakespeare shows the inherent character of the king who can make such a division. This possibly lurks unborn in the legend, too; but the poet sees it and brings it to light; then we all can behold it.

The impression left upon the mind by this drama is that of terrific grandeur. In it is found, probably, the strongest language ever written or spoken by a human being. Dante has passages of fiery intensity, Æschylus has strains of wonderful sublimity, but nothing in either of these poets is equal to the awful imprecations of Lear. The grand characteristic of the play is strength—Titanic strength—which can only be adequately compared to the mightiest forces of Nature. There is a world-destroying element in it which oppresses the individual and makes him feel like fleeing from the crash of the Universe. The superhuman power, passion, and expression can only be symbolized by the tempest or volcano; it is, indeed, the modern battle of the Giants and the Gods. Shakespeare, like other poets, seems to have had his Titanic epoch, and his *King Lear* may well be called, in a certain sense, the most colossal specimen of literary Titanism. Not without a touch of the deepest kinship with Nature is the storm introduced—the fierce violence and struggle of the elements.

Yet the tempestuous character of the play is but one phase of it; there is also a mildness, sweetness, gentleness, charity in it, which belongs of necessity to the complete theme. A one-sided treatment is not the highest; if there is a getting into a storm, there is also a getting out of it. From the Fourth Act the passionate upheavals begin to cease, the work of peace and reconciliation starts, there is a gradual calming down of the volcano, the style has a softer touch; though there still be war and discord, we feel in the very language that they are in the process of being overcome. Two styles, we might say, are employed in the drama, with the subtlest adjustment to the subject-matter. This transition in style is doubtless felt by careful readers; but it must be seen to be in perfect harmony with the transition in thought.

It will be noticed that the action of the play lies mainly in the sphere of the Family, and portrays one of its essential relations—that of parents and children. The conflicts arising from this relation involve also brothers and sisters in strife. The domestic side of life is thus torn with fearful struggles, and its quiet affection and repose are turned into a display of malignant hate and passion. Each element is present. There is on the one hand the most heroic fidelity, and on the other the most wanton infidelity. The parents are both faithful and faithless to their relation; so are the children, taken collectively. Such are its contradictory principles, and hence arises the conflict in which the offending individuals perish, since they destroy the very condition of their own existence, namely, the Family. But those who have been true to their domestic relations, and have not otherwise committed wrong, are preserved. It is essentially the story of fidelity and infidelity to the Family.

Still we must note that the action has a tendency to burst the limits of the Family, and to rise into more universal relations. A commonwealth is also involved, Lear is monarch as well as parent, his children, too, are rulers; thus the political element is whirled into the domestic cataclysm, and the wrong of the home becomes the wrong of the government. The classes of society are also infected, as we may see in Gloster; indeed, it is not too much to say that this drama presents a condensed picture out of the World's History; the decline and corruption of a State, and its process of freeing itself from that corruption, through war and tragedy, till final restoration. So the family of Lear, in its domestic limits, is made, by the cunning of the poet, to cast an image of the Universal Family.

The spirit of *King Lear* belongs emphatically to Shakespeare's own time. The play takes its mythical setting from pre-historic Britain, "before the building of Rome," says Holinshed, the chronicler, from whom the poet, in part at least, derived the story. But the drama, as it now stands, reaches to the very heart of the age of the Tudors and Stuarts, and reveals to us the disease of absolute authority, showing how such an authority wrecks society on the one hand, and, on the other, wrecks the monarch who exercises it. In this sense the present drama is historical, and Shakespeare shows himself the poet of the English, and indeed of the whole Anglo-Saxon consciousness, whose history is largely made up of the attempt to put legal limits upon an absolute sovereignty.

There can be no greater mistake than to explain *King Lear* by referring it to a barbarous period. It is Elizabethan, even in its most revolting incident, the putting out the eyes of Gloster. Its manifold anachronisms we never think of, except by an effort of erudition; then the entire play becomes one monster of anachronism, which swallows all the rest. The poet himself, in a passage suspected by some editors, laughs at his violations of chronology: "This prophecy Merlin shall make, for I live before his time." Still, the setting is mythical and not historical; the poet takes his mythus from a time before history, and pours into it the thoughts and feelings of his own age.

Besides drawing from the story in Holinshed, Shakespeare undoubtedly took dramatic materials freely from an old play, which also went under the name of Lear. This old play is wholly without the part of Gloster and his sons, but is confined to the story of Lear, which furnishes incident, suggestion, and skeleton to Shakespeare's work. It has a happy end. Lear is restored to his kingdom and Cordelia lives; it is, therefore, not a tragedy. Shakespeare has changed its very essence; we can see that he consciously made Lear and Cordelia tragic, contrary both to the old play and to Holinshed, his two main sources; and it is curious to note, that Tate, in re-modeling Shakespeare's play, went back to its primitive form, and saved Lear and Cordelia. So we are forced to ask: What grounds had Shakespeare for making these two characters, especially Cordelia, tragic?

Such a question, however, must be deferred for the present, in order that we may look at the second story which the poet has interwoven into his work, the story of Gloster. This has also the mythical form originally, and is taken from Sir Philip Sidney's *Arcadia*, in which is told the tale of the Paphlagonian unkind King, who has two sons, legitimate and illegitimate, faithful and faithless, and who treats them and is treated by them in the same way that we find in the story of Gloster. Moreover, Sidney's narrative breathes the very soul of compassion, and one thinks, in reading it, that Shakespeare may have drawn thence his germinal idea of that world of charity which envelopes and supports the tragedy of *King Lear* with all its terrible sufferings.

Now to bring these two stories together, and to knit them into one action and one idea, manifestly requires a conscious planning on the part of the poet. Here we can catch a glimpse of him in his workshop; at least we see his raw materials and then we see his finished product. An outer link connects the two stories, the relation of parents and children, but also an inner link connects them in a common idea, in a common charity and uncharity. These two stories give the plot and underplot, or, as we shall call them, the two threads of the play.

The drama presupposes in these two stories, two deeds, done by two men, Gloster and Lear, which deeds by time have solidified into character, and have been built into the temple of life itself; that is, they have hardened into the spirit's boundary within, and have become the world's environment without, for these two human souls. Gloster's act of incontinence, at which he once blushed, though now he is "brazed to it," has entered not only his outward existence, but has wound itself into his very soul and transformed that, during a score of years and more, till it becomes the source of his punishment. Lear's arbitrary conduct, continued long, till it has ossified into character with age, has made for him a world in which he has to live and take the penalty of his action. Thus man's deed is seen to be the architect of the outer edifice of life, as well as the moulder of the inner spirit.

Authority is excellent and may bring forth the highest offspring of human conduct, but it runs always the danger of giving birth to a demon, insolence, which has no charity. Lear, the man of authority, has begotten its two sides in his two sets of children; he has the good child, yet he is father of the demon also, nay, of two demons, who thus show him the parent of more evil than good. Gloster's act, too, has begotten a demon in a son, Edmund, who destroys him, yet inside the family it is good and begets another son, Edgar, who saves him. Such is Shakespeare's dramatic portraiture of the deed; in its image, cast into a brief play, he shows the whole cycle of human action.

Character, then we behold here in its deepest significance, as it stands in relation to the ethical institutions of man. An individual flings his deed into the roaring stream of Time, he is never the same thereafter, that action is transforming him. But we must rise to the supreme standpoint of the poet; he is not simply depicting single characters, he has his last look upon the society, the totality in which the individual moves, which we may call a world, of which the individuals are but the atoms. This world the poet portrays, showing its rise and fall, the corruption and the recovery, a grand revolution in the spirit's solar system, the process of ages compressed into a three hours' spectacle. Yes, we must rise to this point of view in order to see from the altitude where the poet stands, and look with his vision on what he sees.

Accordingly we shall behold the entire drama

separating into two parts or movements, the first of which embraces three Acts and shows the breaking up of the Institutional World by an inner disease, which has been introduced by Lear and Gloster. The very persons who have violated institutions have obtained control of them and are administering them, in order to banish and destroy those who have shown most truly the institutional spirit. It is the mighty collapse of society, in which the individual and the social order around him fall into complete discord. This is the Perverted World, in which the wrong ones have the right, and the right ones have the wrong. But with the Fourth Act, the return out of disorder begins; the shattered Institutional World purifies itself in the fire of war; the faithful ones assert their right of control, and the faithless ones become faithless to one another, while their power disintegrates of itself. Such is the second Movement showing the restoration, and the whole drama is a grand social cycle, including the essential process of history, giving a picture of a world destroyed and then restored, the tragedy not merely of individuals, but of institutions, yet with the recovery of the latter from their malady.

Such are the two organic Movements of the play, which, however, pass into each other by the finest and most intricate net work, showing a double guilt and a double retribution. The First Movement exhibits the complete disintegration of the Family, with the first guilt and the first retribution—the wrong of the parents and its punishment. Lear banishes his daughter; his daughters, in turn, drive him out of doors. Gloster expels from home and disinherits his true and faithful son, in favor of the illegitimate and faithless son, and is then himself falsely accused and betrayed by the latter. Thus the disruption is complete,—the parents expelled, the false triumphant, the faithful in disguise and banishment. Such is the First Movement in its domestic phase—the wrong done by the parents to their children and its punishment. The Second Movement will unfold the second retribution springing from the second guilt—the wrong done by the children to their parents and its punishment. It must be observed, however, that the deeds of the faithless children, which are portrayed in the First Movement of the drama, constitute their guilt. On the one hand, they are the instruments of retribution, but, on the other hand, their conduct is a violation of ethical principle as deep as that of their parents. They are the avengers of guilt, but in this very act become themselves guilty, and receive punishment. The general result, therefore, of the Second Movement will be the completed retribution. Lear and his three guilty daughters—for we have to include Cordelia in this category—as well as Gloster and his guilty son, perish. Such is this terrible tragedy of the Family, with its double sweep of guilt and penalty; but just through this tragedy comes the purification as well as the restoration of the Institutional World.

The Threads of the drama are fundamentally

two, which, however, are differently arranged in the separate Movements. For instance, in the First Movement the one Thread is plainly the family of Gloster, the other is the family of Lear. Both rest upon the same ultimate thought; the one can behold its features in the other, as it were, in a mirror; the drama gives a double reflection of the same content. Both fathers cause a disruption of their families by their uncharitable passion; they drive off the faithful children and cherish the faithless ones; they hand over to the latter their property and power; upon both falls the penalty. There are, however, many differences of character, situation and incident between the two Threads; at the heart there is unity, on the surface there is variety. The one father has only daughters, the other has only sons; each represents thus a side of the Family. Lear is king, Gloster is subject; both taken together show that the conflict is not limited to one rank, but pervades the chief classes of society. Lear is arbitrary, Gloster is superstitious, both are uncharitable. It is a curious fact that the wife of neither appears; long since she dropped out of this world of domestic discord, possibly was its first victim.

In the Second Movement which is the way out of the conflict, there are still two Threads, but they have to be ordered differently. The faithful of both families come together, in their banishment, in order to protect their parents; this is the First Thread, which, as we shall see, has two quite distinct strands, that of Edgar and that of Cordelia.

The Second Thread of this Second Movement is made up of the faithless of both families, who now coalesce; they triumph in the battle, in the external conflict, but there necessarily arises an internal conflict, a struggle among themselves; for how can the faithless be faithful to one another? (The jealousy of the two sisters leads to a conspiracy which ends in their destruction; Edmund, faithless to both, falls at last by the hand of his brother, whom he has so deeply wronged.)

On these organic lines we are now to study the play, and unfold the psychological changes of character, which touch almost every note in the gamut of the human soul from sanity to madness. Particularly the grand transitions must be noted and accounted for, since everything is in process—not only the individual, but also the entire group and the entire drama; as in life itself, the part moves and the totality moves. Development is here, organic development; in fact, this play may be taken as the type of the poet's structure of a tragedy. If we begin and work out from *King Lear*, we catch more readily than in any other way, the archetypal form underlying the rest of his tragedies. The division into Threads and Movements is more strongly marked and more clearly derived from the primal conception, in the present work, than in any other drama of Shakespeare's. In fact, a statement of its organic parts is, of itself, quite sufficient to reveal the indwelling thought. The two original stories, of which the action is composed, designate the two Threads with perfect clearness, however much the various strands of these two Threads shift about in the course of the play. Quite as strongly marked are the two Movements—the sweep into and out of the storm, physical and also spiritual, wherein, too, both Structure and Idea are seen to fuse together at last, and become one, as they are, in the final synthesis, inseparable.

But this ultimate view we are hardly yet ready for, it must come at the end, not at the beginning. We are still in the sphere of analysis, which, as just given, is intended as a sort of tabular statement to guide the reader through the various complications of the play. If the two distinctions of Threads and Movements which have been above unfolded are not carefully thought out, they may become a source of confusion, instead of a means of comprehension. Let it be borne in mind that the Threads divide the drama lengthwise, while the Movements as before explained, divide it crosswise. Each Thread in each Movement will be elaborated in proper order. But the notion must not be entertained that these distinctions are external and arbitrary; on the contrary, they are organic; they reveal the essential members of the dramatic Whole, all of which must be finally seen springing from the structural thought.

I.

We shall now follow out the First Movement, which is the fuller and longer of the two. It shows the process of society toward wrong, peversion and dissolution, symbolized by the transition into the storm of the Third Act. The social framework is falling to pieces; a disease, which is bringing death, has taken lodgment in the body politic. Now, if we should name the disease, we would call it the want of charity in human character—charity in its universal sense. There is a tendency to selfishness, and therewith to revenge, which, in the ruling class especially, undermines social order; no patience, but intense passion, which seethes up in volcanic fury at any restraint or limit; we behold a world in which there is no endurance of others' weaknesses or wrongs, at least on the part of those in authority.

Charity is a well-known religious doctrine; it inculcates long-suffering, alms-giving, and a humane regard for our fellow-man, chiefly from the emotional side of our nature. But now we are to extend our insight into its meaning till we see it based upon the deepest foundations of reason; human conduct becomes a contradiction without it; nay, man's freedom is impossible, if he have not charity. For revenge drives us to act, not through ourselves, but through what somebody else has done, which action we are going to requite. Reason, turning preacher for the nonce, thus exhorts, out of the heart of this play: Do not let others place their limits upon you, maintain your freedom. Be charitable, and no man by doing wrong or being hateful, can make you do wrong or be hateful. But if you have the spirit of revenge, or even of requital, then you say: Because he has done that wrong or meanness to me, I shall do it to him, I shall pay him back. Therein, however, you will always get the worst; you lose your charity, and with it you lose your freedom. For you permit your deed to be determined by his deed, your conduct is directed by the person whom you despise, by the very action you reprobate; and so your action stands as your own everlasting judgment of yourself against yourself. For have you not condemned his deed? And yet you turn around and repeat it; you let your enemy rule your life, you surrender to him your soul. Opposed to requital is charity who suffers long, and still more, preserves to man his freedom—that is, the determination of his life from within, and not from without. True charity is universal, not destructible by any outside power, least of all by its own enemy.

It is the function of Institutions, especially of the State, to bring home to man his guilty deed, but it is not the function of the individual. The relation of man to man is that of Charity, Recognition. Justice, indeed, the world must have, being based upon the return of the deed to the doer; but I am not to bring that return, but the world, through organized order, else it is revenge. Every man must have his punishment voiced by the Universal in some form, not by an Individual, otherwise it is his own guilty act over again. Vengeance is mine, saith the Lord God; surely it is not yours.

But thus it is not asserted that non-resistance is always the way to meet conflict. The individual has the right of physical self-defense, upon which life hangs, but not the right of revenge, which is the giving back what you have received, because you have received it. To prevent character or life from being destroyed, instant resistance may be necessary; but to requite personally the wrong which another has done, is a different matter. The deed accomplished is no longer subject to the private tribunal, it is then the world's.

This idea of charity is the test by which the leading characters of the present play are gauged. But we are not to infer that the poet is the moralizer as such; he is the artist, and specially the dramatic artist, who holds up before us the human deed. Still the test of the deed, whether in life or art, is ultimately ethical, ethical in the broadest sense, which includes not merely correct moral conduct, but the relation of man to the highest institutions.

1. We shall now take up the First Thread, that of Gloster, and carry it through the First Movement of the action. The play opens with the conversation of Gloster concerning his family relations. He speaks of his incontinence with light-hearted frivolity. The fruit of it is a grown-up son, who has come to visit his father after a long absence, but must be sent away again. That son hears his own shame from the lips of his indiscreet parent, and we can well imagine the bitterness in his heart, and his resolution to thwart his father's purpose. Here is indicated the crime of Gloster and the instrument of his retribution. He has

committed the deepest wrong against the Family; he has called a social contradiction into existence, which it is impossible to heal. A son, and not a son; a child by nature, yet a child which the Family rejects, disowns, banishes, though it is the special function of the Family to rear and cherish the child. The wrong of Gloster is, therefore, double. He has wronged the Family, the conditions of whose existence he has trampled under foot, and, at the same time, made it the instrument of the direst injustice against an innocent being. But his wrong against his own child is still greater; it is a born outcast from the institutions of society. If guilt is ever requited at the hands of the injured, that father is bound to receive punishment from that son.

But here is the son speaking in his own person; let us see how he feels. He invokes Nature against the plague of custom, for by Nature he is, in every way, as good as his legitimate brother—indeed, he is better. Therefore, he will have his rights, particularly his share in the paternal estate, even if he assail and destroy everything high and holy in his attempt. His course and character are simply the logical result of his situation. He must turn against all institutions, for they have made him an outcast from society and deprived him of his just inheritance. Yet it is from no fault of his own that he thus finds himself punished for crimes which he never committed. That which is called morality shuns him, scoffs at him, tramples him into the dust. All the safeguards which have been built up to protect the individual, as Family, State, Law, are turned to his degradation and destruction. The illegitimate child, therefore, is the natural villain—hostile to the Family, to Society, to Law, to Morality; in him institutions become contradictory to their purpose, and he must bear the sting of their wrong. Hence he worships Nature, for there alone he is the peer of all. He is thus not without adequate motives for his conduct; still, he is a villain, for such every man must be called who deliberately and persistently assails the ethical principles of the world; yet, if he follow these principles, they crush him. Edmund has taken his choice; he prefers honor and distinction through villainy, to shame and degradation through virtue. But still, the fatal outcome of his career, whatever may have been its cause, cannot be averted.

Edmund, accordingly, begins to work out his schemes. He turns against his legitimate brother, because the latter is the bearer of all those ethical elements which crush him. He turns against his father, who was the original author of the wrong—the evil consequences of which, however, the child must endure. Still, filial affection is his duty, under all circumstances; moreover, he has been given an education, and is beloved, by his father. Here the theme can be seen to be the same as that of Lear—filial ingratitude and parental wrong. Edmund finds his father just in the mood to be successfully deceived, for the latter is excited over the occurrences at court, especially over the banishment of his friend Kent. It is the season of treachery, Gloster thinks, and the son proceeds to inject into his mind the deadly suspicion against the brother Edgar, and, at the same time, artfully conceals his own motives. Gloster is superstitious fundamentally; he sees in Nature, in the eclipses of the sun and moon, the collisions of the moral world; he is always ready to assign to blind physical causes the obliquities of man's action. By thus ignoring human freedom, he would seem to try to get rid of his own guilt. But Edmund is just the opposite in this respect; he does not believe in these external influences, but announces, in the boldest terms, the self-determination of man. He is the conscious villain, and takes upon himself the full responsibility of his own act. He quickly perceives the weakness of his father, and uses it to his own advantage.

Equally well does he grasp and utilize the weak side of his brother Edgar's character, with whom he is next brought into contact. At first, however, he touches the same chord which lay so deep in the paternal nature, namely, superstition. But the plan does not work well. Edgar is not superstitious; but he is wholly unsuspecting. Accordingly he does what Edmund urges him to do—avoids his father. Both Edgar and Gloster have, therefore, credulity, and that, too, credulity of such magnitude that it requires some share of credulity in the reader to follow the poet. But they reach it through different channels. The father is superstitious—hence credulous; the son is simple-minded and unsophisticated—hence credulous. Either form will do for the wily villain.

Edgar is at first concealed by his brother from the wrath of the parent, then is inveigled into making the pretended assault upon the latter, after which he betakes himself to flight. He must be imagined as possessing a primitive innocence which knows of no such thing as deception in the world. Upon this utter guilelessness Edmund relies with success. Again the latter touches skillfully the old chord in his father's bosom, which he knows will be most effective, namely, superstition:

> Here stood he in the dark, his sharp sword out,
> Mumbling of wicked charms, conjuring the morn
> To stand auspicious mistress. —

Evidently the most startling words in the ear of old Gloster. Each is, therefore, wrought upon through his peculiar weakness. But we shall hereafter see that Edgar passes through a course of severe instruction, and learns something. From his present innocent state of mind he is to come to a knowledge of evil, in some of its varied manifestations.

The honest and faithful son has now been driven from home. The true and ethical relation of the Family has been annihilated by the faithless and immoral one. But that is not all; Edgar is pursued as a murderer, is outlawed, and a price is set on his head. The institutions of society are invoked to destroy him. Though true to both, yet Family and State have turned against him in favor of one who is false to both. The ethical order of the world is reversed, just as was declared by

Gloster himself; and yet he is the author of the present condition of things. But what is to become of poor Edgar? Without domestic, or even civil protection, he has to flee, and in some way to avoid the oppression of society. He can only assume the meanest and most loathsome disguise, and wander over the country feigning both madness and beggary. For are not the institutions of man, through which alone personal security is possible, directed against him, and must he not get out of their reach? Still, he will remain faithful to his parent in spite of his wrongs, for fidelity is ever faithful. Nor will he go mad, like Lear, from his fall, though he descends from being a nobleman's son to the lowest depth of humiliation. Innocence, therefore, dares not show its face in this perverted world, but has to hide itself under the garb of insanity, Fidelity, too, must disguise itself from the clutches of the faithless.

The disruption of Gloster's family is now complete. That which the eclipses foreshadowed to him has come to pass—father against child, child against father; yet it was the consequence of his own innate disposition which was thus predicted, the presentiment of his own character. He had within himself the possibility of these events—that is what he saw in the stars. The signs of nature were to him an unavoidable fate, because they were simply the image of his deepest self. The bad son is infinitely the intellectual superior of his father, for he believes in mind and relies upon thought. He knows that the individual is determined through himself. Hence comes his success; he works through intelligence. But he, too, makes a mistake; he imagines his stand-point to be absolute, whereas it also is limited. He thinks that the world is moved solely through that form of intelligence called cunning; he, therefore, ignores the eternal ethical laws of the universe. To employ the technical language of philosophy, his faith is in his subjective intelligence alone, but the objective world of spirit he neither believes in nor cares for; he, accordingly, collides with it, and perishes.

But the deepest stroke of villainous cunning is still to come. Edmund has succeeded in getting rid of the presence of his brother; now he must have the property of the family. His next scheme is to work subtly upon his father to this end. But here arises a great difficulty, which the intellectual rogue perfectly comprehends, and carefully prepares for. While he is instilling suspicion, how is he to avoid suspicion against himself? He is seeking his brother's patrimony by exciting mistrust; will he not be himself mistrusted of doing that very thing? This is the logical consequence of such conduct; a man who tries to arouse suspicion will be apt to be suspected; it is his own action returning upon him, for his principle is suspicion. Only the most adroit villain can make the synthesis of these two contradictory sides. Perhaps Gloster is not hard to deceive; at any rate, Edmund succeeds admirably. His method is to declare openly the suspicion to which he is liable, and which is really true of him. Here is his language to his father:

> " I threatened to discover him, he replied—
> 'Thou unpossesing bastard! dost thou think
> If I would stand against thee, would the reposal
> Of any trust, virtue, or worth in thee
> Make thy words faithed? . . .
> And thou must make a dullard of the world,
> If they not thought the profits of my death
> Were very pregnant and potential spurs
> To make thee seek it.'"

"Edgar said that I would be suspected of plotting for his inheritance, and, therefore, nobody would believe me." All suspicion is thus anticipated and destroyed in the mind of the father. Edmund appears to be the faithful son without property, and Edgar the faithless son with property. Gloster at once makes an adjustment; he says to Edmund—you shall have my estate. Edgar's offense is made to spring from his being heir; of the heirship he is deprived.

The reader will notice that the crafty rogue announces here the very thing of which he is guilty; he *is* seeking the patrimony of his brother. Hypocrisy and falsehood are now carried to their climax; hypocrisy hypocritically condemns its own plan; falsehood falsely laments falsehood, and just therein is the more false. Edmund declares his own nefarious scheme as something of which he might be suspected. Thus, however, he destroys suspicion. A careful concealment would be certain to arouse it; but, when a person finds his most secret misgivings openly announced by the one who is suspected, suspicion is apt to take its flight. Gloster might suspect that Edmund was deceiving him and trying to be his heir, but the latter puts this very suspicion into the mouth of Edgar as the ground of mistrust against himself. Thus its foundation is brushed away, for it is the nature of suspicion to rest upon its own secresy; let the villain destroy this secresy, and he is generally successful. Suspicion seems to take for granted that the motives of a scamp must always be hidden. To avoid suspicion means, usually, to be open, without concealment. The above mentioned trait of Edmund, Shakespeare has given to other villains, notably to Iago. Villainy is full of the reproof of villainy, and thus seems honesty, which is just that which it is not, but it is a still deeper villainy.

Edmund is, however, not satisfied; he is not willing to quietly wait for the succession, but his father must be got rid of too. Gloster sympathized deeply with Lear, and, therefore, incurred the enmity of the ruling powers. He has received by letter information of the invasion of Cordelia; his leaning is decidedly toward her party. He expresses this inclination, and also imparts the news which he has received to the son whom he supposes to be faithful. The son at once betrays his father, and is made Earl of Gloster. Edmund, who had previously been taken into the service of the faithless daughters of Lear, has now obtained all that his family possessed, along with the ancestral titles, and has reached the goal of his first ambition. But a new and higher sphere has been opened to him, namely, the possession of the State.

The fearful retribution of Gloster speedily follows. He has not seen that he has been doing to his own child what Goneril and Regan were doing to their father. The old man is seized, his eyes are plucked out, and he is thrust forth to grope his way in the world. Like ancient Œdipus, he did not see when he had eyes—the result is, he loses them. He learns, however, that Edmund is the informer who has brought upon him the present calamity, and at once the whole truth flashes upon his mind. He has pursued an innocent son with murderous wrath and outlawry; he is himself now driven forth houseless and homeless, and he, too, has a price set upon his head. Another son he has brought into the world of institutions, under circumstances which produce nothing but wrong and degradation; that son is the necessary instrument of his punishment. He has destroyed the rational principle of the Family by his act; his own family is disrupted and turned against him. The consequences of his deed are upon him.

In looking through the career of Gloster we ask, naturally, what is the origin of his habit of holding the planets responsible for man's delinquencies? We see that this habit has grown into the very fibre of his character, and is that through which he is moved. That little talk of his at the beginning of the play, gives the germ: he has been guilty of a wrong, and has tried to shuffle off the responsibility for his act from himself by "making guilty the sun, the moon, and the stars." The result is, he becomes superstitious, a believer in the doctrine that man is governed by external agencies, is not a free being, and hence not accountable. It is the attempt to smother conscience by self-excuse, till he succeeds; it is the lie which he tells to his own soul so often and so long, that at last he comes to believe it—the source of all his calamities. He does not manfully take his wrongful deed upon himself, and purge himself of it by repentance and a clear life thereafter, but he ascribes it to something over which he has no control. Nature did it, not I; do not blame me. In this way he has prepared himself for deception first, then for punishment; it is the channel in which Edmund works with such terrible effect. Many years have passed over Gloster with this falsehood rooted in his soul, as is shown in the grown-up son. As Lear is hardened in arbitrary authority, so Gloster is hardened in the habit of self-excuse; Edmund sees the case and states it to be "the surfeit of our own behavior, as if we were villains on necessity, fools by heavenly compulsion, —and all that we are evil in, by a divine trusting on."

Another result we must notice: Gloster, in releasing himself from moral responsibility, releases himself from inner control, and gives himself over to passion, as he gave himself over to the external powers of the planets. Thus he shows no patience, no charity, and herein he is again like Lear. He boils over at a mere word of suspicion against his absent son Edgar. Yet if Edgar were guilty of all the offences falsely laid upon him, the father's conduct is, nothwithstanding, wholly wrong. He lacks love, he should never treat even a wicked son in such a way; he lacks charity, he should never treat a human being in such a way. To self-defence, if attacked on the spot, he has a right; but not to revenge, least of all against his own son. His spirit is that of requital, like for like; he is deceived, it is true, though his deception comes through his own deed; still, if what he believed were true, he would be in the wrong. Then think! if he could only be charitable and not vengeful, he would not be deceived; or if deceived, the deception would be of no effect. Edmund's plans rest upon the fact that his father is first superstitious, then vengeful. An outer Fate, that of "the sun, moon, and stars," as well as an inner Fate, that of passion and caprice, are holding Gloster in their double chain.

It will now be seen that the characters of both Gloster and Lear reach down to one point: both are uncharitable, in the large sense. Both bring about so much evil in Family and State by a want of that quality, which endures, forgives, assumes the limits of others. They pursue with revenge their own children, they have no true love which dissolves all short-comings, antagonisms, misunderstandings, and restores the harmonies of existence. Both are at the head of institutions; these they will pervert and turn into instruments of caprice and passion, and thus lead the way to the grand perversion of the whole Institutional World. Both, too, have begotten their like, they have children who will act in the spirit of the parents toward the parents, and who will bring home to them this lack of charity.

2. It is now time to go back to the beginning and trace the Second Thread of this First Movement, namely, the family of Lear, to a similar disruption. The general offense of both Gloster and Lear is the same—violation of the right of the Family. Their conduct is fundamentally the same; they trust their faithless, and banish their faithful children. But the origin and special form of their offenses are very different. The play presupposes in Gloster the act of incontinence; in Lear, the tyrannical disposition which overbears and destroys all individual right. With this latter character we are now prepared to begin.

The central figure of the Second Thread—in fact, of the whole play, is the King. The three essential circumstances pertaining to him are his time of life, his long rule, and his absolute power. They make him a tyrant, but a tyrant of a peculiar kind. He is introduced to us with a character long since formed, and now hardened and stiffened with age. He has been, and is still, the absolute monarch whose mandates are not to be questioned. This unlimited authority has fed his temper till it is wholly unyielding and wholly uncontrollable. Any restraint put upon his caprice causes him to boil over with the most intense passion; irascibility has, therefore, become one of his most marked characteristics. The course of the drama will exhibit the various limitations placed upon him, one after another, and increasing in severity, till the absolute monarch, who prescribed to all his people their bounds, becomes the outcast—the most limited of mortals. Old age, long rule, and uncontrolled power combined can alone produce such a man.

Now this King, whose character springs from, and rests upon unlimited authority, is ready to surrender his sway—that is, surrender the very ground of his existence. Tired of the cares of government, yet not weary of its pomp and outward show, he proposes to resign the reality of power and yet retain its appearance—to play the king and yet be freed from the troubles of kingship. He will thus reduce himself to a mere semblance. His desire is to seem to possess authority, while, in truth, he wipes out its last vestige. Such is the contradiction which he deems possible to be realized. The logical result is manifest; the shadow must prove itself to be shadow, and not substance; the show of authority must go where authority actually resides.

This will be a leading phase of the progress of Lear in the Second Thread before us. He will pass from semblance to nothingness; there is no help for him, since he is fighting for a shadow, and has thrown away that which might assist him, if anything could, namely, authority. Every remnant of power will be stripped from him; the ensigns of royalty will also be taken away; he will descend from the palace to the hovel, from the crowned king to the unclothed animal of the forest. In general, from the absolute monarch he will become the most limited individual—a transition which is wholly involved in his choosing the shadow for the substance of authority.

How has it come to pass that Lear has reached such a condition, taking substance for shadow, and shadow for substance? It is the disease of authority; he has used arbitrary power till his individuality is inflated to the size of the universe; he regards himself as greater than institutions. The State and I are one—*l'etat, c'est moi*, a modern monarch once said. The grand development of the State in history has been, mainly, to separate the personal element from the institutional, to place the will of the monarch under law. But Lear has confounded the two elements: his personal whim he cannot distinguish from the highest law of the world. His momentary crotchet or passion he utters as the voice of the nation. Truly, he has taken the shadow for the substance of authority.

Here we may see the ground of his resignation of power. This individual, namely, himself, he deems just as valid, just as mighty, without the institution as with it; his authority, he imagines, comes not from the State, but from his personality. Hence he flings the State lightly away, thinking it to be nothing for him. Lear's act shows absolute pride, it declares that his Ego, of itself, unfilled with the institutional world, is still sovereign. His unlimited rule has thus led him to despise the very institution which is its source. But the play will reduce the mere individual, though he may have been monarch, to the lowest terms with an appalling rapidity.

Furthermore, absolute power will recognize no limits to itself through others; it will endure no restraint, no advice. "He hath ever but slenderly known himself," said one who had felt his authority. He will overbear every individuality that meets his own in any shape; his Ego is absolute against every other Ego. He will endure no love except that which is servile; he will banish and curse his own children, if they set up a limit against him; he will have no charity which regards the other as itself. Thus he nullifies both the individual and the institution in his all-destroying pride.

We have to think that, in this frightful picture, the poet has shown the disease of absolute authority, and has held the mirror up to his own time. Both the monarchs, Elizabeth and James, cherished notions of arbitrary power; but the English people were determined upon limiting the royal prerogative. The conflict was opening, to break out into civil war less than a generation after the death of the poet; to a degree he is the prophet of his people, he shows them the effects of unlimited rule both upon the monarch and upon the State. We do not think that the poet was conscious of any such intention; but he wrote out of his heart, which was the heart of the hearts of the English people; he could not help telling what they felt and foretelling what they were to do.

Lear's temper, therefore, has been fed by absolute authority till he has come to consider himself all and institutions nothing. Now he is to find out what institutions are for the individual, even for so great an individual as the King. Take them out of man, and he is an animal; so Lear descends to an irrational naked denizen of the forest. He will pass from sanity to madness, which transition is involved in that first deed of his. Domination, unopposed and uncontrolled, is the basis upon which the spiritual nature of Lear reposes; destroy the basis and one prop of his mind is gone. He is too old and too stiff to adjust himself at once to such a sudden and overwhelming change in his outward circumstances. He is also the creature of external form, his thoughts rest upon them; when they are gone, he has begun to lose the content of his existence. Yet we must not consider Lear insane at the start; an act of folly does not constitute a case of insanity, else the world were one great madhouse.

Along with this transition from sanity to madness, there will be going on a volcanic struggle within, between Passion which boils up in red-hot fury against all limits, and Patience which tries to endure them, to restain the rising wrath and tumult of the soul. Still further, Lear will seek to control not merely feeling, but action; he will curb Revenge and try to turn to Charity. With limit after limit put upon him, he will learn forbearance; he will make the acquaintaince of Charity whom he has never known before. He will have daughters who will treat him uncharitably, just as he has treated men, not taking into account their short-comings, but requiting them. Now he is the sufferer, and he comes to know Charity by the want of it toward himself, though "<u>more sinned against than sinning</u>." Yet the other tendency will be present in terrific energy; he will burst out into tempests of Revenge, will curse and rave; between the two extremes his spirit will sway so fiercely as to shatter him physically and mentally. The way of Charity leads him to sanity; the way of Revenge leads him to madness. So he careens from one side to the other with tears, convulsions, fierce vengeance and gentle forbearance, and the outcome is insanity.

We may notice, too, how arbitrary power has affected Lear's emotional nature. He, though absolute in authority, is still the most needy of human beings; he feels the necessity of love. But love is an equalizer, demanding that every external distinction vanish before its right. The higher the ruler places himself over love, the more he needs it, but the more uncertain he is whether he has it or not. Fear, self-interest, etiquette may make a show of affection to the monarch. Lear is the tyrant in his love, he will compel it, hence it becomes largely an outward appearance. Lear's love is not sacrifice, but demands sacrifice, to feed his monstrous individuality. In love he gave away all his power, yet did not, but expected to keep it still. There is the same contradiction in his love that we see in his surrender of power; he deems himself greater than love, as he deems himself greater than authority, yet both are what he most needs.

Such is, in general, the character of Lear. Let us now consider its effects upon those around him—upon his family and court. What will be the results of long years of arbitrary rule? Two classes must arise—on the one hand, the hypocritical and faithless; on the other, the rigidly true and faithful. The former class is composed of the sycophants of power who administer to the caprices of rulers—who flatter and fawn in success, but are ready to desert, and even to strike, in misfortune. They are the product of a forced external conformity, full of intrigue and treachery. Lear's court is mainly composed of such characters, at the head of whom stand Goneril and Regan; yet even his own chosen companions—his knights—seem no exception. But the second class will also be there, made up of the virtuous few, who, by a kind of reaction will be the very opposite of what they see around themselves. They must possess strong, even stoical natures to resist the current. Instead of the glib and guileful phrases of the courtier, they will be blunt and direct in speech. The prevailing corruption will only increase the stern code of their morality; but, chiefly the utter faithlessness of the time will engender in them the most heroic fidelity. In Lear's own family this class is represented by Cordelia; in the court by Kent, in a still different relation, more fully to be explained hereafter, by the Fool. These two classes, therefore, spring directly from the character and situation of Lear. Moreover, since he has chosen the semblance, and rejected the reality, his course must be to retain the false flatterer and drive off the true friend. Hence the second class will soon be compelled to fly from his presence.

The tyrannical nature of Lear, therefore, seeks to reduce everybody to an apparent submission and outward conformity. His first collision is with the true and honest people of his court, whom he banishes. Having thereby made the world around him a semblance, he concludes to become semblance himself. Lear is about to manifest in his action various phases of one grand transition, all of which are the direct consequences of his character and situation; he will pass from wrong against his daughter to wrong from his daughters; from unlimited power to the most limited existence; from sanity to madness—in general, from appearance to nothingness. That is, the negative sweep of his deed involves in one common destruction the inner and outer rational existence of man.

We shall now take up the incidents of this Second Thread, and follow them to the end of the First Movement. They are a series of Oceanic fluctuations in the soul of Lear, which toss that little ship of his body, up and down, till he is wrecked in the tempest.

(1.) First comes the division of the realm, together with the test of his three daughters' love, wherein we behold him in his two relations—as monarch and father. This scene has been often censured, and sometimes defended, upon a misconception of its meaning. We are to see in this primal act of Lear the germinal point of his character; he gives away the State, yet thinks that he has it still, he deems himself all-sufficient without the institution. It is the disease of authority, "the imperfection of long-ingraffed condition," the pride of individuality in its absolute expression.

From the same source flows Lear's next action: "Tell me, my daughters, which of you doth love me most?" Absolutism has most need of love, because placed apparently so far above it; Lear must have at least the external manifestation of it around him. Moreover, we have seen that the life of Lear has come to rest more in the outward form of things, than in their inward essence; already he has chosen the semblance of power for its reality. It is in perfect keeping with his situation, and strongly indicative of his character, that he lays more stress upon noisy and exaggerated expressions of love than upon genuine, but quiet affection. Goneril and Regan both declare, in formal phrase, their unfathomable, unspeakable devotion, and receive their share of the kingdom. Their extravagant speech echoes the hollowness of their hearts; one feels, in the stilled words, their insincerity.

(2.) Now Lear is to have the first limit placed upon him, it comes from the third daughter, Cordelia. She belongs to the strict and faithful set at court; she will be the opposite of her sisters, who have falsely flattered the old man; she will also be direct in speech. "I love your majesty according to my bond, no more, no less." Duty with her is higher than love: "You have begot me, bred me, loved me? I return those duties back." She will requite duty. Still more strongly does she draw the limit:

> Why have my sisters husbands, if they say
> They love you all? Haply, when I shall wed
> That Lord whose hand shall take my plight shall carry
> Half my love with him, half my care and duty.
> Sure I shall never marry like my sisters
> To love my father all.

This is, of course, sophistical; she can love both father and husband all, their loves have no such mutual exclusion as she implies. Then Cordelia is a little proud of her virtue here, a little self-righteous, in pluming herself upon her superiority over her sisters. We begin to see that she is also a true daughter of old Lear, even in her excellence. But the father boils over with anger at the limit; he curses and banishes his daughter; in a terrific imprecation he renounces fatherhood; he, too, has no true love, he commits the crime against his own family, and his curse will be literally fulfilled upon himself through his other daughters.

Here we shall have to take a glance at the character of Cordelia, which has received such universal commendation. It is not well to pick flaws, but we must see what the poet has done. He has portrayed her devotion to duty; also she is a worshipper of truth.

> *Lear.*—So young and so untender?
> *Cord.*—So young, my lord, and true.

Her truth, not her tenderness, is her pride. Now duty and truth are excellent; but Cordelia, resting upon them, loses the lustre of love, she becomes uncharitable. She disregards the age, weakness and temper of her father, and hands him over wholly to the two sisters, whose characters she well understands: "I know you what you are." She seems ready to sacrifice her share of the kingdom, which might be the protection of her parent in the future, to what she deems truth and duty. So, often the obstinate adherence to a moral punctilio jeopardizes the greatest interests, even institutions. As her conduct is undaughterly, so it is unsisterly, when she sarcastically bids farewell to her sisters: "Ye jewels of our father—with washed eyes Cordelia leaves you." Cordelia's act is thus the source of the terrible calamities which befall Lear and the State; with all her virtues she has not yet reached the highest, which is charity.

But she will reach it, and this is the interest and beauty of her character; she develops, she has an indestructible element of goodness in her nature. Truth is not love, but leads to love. When we meet her again in the Fourth Act, we shall find the change complete; she returns to her country, full of contrition and pity, and tries to undo the evil consequence of her deed, by restoring to her father a daughter's love. What is the ground of this change? The poet has indicated it in the wooing scene between France and Burgundy; the latter is the false suitor who seeks a bride for her dower, not for love, and so is rejected. But France is the true suitor and true man, he takes the dowerless daughter.

> Fairest Cordelia, that art most rich being poor,
> Most choice forsaken, and most loved despised,
> Thee and thy virtues here I seize upon;
> Be it lawful, I take up what's cast away.

Such is the husband with whom Cordelia is to live henceforth, and to experience love; the atmosphere of his court will be far different from that of Lear's court; she enters upon a new life, in which a brighter jewel is added to the crown of her virtues. This wooing episode thus weaves itself into the heart of the action, and does not remain an external appendage.

(3.) The next limit is that which Kent undertakes to place upon the old King. It is merely a strong piece of advice against the present course of Lear; the result is just what might be expected from the aged and absolute ruler—his rage swells at the audacity, and Kent is banished. Kent goes off with apparent indifference, saying: "Freedom lives hence and banishment is here;" in him honest counsel and courageous utterance take their departure from court. Kent praises Cordelia as one "who thinks most justly, and has most rightly said;" yet he will return at once and surpass her.

Fidelity is ever faithful; that of Kent is stoical, the deepest principle of his nature. Whatever be the wrongs which he may suffer as an individual, he will remain true to his allegiance. His loyalty is not determined by the treatment he receives; it is self-centered, loyal under all circumstances. He will come back and serve his King in disguise, when he cannot do it openly; such is the last necessity of his nature, though he be a little rough in manner and blunt in speech. He has reached charity in those deep-toned lines:

> Now, banished Kent,
> If thou canst serve, where thou dost stand condemned,
> So may it come, thy master, whom thou lovest,
> Shall find thee full of labors.

This is the highest stand-point of the poem. It shows the man charitable, free; the man who is ruled by the good, not by some wrong action of another man towards himself. Kent has no revenge for what he has suffered from the King, has not even indifference after such treatment. Injustice drives him not to requital, but to the more active charity; here he over-tops Cordelia, and places himself upon the summit of human conduct. From this altitude we can look down upon all the other characters of the drama, and behold them at various stages of the ascent. Such is, clearly, the standard of the poet, which we, too, must have in mind for measuring his work.

Lear has now succeeded in getting rid of every species of fidelity—fidelity to parent in Cordelia, and fidelity to King in Kent—fidelity to Family and to State. The world of appearance is everywhere triumphant. He has completely realized his principle; he is himself a shadow; all are shadows around him; they seem what they are not. Even fidelity must conceal itself; it dares not appear in its real form, hence Kent has to put on a deceptive guise in order to be faithful. Wisdom also can show her face only in the garb of folly; the sagest counselor of the King is his Fool. The same result was observed in the preceding thread concerning the family of Gloster. Edgar, the innocent and true son is compelled to flee and assume the guise of a madman, while the false, base-born son, is triumphant in his wildest schemes. Society is a grand masquerade, where each person seems to be what he is not; the world has become one immense deception.

When such a state of things become universal, the logical result begins to make itself manifest; falsehood must be false to itself, and will turn upon and destroy itself. The sham-king Lear must have his semblance stripped away, and be reduced to what he really is, though this be done by his false daughters. The world of monsters is always self-devouring, and the process now opens. Hitherto, Lear could bear down every person with his absolute power, as we have just seen in the case of Cordelia and Kent, but now there is to be put upon him the limit which he cannot brush away, but to which he, apparently for the first time in many years, has to yield.

(4.) This is the work of Goneril, his eldest daughter, who now has authority. She bowed to it while she was a shadow; yet she has been trained by her father's example to arbitrary use of power without charity. Lear's turn has come, he must follow the logic of the situation. Moreover he has banished his faithful daughter, why should his daughters be faithful to him? We are to see that it is his own deed returning to him through his family; he has prepared the very instrument of his own punishment, he has made the hell in which he is scorched. Nevertheless, the devil who tortures him is not to be excused; Goneril's wickedness remains the same, she is false to her agreement and undutiful to parent.

But Lear will not receive any limitation without the most terrific convulsion. His whole nature, physical and mental, will rise up in a gigantic rebellion against the barrier. When Goneril complains of the license of his retinue and threatens to take redress into her own hands, Lear is beside himself with wrath, and thinks, "This is no Lear," and asks: "Who is it that can tell me who I am?" But Goneril persists, she asserts her power:

> Be then desired
> By her that else will take the thing she begs,
> A little to disquantity your train—

Whereat Lear orders his horses for departure, but before he leaves he launches another and deeper curse against a daughter. He prays that she may never have offspring; or, if she have, that it may be a monster. Therein he curses his own generation; his imprecation is that his own tribe may perish. It will be fulfilled to the letter. The curse invokes the governing principle of the world to requite on individual grounds some personal affront; such a curse comes home to the curser and the cursed.

Thus Lear has had the first limit placed upon himself which he cannot sweep away. He is now in the full process of his deed; he surrendered his power, yet retained it in his pride—the primal fact of his character stated in those sharp lines:

> Idle old man
> That still would manage those authorities
> That he hath given away.

But with this limit is the beginning of an inner change, of a spiritual transformation. He now reverts to his conduct to Cordelia, and can say for the first time: "I did her wrong." That is the little ray of purification which beams out of his terrible discipline. The haughty individuality which held itself All and the State nothing, has taken a lesson. But the shock, both physical and mental, is that of the earthquake; will he endure? Look at his body; it, too, seems an absolute tyrant, shakes and swells at the limit put upon authority, sympathizes most deeply with its royal occupant: "I am ashamed that thou hast power to shake my manhood thus;" but he can no more control his body than his mind. Hot tears break out of old fond eyes, which he threatens to pluck out, "and cast you with the water that you lose to temper clay." He tries to suppress his physical agitation, but cannot; nor can he endure mentally, but flies off to the thought of revenge: "I have another daughter, with her nails she will flay thy wolfish visage." The mental break, too, he begins to fear:

> O let me not be mad, not mad, sweet heaven;
> Keep me in temper: I would not be mad.

Yes, unless he can restrain his temper, his passion, his revenge, he will go mad, and he knows it. But if he can draw from his discipline the healing thought, and continue to say: "I did wrong," then he will become saner than ever in his life before.

But this world of disguise is not one of utter falsehood and wickedness, for fidelity is also here in disguise. We have already mentioned Kent, who takes service as a menial; sincerity itself must be insincere; truth has to assume the form of deception. To this pass has Lear reduced his whole court. If the honest man must become dishonest in order to be true to his nature, what of the naturally dishonest? Kent acts as servant to his master; his duties are of the lower kind; he cannot appear as the adviser of the King, since the latter will suffer no advice. He is messenger, and zealously defends the royal honor against the malign attacks of Oswald, the unprincipled and ready tool of the wicked daughter, Goneril.

But the complete and conscious reflection of this world is in the Fool. He, too, is in disguise—seems to be what he is not, and thus is a true representative of his time. But his peculiarity is that he sees beneath the masks of all around him, and knows their acts and purposes. He is the intellectual man, yet his intelligence must also be disguised; wisdom casts an inverted image in the waters of untruth. The contradiction is that the wise man of the company is the Fool. His theme is the folly of Lear's conduct; he offers the latter a coxcomb—the symbol of his own profession. Knowing the character of the two daughters, he sees the situation and anticipates the result. He alone appears to comprehend adequately the act of Lear in surrendering the kingdom, and he alone can assume disguise sufficient to tell to the old King the nature of that act without being banished. Thus wisdom, at the court of Lear, dares look only through the mask of folly, and good counsel takes the form of nonsense. In this way, however, no insult or reproof is given to the haughty old King, for, when a fool says anything, it is supposed to be foolish. But, if the truth should assume the form of grave advice, it would imply the lack of wisdom on the part of the ruler. Hence the absolute monarch has his critic, but this critic must take the form of a fool—then the royal vanity is not touched. Thus it will be seen that not only fidelity and truth, but even intelligence, must seem to be what they are not, when semblance is the universal principle. The Fool accordingly becomes a necessary part of this world of appearance.

The First Act ends with the flight of Lear to his second daughter; he flies to get rid of limits which he now finds are made valid against him. But he will not escape them, he will meet them everywhere. Father and daughter are alike, in that each has no charity, which holds the fellow-man, not rigidly to his weaknesses, but takes them up into its completeness, in which they vanish. The very fact of Lear's failings ought to excite in the daughter not the wish to collide with them, but to bear with them, to take them, as it were, upon herself, and thus obliterate them.

Passion versus Patience is now the antithesis

in the soul of Lear, as expressed in the terms of the poem. Nor are we to neglect the sympathy, or, more properly, the symbolism, of Lear's body, in response to his soul. In his Passion, "this mother swells"—he calls it *hysterica passio*—the inwards of the man seem to rise and seek to rush outwards, as if to get beyond their center within. Then Patience is not only a moral but a physical return to the center: "down, thou climbing sorrow." What an immediate response is always given by nature to Lear's disturbed spirit! Here the actor has his field.

(5.) In the Second Act, Lear passes to Regan; he will meet with almost every kind of limit in his passage. The servants, headed by Oswald, show him disrespect, which calls forth Kent to the defense of the King, and to a conflict with Oswald. The result is, Kent is put in the stocks, but he is equal to any fortune: "Some time I shall sleep out, the rest I'll whistle. * * Fortune good night, smile once more; turn thy wheel." Then Cornwall, husband of Regan, refuses to see Lear, who again shows the struggle between Passion and Patience: "Tell the hot duke that—No, but not yet—I'll forbear." Still he cannot curb himself: "O me, my heart, my heart, my rising heart. But down!" So he lurches from side to side.

(6.) Then Regan appears, and the old man appeals pitifully to her for sympathy. But her words freeze while dropping from her mouth: "O, sir, you are old, you should be ruled and led." The Fool foresaw what the supposed wise man, the King, did not; the dispositions of the two daughters are alike, "as a crab to a crab." But this time Lear restrains himself, he does not curse Regan as he did Cordelia and Goneril. He even sees in her a certain mildness, a "tender-hefted nature," and eyes which "do comfort and not burn." Not revenge, but kindness he shows; certainly he is advancing. But just at this juncture, who comes here?

(7.) It is Goneril; she has hastened to support her sister Regan, who, in strength of will, seems to have been the weaker and less aggressive of the two women, and strongly influenced by her more determined sister. The presence of Goneril again disturbs the balance of Lear, and begins to make Passion overbear Patience:

> O, Heavens,
> If you do love old men, if your sweet sway
> Allow obedience, if yourselves are old,
> Make it your cause, send down and take my part.

Then that chilly Regan sends an icy blast: "I beg you, father, being weak, seem so." The two daughters now begin to rival one another in putting limits upon the old King. Goneril cuts off half his train; his rage first rises, then drops, and he can say: "I'll not chide thee—I can be patient." Safe again; but Regan overtops her sister, and says "but five and twenty" knights she will receive; Goneril then outbids Regan: "What need you five and twenty, ten, or five?" Then hear the last limit uttered by Regan: "What need one?"

Lear is at first calm, and draws swiftly the logical conclusion:

> O reason not the need; our basest beggars
> Are in the poorest thing superfluous.

The two daughters have indeed reduced him to the basest beggar in thought, which thought will soon be fact. He sees clearly what he needs in this ordeal:

> But for true need,
> You heavens, give me that Patience, Patience I need.

Yet his physical nature is bursting over all restraint; "woman's weapons, water drops" are again staining "his man's cheeks." But will he endure the mental strain—will he keep that Patience he prays for? Listen now:

> No, you unnatural hags,
> I will have such revenges on you both
> That all the worlds shall—I will do such things—
> What they are, yet I know not—

Patience is gone, Revenge has the control, he will not weep in his scornful pride, even if "this heart shall break into a hundred thousand flaws." Hence his final cry: "O fool, I shall go mad." And he will go mad, if he cannot get rid of that seething crater of passionate revenge in his soul. Whereat he runs out into the storm.

Like Lear himself, this storm is both physical and spiritual; the last mark of royalty is stripped from him, he is driven out of the protecting institutions of the world, Family and State, into the rude elements of Nature. The Fool declares that the greatest folly is now fidelity; it were wisdom to let go a great wheel running down hill; yet he will remain fool and faithful. Goneril can only say: "'Tis his own blame, and must needs taste his folly." In the same spirit Regan declares:

> O, sir to wilful men,
> The injuries that they themselves procure
> Must be their schoolmasters.

It is a world without love; man would perish in his babyhood, if injury were to be his schoolmaster. "Shut up your doors," as you have shut up your hearts; "'tis a wild night—come out of the storm," and leave the others, even the parent, exposed to its blasts.

(8.) The Third Act is this storm, it shows Lear with the entire world of institutions closed against him; he is driven forth to the woods in a tempest, without civil protection, without shelter, and finally without clothing. Those institutions which he deemed nought, and that individuality which he deemed all, are getting to be in strange contrast.

But even here Nature with all her might is trying to put a limit upon him. So he defies her with her winds, and cataracts, and thunderbolts; he is unsubdued. Yet he will not "tax with unkindness" the elements which assail him so ferociously, they are not his daughters. Still, he calls them "servile ministers" that conspire with his children against him, who is now

> A poor, infirm, weak, despised old man.

Surely he begins to see himself, and still he struggles with his rising Passion: "O, O, 'tis foul!" Then the lurch to the other side: "No, I will be the pattern of all Patience, I will say nothing." He is, however, aware that his "wits begin to turn" in this conflict.

Kent tries to bring him under the shelter of a hovel. But the outer tempest scarcely touches him; it is the inner tempest which is tossing him —"the tempest in my mind doth from my senses take all feeling;" now we are to see again the swayings of that mental tempest. "Filial ingratitude! But I will punish home! No, I will weep no more." Revenge on the one side, endurance on the other, so the battle rages. "In such a night to shut me out!—Pour on, I will endure." Yet he cannot endure, but surges back: "In such a night as this! O Regan, Gonerill! your kind old father whose frank heart gave all—." Then he recovers himself: "O that way madness lies; let me shun that."

But it is wonderful what purification Lear has reached, he seems on the verge of becoming self-centered, and of attaining the true view of human conduct. For now he becomes charitable, he thinks of the poor and wretched, "that bide the pelting of this pitiless storm," and in self-reproach he exclaims: "O I have taken too little care of this!" Now the regal show is quite gone: "Take physic, pomp." His own sufferings have brought him to think of others, which he has not done before, and to think of them with compassion. Shall we not forecast that he will recover, a new man through his trials? Certainly he has mastered the tempest and drawn from it the grand lesson.

(9.) But what is this sudden, new appearance, which whirls Lear back into the way of madness? It is Edgar, disguised as mad Tom, quite naked. We at once see that Edgar's insanity is simulated; it is madness learnt by heart, and pretending to spring from crime. Its very exaggeration reveals it to the sane judgement, but to the shaken mind of Lear it is a wrench backwards, and throws him again into his fixed idea: "Didst thou give all to thy daughters?—What, have his daughters brought him to this pass?" He connects this assumed madness with his own case, ascribes it to the same cause; he sees his own future and the image of himself in mad Tom, it drives him forward, he is going over the bound of reason: "Now all the plagues that in the pendulous air hang fated o'er men's faults, light on thy daughters." Revenge he turns to once more, he can have no charity for "those pelican daughters." Shakespeare evidently knew the fact, now recognized in the treatment of the insane, that the presence and example of a crazy person may drive a patient trembling upon the borders between reason and unreason into insanity. He also seems to have known another fact: an outer disturbance, like a tempest, has the tendency to help forward madness in a mind predisposed to it.

So Lear will be mad as Tom himself, not only mentally but in external appearance: "Thou art the thing itself; unaccommodated man is no more but such a poor, bare, forked animal as thou art;

off, off, you lendings! come, unbutton here!" and he tears away his garments. Now he is reduced to the individual of Nature; every product of man's intelligence, from the highest institutions to the humblest contrivances, even clothing, he has thrown away; in other words, he has got rid of the whole content of his rational existence. The result is he is irrational; from the king he has descended to the animal. He has experienced to the full, what that first resignation of authority means; he cast away institutions in the pride of individuality; no family, no state, no society, not even shelter and clothing—a wild man of the woods. But even here he might maintain himself, as Edgar does, in the very dregs of calamity, could he keep his inner freedom, and not be determined to Revenge. Let us note this final phase of Lear in the present Movement.

(10.) We find him engaged in the imagined trial of his daughters: "It shall be done; I will arraign them straight." Kent, who is seeking to calm him, reflects the situation to us in his words: "All the power of his wits have given way to his impatience." No more Patience, no more resistance to his Passion, the barrier is broken down. Imagination controls him, he tries his daughters in Revenge, and Kent exclaims with despair:

> Oh pity! Sir, where is the Patience now
> That you so oft have boasted to retain!

The light of Reason goes out in Revenge, and sleep at last draws a veil over the mental ruins of the lofty monarch.

The divine view of the world is to recognize the mortal as limited, finite; still, he is not to be destroyed, but saved even in his shortcomings. The old saying runs that if man had met with justice, merely, he would long since have perished; but charity in the divine nature rescues him. Self-pride avenges every small injury or affront; it demands that the world recognize it as infinite, which the world cannot do, without its own annihilation. In the present play, we behold the poet taking this highest stand-point and looking with the divine glance upon man and the world.

Lear reaches charity for mankind, he learns the inadequacy and failure of his own life, though he be a King. But he cannot reach charity for his daughters; filial ingratitude he cannot get over, he will revenge it, and so goes mad after becoming more sane than he had ever been. When he seems to be ready, after his bitter trial to live the regenerate life, he drops back to Revenge, he seeks to requite his daughters' wrong, and just at that point he breaks. He is not yet cleansed; he is unable to rise into the realm of universal charity, where the hateful blow falls harmless because it cannot touch the inner freedom of man. Could he let the unkind deed pass over him and not determine him to like unkindness, he were indeed saved. But not yet; he must have another dip, which sends him to the very bottom of the stream of human trial, into the oblivion of insanity, last before death; let him then be taken out, restored to reason, and be tested again in a new and even more terrible ordeal.

The insanity of Lear has attracted a great deal of attention in recent years from physicians, whose specialty has been the treatment of insane people. The truth of the poet's work has been generally admitted, it is a great study on the subject. Still the matter must not be carried too far; Lear's insanity cannot be called organic; he gets into it and comes out of it; it is a mental derangement whose possibility exists in every man. It has even its good side, it has in it a process of purification, a strange attempt of Nature to throw off a deep-seated spiritual disease, by plunging the soul for a time into the Lethe of irrationality, whereby the worst evil to man is transformed into a means of the spirit's ascent into a new life.

And can we not see that Lear and Gloster have made their own Inferno, and have created their own means of punishment? That primal deed of each becomes character, and it becomes environment. Goneril and Regan, and likewise their court, are Lear's own product; even Edgar, disguised as mad Tom, upon whom Lear seems to come by accident, is really a result of this society, and the accident of meeting him is Lear's necessity. What Lear has done, thus becomes his outer crushing situation, as well as his inner impelling power. Yet even his career, as well as that of Gloster, reveal a compensation; they show that this world is but a probation, and those who can digest wrong, and sin and misfortune, can be redeemed. Both of these sufferers go far on the path, but do not quite reach the goal.

Let us grasp the complete picture of this society—this Perverted World, as it may be called, and its characters. First in order come Edgar and Lear, now reduced to the same outward condition, and from the same general cause. Both have touched the very bottom of human misery; both are in a deadly struggle with the spiritual and with the physical world—with quite the sum total of being. The Family has turned against them, the State has driven them forth from its protection, and Nature herself has assailed them with her terrific forces. Such is the outcome of man in hostility with institutions. Still, neither Lear nor Edgar are conquered; in spirit they hold out—are even defiant. The unconquerable will—the subjective independence of man—could not be asserted against an opposition more destructive. But Edgar is sane; his madness is only simulated, while that of Lear is real. Lear has been deprived of what constituted the innermost essence of his nature. But the mind of Edgar had never become so interwoven with his rank and power that separation from them would destroy it. He is also young and supple; he can bend without breaking.

Gloster is also present in these wild scenes, deeply sympathetic with Lear, and incurring danger for the sake of the old King. But his own sympathy condemns him. Before his eyes stands a man—his faithful son—whom his wrong has reduced to a condition as miserable as that of Lear. Every word which he speaks against the unkind daughters is a judgment against himself. That judgment is executed upon him in a manner which every humane feeling cries out to be too severe.

Kent, the picture of fidelity, is also present in the storm; for he is going to follow his master through every grade of calamity. Still, his fidelity must remain in disguise, in order to accomplish itself. It dares not, even now, assume its native form. The world of appearance has, however, reached its climax; it is rapidly dissolving. Lear, its original source and supporter, has himself become, not merely the shadow of a king, but the shadow of a man. Reason has taken its flight, and the erect animal shape alone remains.

The Fool, too, is present in the tempest, trying to divert the King from his thoughts, and to jest away his approaching insanity; but it is to no purpose. Wisdom—though, to effect its design, it has assumed the garb of folly—has not succeeded. The Fool, therefore, drops out now; his function must cease when Lear is no longer rational, but has himself turned fool. It was his duty to reflect the acts of the King in their true character, so that the latter might behold what he was doing. When intelligence is gone, this is impossible, and folly, too, becomes tragic. Deepest sympathy the Fool shows amid all his jesting; he, also, has a disguise, under his folly he hides a breaking heart.

There never was painted such a picture as this of the Third Act; it is the world turned upside down—morally, mentally, physically. To give it greater strength and terror the two Threads of the action are now brought together. There are the faithless, protected in their wrongs by institutions, and sheltered by their palaces from the raging elements. There are the three disguises—that of innocence, that of fidelity, that of wisdom—seeking to be true to their own nature under the most alien forms. Then there is the parent of these false appearances, himself now the shadow of a shadow. Finally, there is the storm without—one of the warring principles in itself, and, at the same time, symbolical of the storm within. It is the Perverted World; it seems quite to reach the extreme negative point short of annihilation.

The consequences of Lear's conduct and character are now complete; they have produced their legitimate fruit. The semblance of absolute authority has vanished; he is now the humblest of mortals. At the same time he has passed from sanity to madness. The unlimited monarch has descended to the most narrow existence—has become, in fact, a beast of the forest. But, above all, his wrong against the Family has met with a retribution which seems but too harsh and horrible. The fate of Gloster, as before remarked, is in every essential respect similar, for he, too, is sent forth an outcast, deprived of title and possessions— dazed, if not crazed, by his misfortunes. The two Threads have thus been brought down to the time of the disruption of the two families, and of the punishment of the two parents. Now the reaction must be portrayed, which will vindicate and restore the shattered institutions of the world, bring the false and guilty to justice, and cause the triumph of the faithful and innocent.

Such, then, is the First Movement. We notice that it has been a great movement or development of characters, also that it has been a great movement of society, which has become for man a Perverted World. Those who have violated institutions, and who ought to be punished by them, are not only protected by them, but are actually administering them; and those who ought to be not only protected by institutions, but to administer them, are driven out and punished by them. With this grand perversion of the institutional world, we have touched the lowest point in the sweep of the dramatic action.

II.

We have now reached what may be called the Second Movement of the play, the Movement which will set forth the reaction against the successful, but guilty children, and show the completed retribution. The Ethical World is lying in ruins—falsehood triumphant, honesty banished, moral ties destroyed, Family disrupted, State perverted. Truly, chaos seems to have come again, and social order to have passed into a period of dissolution. But from the chaos those elements are beginning to separate and to coalesce—which will restore order and bring back to man his violated institutions. We have seen how the faithful children were unjustly cast off by their parents, and how the latter received the penalty of their wrong. But thus a new guilt has arisen, that of the faithless children, whose punishment also must now be portrayed; for, in their case, it is the same law of retribution —the return of the deed—which was observed in the case of their parents.

But who are to be the instruments of their chastisement? These are the faithful children, who will return and seek to punish the wrongs and recover the rights of themselves and of their parents. This Second Movement, accordingly, proceeds on the line of restoration; it is the attempt to restore the disrupted Family, and the perverted State. Thus the circle of the action is complete; it begins with the wrongs done to the faithful children, and ends by putting into their hands the means of justice, and of social recovery. But the parents cannot be completely restored to a society which is seeking to heal itself of their deeds; they are tragic in a world which they have made tragic.

Between the First and Second Movements the reader will note many differences corresponding to this difference of thought. There is a change in tone, color, style; the volcanic, defiant, wrathful energy of speech becomes calmer, more soothing and compassionate; the First Movement passes into a storm, the Second gradually passes out of it into a clearing-up; Passion and Revenge are turned to Patience and Love; in the one part, limits are placed, in the other, limits are taken away; the one seems to share in the curse, the other in the blessing. All undergoes transformation, from the outer garment of language to the soul within. But the chief of these changes, and the one to which we must reach down as the ground of the others, is that of institutions, which are broken, shattered, perverted in the First Movement, and then in the Second Movement rise toward recovery. The play shows, not some man or some men, but a society, a world going to pieces, then restoring itself by getting rid of its destructive characters. Thus we behold in the total action the process of social regeneration.

The structure of the Second Movement will, of necessity be somewhat different from that of the First Movement. The good people must separate themselves from the bad, and then unite; such is always the process of purification from social disorder. Hence there will be two main Threads still, but differently arranged. In the First Movement these two Threads were the families of Lear and Gloster; but now the faithless members of each family, have coalesced into one party, and the faithful members of each family are brought together into a union of symyathy, if not of action. We have already seen how Edmund has gravitated toward his like, Regan and Goneril; on the other hand, Edgar sympathizes with, if he does not aid, Cordelia. These two sides are brought into collision; the faithless children are victorious in the external conflict, as they, under the leadership of Albany, are fighting for the State, but the daughters perish in a struggle among themselves, and Edmund falls in single combat with his brother. At the end, all the characters who have introduced disorder and conflict into the institutional world are eliminated, while the positive characters of the drama remain to build up anew the shattered society. These two Threads we may now follow out more fully.

1. Beginning, therefore, with the first Thread, we observe that it is composed of the faithful children, Edgar and Cordelia, together with the groups of which each one is the central figure. Both are similar in conduct and character; both bring aid and solace to their afflicted parents, who, however, have done them the deepest wrong. But their fidelity never falters, it is self-centered, determined in itself; their duty cannot give way to revenge or indifference. Such has been their trait from the start, yet both have developed wonderfully in the course of the drama. This development must be specially noted; it is one of the grand facts of Shakespeare's procedure; his characters are not generally a dead result, but an unfolding. In the present case, the two fathers are to be brought back, through their faithful children, to their previous circumstances of honor and power, if possible; at least, they are to be solaced, comforted, and restored in mind. Accordingly, there is a great change in the literary atmosphere of this portion of the drama, as we have already noticed; the tremendous upheavals of passion cease, to a great extent, and, in their stead, the tenderest emotions of love and pity stir the breast. The action becomes more quiet and pathetic, tears succeed to wrath, loving devotion to ingratitude.

This Thread, moreover, divides of itself into two distinct strands, which often touch each other, but are never firmly twisted together. We are, therefore, compelled, if we follow the organic characteristics given by the poet, to unfold these two strands separately.

(*a*) First, then, let us trace the career of Edgar and his father, who are, from the Fourth Act, joined indissolubly together. Edgar is a grand development from blank innocence to a complete knowledge of the world. We saw how simple-hearted he was, and how easily deceived; that simple-hearted honesty is the mother-soil which will bear the richest fruits of character. The wrong of institutions towards him has never made him faithless to them, as it has his brother, though he endures more from them than his brother. From this primal, indestructible germ of fidelity he is to unfold into the complete man through a long and terrible outpour of sufferings. His training is, indeed, severe; in his own person he has felt the perversion of the Ethical World; if he, nevertheless, will not fall out with institutions, but keep his faith in them, in spite of their perversion and wrong toward himself, he will become a strong man indeed. If he can take up the very injury of society into himself, without losing his duty to it or his love towards man, he will have everything that the world can give him—a soul filled with all the wealth of human experience; he will have charity.

Let us look back at what he has passed through in his discipline. First, he had to flee to the woods and disguise himself as a beggar—

> And with presented nakedness outface
> The winds and persecutions of the sky.

Next, a deeper disguise he assumes, he simulates madness, in order to preserve life and with it the unquenched spark of character. But under this disguise, taken for self-protection, now rises compassion for others, when he sees Lear in the storm: "My tears begin to take his part so much, they mar my counterfeiting." Therewith comes to him a relief:

> How light and portable my pain seems now,
> When that which makes me bend, makes the King bow,
> He childed as I fathered!

It is the relief which its own charity gives to the charitable soul; truly he is getting the discipline of adversity. When we meet him at the beginning of the Fourth Act, he can say: "Yet better thus, and known to be contemned, than still contemned and flattered." He would choose the reality, however bitter, to a false appearance, however agreeable, so deep is the truth and sincerity of his nature. To be the lowest thing in fortune "stands still in esperance;" no despair, no bitterness or misanthropy; he has become the self-centered man to whom insanity is not possible, he has received the full training of misfortune into an inner freedom.

But who is this wretched, mutilated man, who meets him here upon the wild heath? It is his father Gloster, blinded, fleeing from the cruelty of the other favored son, accompanied by a faithful tenant as a guide; this tenant is a momentary shooting-star of hope that darts across the dark horizon, and prognosticates the coming dawn. Edgar beholds his parent who has so wantonly wronged him; no malice or revenge, but a deeper pity: "I am worse than e'er I was." Yet he recovers at once; low though he be, he might be worse: "The worst is not so long as we can say, "'This is the worst.'" Thus he is prepared to be the Healer of his father, whom calamity has humbled into despair—which it could never do with the son.

We noticed that Gloster saw the wrong which had been done to Lear, but not the very similar wrong which he had himself done. Again he shows himself the superstitious man, who beholds not his own delinquency, but ascribes it to the sun, moon and stars; thus he cannot see his own deed, though he sees another's deed. Then follows the penalty, his eyes are put out: "I stumbled when I saw," and he comes to know the faithful and the faithless son: "O, my follies! then Edgar was abused." Now he thinks of his injured child, nay, his sympathy becomes universal, and like Lear, calamity leads him to charity:

> Heavens, deal so still!
> Let the superfluous and lust-dieted man
> That slaves your ordinance, that will not see
> Because he does not feel, feel your power quickly;
> So distribution should undo excess
> And each man have enough.

Such is the prayer, in which he seems to justify the discipline of Heaven. Gloster, too, has received the training of adversity; he shows contrition for his wrong, he has reached an inner reconciliation with his son, he has come to a universal charity. As in the case of Lear, we think that he, too, is saved; but like Lear, there is in him a counter-current which drives him forward in the opposite direction.

This is his despair, he believes that he is the victim of an almighty, yet cruel power above:

> As flies to wanton boys, are we to the Gods;
> They kill us for their sport.

Such a creed is the fruit of superstition, of a belief in external determination, which belief, in turn, springs from his original guilt. It is manifest that, if the Gods are the immediate cause of all events, the misfortune of Gloster comes from them directly; calamity is divine persecution, and hope is impossible. Gloster, then, is still bearing the mental consequences of his primal sin; his discipline has brought him far, but has not yet reconciled him with the world-order; he still attributes to external power the evil which he has brought upon himself. It lies deep in the characters of Lear and Gloster that the one sinks down into insanity, the other into despair.

Gloster, accordingly, wishes to end the unequal contest by ending his own existence, and from this comes his desire to reach the precipice of Dover. But it is the object of Edgar, who now acts as leader instead of the aged tenant, to rescue him from despair and to reconcile him to the world. Edgar has been trained by his experience to be the soul-curer of his father, for has he not passed through despair himself and come forth sound? Moreover, he has learnt disguise in order to escape evil; life has, indeed, given him her full instruction upon this point. We find him assuming four different characters in these last two Acts—true always to the highest principle, yet subtly adapting himself to the emergency. That guileless, innocent youth of the First Act has learnt somewhat! He seems to know how to combine the two extremes of human conduct: absolute versatility and true steadfastness.

This new skill is shown in the artifice that the son practices upon the blind old father, making him believe that he has fallen down the lofty cliff, that he has been preserved by the miraculous interposition of the gods, that, in fine, he must be the special object of their care and protection. This conclusion is plainly drawn from the incident:

> Therefore, thou, happy father,
> Think that the clearest gods, who make them honors
> Of men's impossibilities, have preserved thee.

Wherein the purpose of the artifice is distinctly stated. Gloster is cured, he is now ready to accept life anew, and to endure every species of affliction. He seems also to abandon his notion of a divine persecution directed against himself. Edgar can well declare in a later passage:

> Met I my father—became his guide,
> Led him, begged for him, saved him from despair.

It is true that the son skillfully makes use of his father's weakness, namely, superstition, to effect his pious purpose; Edgar shows himself a great reader of character, as well as a psychical healer, in the description of the fiend whose eyes

> Were two full moons, he had a thousand noses,
> Horns whelked and waved like the enridged sea,
> It was some fiend—

And truly it was a fiend—despair—which lured the wretched man to the precipice; so Edgar told the truth, though in a mythical form. But ought he to have practiced that deception upon his father that good might come? Pathologists do so without scruple, to cure disease; then we must recollect that Gloster's trouble was itself a delusion, he thought the gods were against him, and, hence, wished to commit suicide; so Edgar simply uses a deception to wipe out a deception, and leaves his father's mind clear and sound. It is the farthest-reaching truth that "the Gods have preserved thee."

Gloster again meets Lear, mad, roaming at large over the country, though Cordelia is trying to get possession of his person, in order to restore him. It is the last time the two ill-fated parents come together; both have touched the lowest depth of misfortune; both are now found and cared for by the children to whom they have done the grossest injustice. The presence of Lear, showing a greater fall, works in Gloster a still deeper cure, a more complete reconciliation with the higher powers, whom he can now address as "ever-gentle gods," and pray: "Let not my worser spirit tempt me again to die before you please." He can now "bear it longer, and not fall to quarrel with your great opposeles wills." Edgar thus has spiritually saved his father; next he saves him physically, he rescues him from death at the hands of Oswald and slays the assassin. The supreme filial action is shown; he has rescued the mind within from despair, and the body without from destruction. He may be said to have restored his parent to existence, the devotion of the child reaches in him its climax. Every word that Edgar says now we delay over with a deep and thoughtful interest; his passing remarks are filled with the richest experience of life. He calls himself

> A most poor man, made tame to Fortune's blows,
> Who, by the art of known and feeling sorrows,
> Am pregnant to good pity. Give me your hand—

Such is his explanation of himself and of his pity, which is born of the discipline of "fortune's blows;" his has been the school unto charity, and he has learnt the lesson. In fact, the whole play represents such a school. Then to his father he says: "Bear free and patient thoughts," for Patience, not Passion, is freedom, as we saw in the case of Lear.

The roar of battle is heard in the distance; Edgar puts his father in a place of safety, and goes out to observe the result of the conflict. He does not seem to have participated in the fight; he keeps aloof from the collision with the State, which is the tragic act of Cordelia, and hence he is preserved at the termination of the play. The great end of his present effort is the personal security and mental repose of his parent, who once more, at the defeat of Lear, drops back into his former condition, but the son drags him out with a word of fortitude: "What, in ill thoughts again? Men must endure," and so Gloster still endures.

But there is a limit to his endurance, and to this limit the drama has come. Edgar, hoping his father sufficiently restored to hold up under the news, reveals himself, and tells the whole story of his pilgrimage. The parent could not endure this last strain, here Patience ends:

>   His flawed heart,
> Alack! too weak the conflict to support!—
> 'Twixt two extremes of passion, joy and grief,
> Burst smilingly.

Gloster cannot be restored to the Family whose essence he has so deeply violated. His heart breaks in the process; his emotional nature cannot bear up under the contradictory feelings of his situation. His inability to make this final reconciliation is the logical necessity of his character; he has been brought into harmony with Providence but not with himself. He now sees, not the sun, moon and stars as the cause of his evil, but himself; he has run upon his own limitation and he dies. Those two sons are the grand conflict which he has brought into the world, and of which he perishes, for both are in him, and the tragic one is the stronger; he is really the victim of his faithless son, since the latter existed not only in the world, but also in the father's character. The sight of his own deed in its complete circuit slays him. Yet Gloster is not so much a bad as a weak character; he is unwittingly made the instrument of the disruption of his own family; if he be restored to it, there would remain the same possibility of his disrupting it again, unless his intellectual weakness be removed by his experience. But he is not strong enough to span this last breach; when he discovers himself, the discovery kills him. Edgar, speaking to Edmund, hints the origin of the father's misfortunes, and shows the full circle of his deed:

> The gods are just, and of our pleasant vices
> Make instruments to plague us;
> The dark and vicious place where thee he got
> Cost him his eyes,—

And it may be added, cost him his life. Edmund, too, recognizes the fact, and confesses:

> Thou hast spoken right, 'tis true;
> The wheel has came full circle;

And he makes the application to his own case: "I am here."

This brings us to the final act of Edgar, the duel with his brother. It has been observed that he is no longer the unsophisticated youth, who was so completely outwitted by the rascal Edmund. He has learned to disguise himself and to assume a wonderful variety of characters; the number and skill of the deceptions which he practices upon his father, to accomplish the most unselfish and pious ends, are startling to the rigid moralist. His education has been severe, but thorough, and when he now comes to meet Edmund, the wily intellectual villain, he is fully prepared. He assumes his final disguise, meets his brother and slays him—destroys the instrument of destruction. The innocent man, accepting life's trials, overtops at last the subtlest rogue. Still, it is harsh that brother should kill brother; it has in it a little too much of individual requital. But Edmund's success in villainy has hardened him, he cannot be transformed till he be struck down; no charity will change him, as it did not change the father, till misfortune smote him. Then comes forgiveness, and Edgar responds: "Let's exchange charity,"—so that in their case, too, we hear the golden words of the play.

Such is the light-giving career of Edgar through all its transmutations; he is the transparent, pure soul compelled to assume the disguises of the world, and to take on the appearance of untruth, that he may be true. Thus he saves himself, saves his father, and puts out of the way the destroyer, rising to the supreme height of the drama. But Gloster, so similar to Œdipus, cannot attain to self-knowledge without becoming tragic; he who was in the habit of thrusting off responsibility for his deed, comes at last to see its full sweep into himself; that sweep is so violent and overwhelming that it kills him. The limit of character has hardened into the limit of life, so that to transcend the one is to pass out of the other; when he has to take the burden of his conduct, he breaks. Self-excuse of guilt has placed upon his soul the limit which makes him tragic.

(*b.*) We have now reached Cordelia again, whose wonderful development since we last met her in the First Act, is next to be considered. Her career is similar to that of Edgar in many respects; she, too, is the faithful, yet injured child; she, too, seeks the internal and external restoration of her father. But she goes a step further than Edgar—she assails the State in her attempt to recover the rights of Lear. She thus falls into guilt, which brings on the tragic end. Her endeavor has three different phases—restoration of her parent to reason, to Family, and to State.

First of all, the attempt must be made to cure the insanity of Lear. He seems to be wandering alone over the country, without care or guidance; his talk, though wild and incoherent, is mainly connected with his lost authority, with the cruelty of his daughters, and, in general, with the utter perversity of both the institutional and moral worlds, which he, in his raving mood, scoffs at and condemns with sarcastic bitterness. The poet has thus intimated the cause of his madness, as well as the means of its cure—restore him to a daughter's love, along with the image of respect and power, and the ground of his insanity is removed. These are just the spiritual medicines which Cordelia administers to him after sufficient physical repose. In the pathetic scene where he awakens, she asks for his blessing with the deepest affection, and assures him that he is again in his own kingdom. Lear is thus restored to reason, and to the Family with its love; the original cause of insanity is taken away.

It is manifest that Cordelia is different from what she was in the First Act; a new element of her nature seems to have developed itself. Previously we saw her rigid moral code and her intellectuality brought into the greatest prominence; now her character, in its softer and more beautiful features, is shown; we behold her devotion to parent, as well as her intense emotional nature, which, however, she is able to keep under perfect control. Still, the germ of this new trait can be found in her earlier declarations and demeanor. In fact, it may be found in her rigid sense of duty, which is the seed that at last unfolds into charity. If the germ of character be sound, it will grow into beauty through the storm and sunshine of life.

Cordelia now finds that love of husband is not a limit to love of parent; she can love both all. She comes back, broken and tender, with a bruised heart: "patience and sorrow strove who should express her goodliest." She, too, has had to have her discipline, she was not perfect at the start. She has tamed her sarcastic speech against her sisters, though under far greater provocation than ever before; once or twice only she expresses a sorrowful surprise at their conduct. An inner, as well as an outer, return is hers—a return to England and a return to love. Her life in France has taught her much, taught her love as the principle of conduct; the French King took her dowerless, for love;

we may suppose, that he has treated her with love, not with doting or irascibility. She is, indeed, a new woman, and she looks back at her former action with some pangs apparently; especially she contrasts her conduct with that of Kent:

> O thou good Kent, how shall I live and work
> To match thy goodness? My life will be too short,
> And every measure fail me.

She seems to place Kent's action above her own; she gives him supreme recognition of worthiness, which is to him the highest reward:

> To be acknowledged, madam, is overpaid.

The new Cordelia has become not merely sound herself, but like Edgar, a healer of the diseased spirit of others; for it is not simply the physical repose prescribed by the doctor, that clears up the clouded intellect of Lear, but it is the presence of the daughter, who brings with her a double restorative—that of her transfigured love on the one hand, and that of institutions on the other. It was the loss of both these, through the conduct of his daughters, that shattered his reason. The return of Cordelia means, accordingly, the return of sanity.

But her third purpose is that which ruins her cause. She brings a French army into England, to secure to her father his right, as she says; it is evident that she means to place him again on the throne. She thus assails the highest ethical institution of man—the State; in defending a right, she unwittingly herself commits the greatest wrong.

The poet was doubtless patriotic; neither he nor his audience would allow Frenchmen to be victorious in England, and the one who introduced the ancient enemy of the nation would be held the worst of traitors. Moreover, Lear had resigned his power and divided his kingdom; he had no longer any just claim to the crown. Her invasion of the country rouses up against her the head of the State, Albany, who was otherwise favorable both to her and to Lear. But he had to defend his own realm, though he hates his associates and loves those who are fighting against him. Had Cordelia been satisfied with the restoration of her father to his reason and to his family, Albany would have given her both aid and sympathy. However much we may admire her character and regret her fate, however indignant we may be against her two sisters, still we must, in the end, say she did wrong—she violated the majesty of the State. In her affection for parent she attempted to destroy the higher principle for the sake of the lower. The result is, she loses the battle, is taken prisoner, and perishes.

The death of Cordelia is often felt to be unjustifiable, and the play was once altered to suit this feeling. But a true comprehension of the nature of Dramatic Art will vindicate the poet. The end of Tragedy is not that somebody get killed, or even that a villain be brought to justice; it must show the collision of two ethical principles, both of which have validity in the reason of man. The individuals who are the representatives of these conflicting principles are brought into a struggle which admits of no mediation. Both, from one point of view, are in the right; and yet both, from another point of view, are in the wrong. The deeper, more universal thought must decide the conflict and must triumph in the end, for strife cannot be eternal. Cordelia's profoundest impulse is devotion to Family—a very lofty principle of action; but she is led by it into a collision with the State—a still higher principle. Undoubtedly, these two elements ought to be harmonized if possible; but Tragedy means that they cannot always be harmonized, and, hence, the lesser must be subordinated by violence and death.

Cordelia is, therefore, a truly tragic character, whom we are compelled to condemn, though we shed tears over her fate. But she is something more—she is the tragic *female* character; for her collision is peculiar to her sex. The Family is the highest ethical principle of woman as woman—at least it has been hitherto in the history of the world, even though we may think that this condition of things will be changed in the future. The readers of her own sex, therefore, will always feel—perhaps, ought always to feel—that she is in the right—that her death is unjustifiable. Let us contrast her action with that of Albany, who is a man, and holds to the other principle—the State. He, too, is indignant at the conduct of Goneril and Regan. He sympathizes deeply with the misfortunes of Lear, and wishes well to the efforts of Cordelia for the restoration of her father. But a

French army means the ruin of his country—at least its control from without; he, therefore, is compelled to make the choice; he takes the State as his ethical principle, though he has to act with those whom he hates and against those whom he loves. Albany and Cordelia, accordingly, collide; it is the collision of man and woman, both of whom are the representatives of the essential ethical principles of their respective sexes. It is also, to a certain extent, the collision between emotion and reason. Our feelings go along with Cordelia—even Albany's feelings went along with Cordelia; for the Family is the realm of affection, and must always call forth the emotions of man. Still, intelligence must control sentiment, and subordinate it to the higher end. The consequences of their actions are seen in the catastrophe; Cordelia perishes, while Albany survives as the ruler of his country.

It may be affirmed very decidedly that Shakespeare makes Cordelia tragic in accord with a conscious principle of his Art. His two chief sources, Holinshed's chronicle and the old play of *Lear* portray her invasion as successful in restoring her father to his throne. The poet must have purposely changed the story in this regard. On what ground? Assuredly not to show the good woman overwhelmed in her goodness; that is not Shakespeare's view of the moral order of things. An innocent person may perish in the world of accident, but not in the ethical world of which Shakespeare gives the picture. Like his tragic characters in general, she is caught in the antithesis of opposing principles; in following one virtue to excess, she violates another; in pursuing one right to an extreme, she falls into wrong. Her tragic pathos is as old as Literature, or rather, as old as woman herself; it is that of Antigone, even that of Andromache, recorded in our first Literary Book, ancient Homer. Family and State collide in her, and she goes down in the conflict.

We have next to consider Lear. His too, is a course of development; we saw him develop into insanity, where we left him in darkness; now he is to develop out of insanity. Of this process we mark briefly the stages. (1). The poet introduces him in his mad fit after waking up; he is playing with kingship, with authority; as judge, he upsets the ethical order, as it has been upset in his own case; the culprit shall not "die for adultery" or other guilt; "none does offend, none, I say." The institutional world is turned upside down; society is as crazy as Lear is; in fact, his mind is now the image of the grand social perversion which comes of the present rulers, Goneril and Regan. (2). Restoration to his reason and to his daughter— both go together—follows in due order. First is his repose, "our foster-nurse of nature;" he wakes, beholds Cordelia, begins to recognize himself as "a very foolish fond old man;" the cloud breaks, "I fear I am not in my perfect mind," a self-cognizance which is the turning-point to reason. But behold now the sun-burst of sanity: "You must bear with me. Pray you now, forget and forgive, I am old and foolish." The revengeful Lear pleads for charity, the unlimited monarch recognizes his limits in full. He is indeed redeemed with a marvelous baptism; having been immersed in the dark river of madness, he comes out a new sane man. (3). Not only reason he has, but love now in its true sense. Fortune turns against Cordelia and Lear, both are taken prisoners. But the prison is no limit; "we two alone will sing like birds in the cage;" he gives himself fully to love without commanding it; the restraint of the jail is no restraint to the man spiritually free. (4). But with the new bond rises the new limit, for upon the permanence of that bond rests Lear's love, his reason, his life. Cordelia is removed by death; what now? The storm bursts again: "Howl, howl, howl, howl!" Lear drops back to Passion and Revenge, Patience and Charity are again lost, this last test was too strong for him. Thence he passes down into insanity, though he wakes out of it for a moment to recognize Kent, and Kent's character; but he reverts to Cordelia, and is at once with her in death.

It is evident that Lear did not attain a perfect restoration, he was not absolutely self-centered, the last trial was too hard for him. Yet the complete man must meet even such a trial. Lear dies with all his daughters, as it were, together; there is something common to them all, which gives the tragic outcome. The first disruption of Lear's domestic ties ended in the loss of his reason, the second now ends in the loss of his life; still, it is his own primal deed of wrong, which reaches through the whole play, and at last strikes the fatal blow.

We must feel, however, that he received his compensation, he attained love, the surrender of that stubborn individuality, which in its pride endured no limits, which at first was tyrant over love, as over everything else. But even here the tragic line is drawn; that love, welded by such a fiery discipline, has become so strong that it cannot now be broken but at the cost of life. The union of father and daughter has reached its tragic intensity; separation means death. That selfhood of Lear so colossal at the beginning he has immolated utterly to the loved object; he can never regain it when she is gone.

Thus Lear's full conscious restoration to his true daughter turns out tragic, as Gloster's full conscious restoration to his true son is tragic. Both impinge upon the limits of their characters; both perish by a breaking of the heart, by a cataclysm of emotion. Gloster, when he finds himself and not the outer power responsible for his own and his son's misfortunes, breaks under the responsibility of his deed; the thought of it kills him, he is the victim of self-knowledge. Lear's very strength of individuality conditions the strength of its sacrifice; lost in love, when love is lost, he is lost; he returns to Passion, his old limit, and is dashed to death upon it. Both reveal limits in their characters—limits which grow and harden from conduct, and which they at last cannot transcend, but by transcending life itself.

2. There remains, finally, the Second Thread of the Second Movement to be considered. The faithless children of both families have come together—similarity of character naturally attracts them to one another. Edmund and the two sisters constitute the heads of this group, to which Albany must be added—though he only belongs to it partially. An external conflict has arisen with Cordelia, the nature and grounds of which have, already been given. In it they were successful, as they happened to be the supporters of the State in conjunction with Albany. But the internal conflict has also arisen, as it must arise under the circumstances. The unity of the faithless cannot be permanent; they must be true to the deepest principle of their character, and, hence, must be faithless to one another. This gives the struggle among themselves, which the poet has also developed to make the delineation logical and complete.

The two sisters have become fired with the most intense mutual jealousy and enmity in their endeavors to obtain the love of Edmund; they are playing false to each other, and Edmund is playing false to both. The principle of them all is falsehood—what else can be expected but mutual treachery? But Goneril and Regan are now shown in a further, yet very consistent, development of character—their faithlessness becomes universal. Having been faithless to their father, they naturally become faithless to the Family in all its relations;

they are now portrayed as violating the great fundamental virtue of the Family—chastity. Infidelity toward parent is deepened into infidelity toward husband, and the very possibility of any domestic ties is annihilated. Their former conduct has adequately motived this final development. For them every condition of the Family is destroyed; daughterhood has long since perished; now wifehood passes away. Union with them is impossible, even for the Bastard, as he himself intimates. What remains? Only death; for every substantial element of existence is gone. Goneril, always the prime mover, destroys her sister with poison, as before she brought ruin upon her father; and, when she knows that her intrigue with Edmund is discovered by her husband, she speedily thrusts a dagger into her own bosom. Such is the end of the two faithless sisters; both perished in a struggle with each other for the possession of an infamous villain who was faithless to both.

But Edmund remains; his success has been without a parallel; he may well believe that his lucky destiny cannot be arrested. Hitherto he has obtained all the honor, titles, and property of the family of Gloster; now his object is the possession of the State. He fights bravely against the French invasion for a crown which he regards as his own, and, to remove every obstacle which might arise in his path after the victory, he orders Lear and Cordelia to be put to death. This conduct brings him into direct conflict with Albany, the present head of the State, whose life he has before sought to destroy. But Albany, according to the spirit of the play, cannot be his slayer; this can only be his brother, Edgar, whose father he has deceived, betrayed, and outraged, and who now appears as the avenger of the Family. The poet is thus careful to make the first wrong of Edmund to return, and to involve him in its inexorable retribution. The base-born son, in the course of his career, has assailed quite all the ethical institutions of man; he believed that the world was entirely controlled by management, and not by principle; hence his sole faith was in his own cunning. His fate, though long deferred, is the necessary consequence of such a character; some one armed with the vengeance of violated right destroys him. Such is the outcome of the three faithless children.

The conduct and fate of Kent, in this Second Movement, seem to be left somewhat indefinite. The poet, however, carefully informs us that it is so intended:

—"Some dear cause
Will in concealment wrap me up a while."

No active participation in the war is manifested by him, though he visits the camp of Cordelia. His devotion appears now to be to Lear as an individual; still, the drama indicates little one way or the other. Some critics have imagined that his death is given in the play, but this is certainly a mistake of a fact, and also a misunderstanding of a principle. The truth is, the poet wishes to preserve all the faithful; but, to do so consistently, he must keep them out of the collision with the State, which was the fatal deed of Cordelia. For this reason the conduct of both Kent and Edgar, in regard to the war, is left in obscurity, though their personal devotion is still brought forward in the strongest light. They, therefore, survive with Albany, who defends the State, and yet, at the same time, respects the Family.

The action has now completed its revolution, and brought back to all the leading characters the consequences of their deeds; the double guilt and the double retribution have been fully portrayed. The treatment of children by parents, and of parents by children, is the theme; both fidelity and infidelity are shown in their extreme manifestation. Two families are taken—that of the monarch and that of the subject; the former develops within itself its own collisions, free from any external restraint, and, hence, exhibits the truest and most complete result; the latter is largely influenced and determined in its course by authority, but an authority which is itself poisoned with domestic conflict. The exhaustiveness of the treatment is worthy of careful study. Regan is faithless to parent; Goneril is faithless to both parent and husband; Cordelia is true to both, yet assails another ethical principle—the State. The two sons and the two sons-in-law exhibit also distinct phases of the domestic tie; they are still further divided, by the fundamental theme of the play, into the faithful and faithless—that is, a son and a son-in-law belong to each side. But it is a curious fact that one very important relation of the Family is wholly omitted—no mother appears anywhere; sonhood, daughterhood, wifehood, fatherhood, are all present, but the tenderest bond of existence—motherhood—is wanting. The poet evidently does not need it, for the action is already sufficiently full and complicated; perhaps, too, the character of the mother may be supposed to reappear in some of her children, as, for example, in Cordelia, who, in spite of certain similarities, is so different from her father. But one cannot help commending the true instinct, or, what is more likely, the sound judgment, which kept such a mild and tender relation out of the cauldron of passion and ingratitude which seethes with such destructive energy in this appalling drama.

But not alone the domestic, but also the social element must be always present to the thought. A history of society in small is shown in the drama; we see how a period gets corrupt and perverted, then how it is purified. A destructive element, a poison is introduced into the body politic, which passes through wrong, convulsion, revolution to restoration. Society is not tragic in Shakespeare, but the individual may be, if he collides with its interest, and persists in his collision. We notice that three men are left, the truly positive men of the play, Albany, Edgar and Kent, who are to build up anew the shattered social organism. Thus the tragedy leaves us hopeful of a purified society, and reconciled with the supreme ethical order, which, we feel, cannot perish, though it, too, has to pass through its periods of corruption and purification.

MACBETH.

The date of the composition of *Macbeth* seems to hover around the year 1604, the period of the union of Scotland and England under James. At that time the English people felt an increased interest in their Northern neighbor, who was to furnish them a ruler, and with whom they were to live in the future. The play gives a typical view of Scotland, and the character of its people, with their superstitions, virtues and vices, and with local touches of atmosphere and landscape. The political relation of the two countries is shown from an English point of view: Scotland, full of revolt, turbulence and crime, is pacified by interference from England. The model of the ruler in the drama is an English King, who imparts his exellence to the Scottish King. The action is more hurried than in other tragedies of Shakespeare; but this hurry lies in the very conception of the work, and may be the poet's art, and not a careless precipitancy in getting his play done, as some have supposed.

This is not an historical play, though the chief personages that appear in it have a place in history.

On the contrary, its soul is mythical, and it belongs to an age of fable as thoroughly as Oedipus. Even in Holinshed, the chronicler from whom the poet derived almost wholly the outer body of his drama, the narrative is mythical, changing suddenly from dry fact into a Marvelous Tale, as we often behold in Herodotus, the Father of History. The Supernatural World plays into the action, and is spun into the characters in the story of Holinshed, which has also the strong ethical element found in Shakespeare's drama. Guilt and Retribution we can feel in the rugged words of the old chronicler, as he dresses up his miraculous legend, and hints the consequences of the wicked deed. But Shakespeare has taken these mythical outlines, and filled them with human motives and actions; moreover he has organized the whole into the structure of his drama, though in the chronicle also the narration often falls of itself into a dramatic form, and seems to be calling for the poet. He must, indeed, have the Mythus, yet the Mythus must have him also, to reach its true completion and fulfilment.

The play, in its whole sweep, reveals a grand cycle in the ethical order of the world. Given the weak, inefficient ruler; he, through his weakness and inefficiency, generates rebellion, which, however, is put down by the strong subject or Hero; yet this very victory over rebellion begets rebellion anew, for the cause still remains, namely, the weak King on the one hand, and the strong subject on the other, who is now mightier than the

King. The great victory, in the subtle movement of History, has a tendency to lose itself in the defeat which it has caused; it coalesces with what it has conquered, and becomes one with the same; it sweeps away the limit against its enemy, and takes him up into its bosom; it is indeed no true victory, unless it includes itself and its enemy too, removing the boundary between the twain; if it cannot do that, the battle will have to be fought over again. It is an old saying, that nations which conquer are themselves conquered in their victory—*Grecia capta ferum victorem cepit.* The triumph over rebellion has not, then, settled the question of rebellion for Scotland, and Macbeth, in putting down treason, has become himself the traitor.

Let us seek to take in the entire orbit of Macbeth's career at a glance. The poet shows in him a man, who, having saved the State, becomes the Hero, greater and more powerful than the King, and who then wheels about at the very point of supreme greatness, and turns faithless to the State and Ruler that he has saved, a traitor to his own heroic action. The drama will show such a man, meted, condemned and executed by his own standard; as he put down rebellion, so he a rebel, will be put down, by the law of his own deed. What he measured out to others in strict justice, is in strict justice measured out to him, with Providence holding the scales, as the World's Justiciary.

Macbeth then, has done the great action, which is also good; but just out of this great and good action is conjured the demon who is to destroy him. For the Great Deed, however worthy, has in it the Great Temptation, or rather it has the Tempter himself ensconced, secretly coiled up in its very excellence. It breeds even in high souls, insolence, a defiance of the ethical world-order, in subserving which alone man becomes truly great. The puny individual, in his success, gets to imagining that he may somehow be above this world-order, that he is mightier than it is, and so he collides with his own Great Deed, inasmuch as he turns to doing that which is its opposite. Out of Macbeth's triumph over rebellion is born the Weird Sister, who lures him into rebellion. But look at the mightiest captains of the world, Themistocles, Napoleon, supreme in victory which defeats them. Yet there is the other class of men the Washingtons, who have done the Great Deed, and have not been caught by its Devil, a class only partially represented in this play by Banquo. The triumphant Hero must find his ethical limit somewhere in King, Country, Providence; let him dare transgress it, and his doom is uttered by his act.

Now, it is just the function of Mythology to shadow forth this mysterious power of evil which hides in the human deed, and perverts it into the scourge of itself, and of its doer. What is witchery, but that which makes this demonic principle corporeal, and gives to it a voice speaking darkly, yet prophetically, out of its world beyond? Hence comes the supernatural tinge which is given to the present drama, and which is always felt to be one of its most effective qualities. It transports us into a world so different from our own that sometimes we are at a loss to explain the acts and beliefs of its characters; still the mystery always heightens the impression. The coloring throughout is the same; it belongs not merely to one person, or to several persons, but it is the atmosphere which envelops the whole play. All move in a world of imagination in which man dwells among, or is influenced by, strange fantastic shapes.

The poet has produced his marvelous effect in two ways. In the first place, Nature, whenever it is introduced, is made to prognosticate spiritual occurrences and conflicts; it seems to exist only as the sign and impress, in which is read the human deed; it is filled with human purpose. This is Nature's enchantment, whereby it is given a tongue and speaks wonders; the raven, the owl, the cricket betoken darkly what is to come; the wind and the tempest "threaten man's bloody stage," while the heavens are "troubled at his act;" Duncan's wild horses (Macbeth and Banquo, let us suggest,) "break their stalls and eat each other." The struggles of men are foreshadowed and aftershadowed in the living picture of the sensible world; the minor characters and the popular mind especially look at themselves in this broad mirror of Nature.

But, in the second place, the converse procedure is far more effective, and, hence, is far more prominent in the present drama—that is, the internal spirit, in excited activity, projects its workings into external forms of its own, which rise up before it with all the certainty of a real object. Such is the air-drawn dagger, the ghost of Banquo, and chiefly, the Weird Sisters. These are products of the imagination of those who behold them, but of the imagination so intense that it does not recognize its own shapes as distinct from actual things. These two processes are the complements of each other, to a certain extent—the one unfolds the internal out of the external, the other unfolds the external out of the internal. Both indicate the supremacy of the imagination, whose great characteristic is to find already in Nature, or to create purely out of itself those objective forms which express the activities of spirit.

It will be seen that man, in such a condition, is apparently controlled from without by the dim forebodings of the physical world, as well as by the phantoms of his own brain, which have, too, an outer reality. A realm beyond human power or consciousness seems to exercise a governing influence over the action of the individual. It may be derided as superstition, but let not the other side be forgotten: it is a genuine attempt of man, in a certain stage of his culture, to find or create some expression for what is truest in himself and in the world. Such a theme is, however, essentially epical, for it is the Epos which exhibits its characters as determined by external powers—by the god or demon, by the fairy or angel. The Drama, on the contrary, portrays man as acting through himself, as ruled by his own wishes, motives, ends, principles; hence in it the abovementioned instrumentalities of the Epos must always be subordinated and explained into an internal element. Shakespeare has, accordingly, shown the inner movement of the mind of his characters alongside of the outer influence of the Weird Sisters; both are, indeed, two different forms of expressing the same ultimate fact. There is thus a twofoldness in the play, a double reflection of the same content; the reason whereof is that characters which are controlled by the imagination are portrayed in this drama, and, hence, it must be shown what they seem to behold and follow in the outward world, and what they really do behold and follow in the inward world. Macbeth, for instance, will see the Witch on the heath, and will see "vaulting ambition" in his own soul; both the "air-drawn dagger" and "the dagger of the mind" will be present to him. The mystery of the play lies in this doubleness of its meaning, veritably oracular, which mystery, however, the reader is to solve in his vision of its deeper unity.

The Dramatic Structure at once reveals the fundamental fact of the play in its external form, as well as hints its inner meaning. The first thing we notice here is that there are two worlds, the natural and supernatural, which run through the entire action, and which, therefore, we shall call its Threads. These two worlds are respectively portrayed in two sets of characters, in which they are wholly distinct, then in one set of characters, in which they come together.

The Supernatural World is that of the Weird Sisters, who seem to enter the action from the outside, and to direct its course; yet they also belong inside and work from thence. They appear in their own independent realm in two scenes, and then they are shown, in two other scenes, connecting with Macbeth, who thus has the two great turning-points in his career marked in the drama; the first time he is incited to Guilt, the second time he is led to Retribution. Moreover, the first time the Weird Sisters alone appear, who are subordinates in this realm; but the second time, Hecate, the queen of the witch-world, comes forth also, who is not only tempter, but punisher as well. Their two appearances thus divide the Tragedy into its two Movements, the one of which unfolds the crime, the other its punishment.

The Natural World, which is the Second Thread of the play, separates easily into two well-defined groups, each of which must be looked at by itself, and then taken in conjunction with the other. The first group contains the three capital personages of the drama, those in whom the Natural and Supernatural Worlds fuse together; they are the three whom the Weird Sisters influence—Banquo, Macbeth, and, less directly and less strongly, Lady Macbeth. They manifest a regular gradation in their attitude toward this magical power: Banquo resists its temptations; Lady Macbeth follows them, or, rather, she brings to their aid her own strength of will; Macbeth fluctuates—entertaining them at first, then resisting, but finally yielding. These three characters unite in the point of showing the influence of imagination; they all have that double element above mentioned, they are impelled both by external shapes and internal motives. This imagination of which we are speaking, is essentially the poetic, the maker of images for the spirit's activities; Macbeth, Lady Macbeth, and Banquo, though not intending to make a poem, are great poets; their language is full of white-hot conception and mighty figurative energy; their poetizing, however, is not a pretty play of fancy, but the rush of the life-blood of their very existence.

There remains the second group of the Natural World, which embraces Duncan, the King, and those around him, the representatives of the established institutions, against whom the Weird Sisters are driving the previous group. These people do not come in contact with the Weird Sisters, nor are they directly influenced by the prophetic utterances of the same; still, they are made to feel the supernatural impulse through the previous set of characters, with whom they are brought into collision, except in the case of Banquo, who resists the demonic influence, and hence, himself conflicts with Macbeth, the instrument of that influence. But this second group, which we may name the institutional group, after being overwhelmed and driven out of Scotland, will, in the second part of the play, return as the supporters of a grand reaction, will punish the usurper, and restore the rightful King. Thus Scotland is brought back to order, not through herself, but through England, which country is shown by her poet to be the great bearer of the institutional world, and this has been and still is largely her function in History.

Such is the general structure, giving the main organic lines upon which the drama moves; this general structure will be further carried out into its details at suitable points in the following exposition. Threads and Movements are the organic lines of the Shakespearian Drama; through them we are enabled to see the whole in its complete process, as well as the development of the several parts, and of the individual characters. Two grand Movements we notice in the play, each being strongly marked by the appearance of the Weird Powers; also we observe two well-defined Threads running through the entire dramatic Action. These outlines we shall now take up in order, and try to fill with the living thoughts of the play.

I.

The First Movement starts with the first appearance of the Weird Sisters, and extends to the intervention of Hecate; it gives the subtle inter-action as well as the mighty crash between the Supernatural and Natural Worlds, in which all the individuals of that Scottish life are, more or less directly caught, being driven step by step, some to the guilty deed, others to flight or death. Society is disrupted, institutions are violated, in fact the whole ethical world is toppling to ruin under the blows of a demonic power.

1. The First Thread is this demonic power, the Weird Sisters, who dwell in a realm of their own, distinct and complete. Three things concerning them are to be noted, their physical surroundings, their corporeal appearance, and their moral qualities. First, their coming is in thunder, lightning, and rain; their home seems to be in the tempest, in the wild convulsions of Nature; their attendants are the lower, and often repulsive animals. Secondly, their bodily aspect appears to represent the Ugly; they are withered, bearded, bony hags, unnatural monstrosities, seemingly without sex, opposite in every regard to the beautiful human form. Thus upon their bodies and upon the very atmosphere which envelops them, Nature has written her suggestion. Thirdly, in correspondence with their looks and their surroundings is their moral character; to them fair is foul, and foul is fair; they are portrayed in a state of hostility to man and what is useful to him; their delight is in darkness, confusion, destruction; malice and revenge' enter deeply into their disposition; in general, they exhibit an inimical power, which is directed against mankind, and their world seems to include the hostile phases of both Nature and Spirit. The storms around them and their own dispositions are equally charged with harmful threatenings. But at present their special element is this rebel hurlyburly, out of which they are to come and meet Macbeth, "in the day of success." So they always do, the temptresses, being born of

victory, and turning it into defeat, "when the battle's lost and won." Mark, too, that they do not mention Banquo, after him they do not come, for a good reason. Still, they will get him too.

So far we may consider them as a type of the traditional witch, the embodiment of malice toward human kind, such as she appears in the popular Fairy-tale. But now comes another attribute, the gift of prophecy, whereby the Weird Sisters get a tinge of the Norns, the three Fates of Northern Mythology. Especially the third Sister is prophetic, though she does not always prophesy in her utterances, nor is she the only one of the three that prophesies. Upon the witch is engrafted the sibyl, whose speech is laden with destiny, and works out its own fulfilment; with prophecy is deeply connected fate. In such fashion the old Norse spirit has woven its strand into Scottish legend.

The prophetic gift is the culmination of their influence upon human conduct—the influence of a prediction which is believed to be true. If the conviction is once settled that the promise will turn out as foretold, it becomes, usually, a wonderful incentive to action; indeed, a prophecy may force its own fulfilment through its sheer power over the mind. When Lady Macbeth says, "thou shalt be what thou art promised," it is manifest that she is going to employ all her energy in making the prophecy of the Weird Sisters a reality. When Macbeth "yields to the horrid suggestion" of the King's murder, he has already imaged the prediction as completed in the deed, and is hardening his thought by familiarising it with the crime. Banquo, too, is powerfully wrought upon by the same influence, but he cannot be torn from his moral anchorage. The Norns are clearly at work upon these souls; prediction is spinning them into the web of destiny; will that web catch them? It depends upon their several characters, as we shall see.

A question is likely to arise here in the mind of the reader—why are such beings endowed with the gift of prophecy? The complete insight into their nature reveals its necessity. They represent the totality of conditions, internal and external, which determine conduct to evil; impart to that totality a voice, and you have the prophetic Weird Sister. Given all the circumstances, the occurence must take place; if then, all these circumstances can find utterance, that utterance must be an announcement of the event which is to happen. The powers which control and impel the individual are united together, and endowed with speech and personality in the case of the Weird Sister. When she gives expression to her own essence, it is a prophecy. Hence the poet has introduced these existences to foretell; we may call this their ultimate principle. It must be remembered, at the same time, that the gift of prophecy is a natural quite as much as an intellectual endowment; the prophet feels in the surrounding circumstances that which is to come; it is not so much a clear, conscious knowledge, as a dark presentiment. Undoubtedly, the present has within it the seeds of the future; let the totality of influences work upon a keenly receptive spirit, gifted with a strong imagination, and we have the Seer. He is not the Thinker who can deduce the future as the logical result of the present, but he is one who feels the whole, and sees in rapt vision its consequences, and expresses them in dark, often high-wrought, symbolical language. With the growth of the understanding, prophecy passes away, for two reasons chiefly: its place is supplied by a different faculty, and it loses its credit through the deceptions practiced in its name. Such was its history among the old Greeks and Hebrews. But the prophet is still found, in degraded form and function, amid the lower classes of civilized nations, and he still flourishes among the wilder peoples who live in close intimacy with Nature.

So the Weird Sister is the prophetic voice of the environment, and her own prophecy is itself an active part of this environment; a personification, we may call her, of the influences which impel the individual to evil; yet this individual must have her shape within him also, to see her and to hear her voice. Now let us search the environment and try if we can find these influences. We have not far to look, for immediately after the first scene, which shows the witch-world, comes the second scene, which shows the actual world in emphatic contrast yet harmony. We see the spiritual hurlyburly into which society is whelmed—a great rebellion, then two victorious generals, also a weak King, who owes his kingdom to their ability and valor, who could not resist their power, were they to turn against him. What situation would be more likely to stir up ambitious thoughts concerning the throne? And it is toward the throne that the prediction of the Weird Sister mounts and ends. One lesser prophecy is immediately fulfiled, when Macbeth is made Thane of Cawdor. But here too, our credulity is not very heavily taxed, for can anything be more natural than that Macbeth should receive the title and estates of the rebel whom he has just put down? It is manifest that these prophecies are written on the sibylline leaves of the circumstances, and they utter the voice of the environment: yet, on the other hand, they find their true echo in the souls of the two heroes, Macbeth and Banquo, as they return from victory.

At this point we must grasp the very heart of the poet's conception: the Weird Sisters are both outside and inside the man. They are twofold, yet this twofoldness must be seen at last in unity, as the double manifestation of the same ultimate spiritual fact. So all mythology must be grasped: the deities of Homer are shown both as internal and external in relation to the acting person. So too Religion teaches: God is in the world, is its ruler, but He is also in the heart of man; still in both He is one and the same. In like manner is the evil principle to be conceived, be it the Devil or the Weird Sister. We must not then say that the Weird Sister is simply an embodiment of an inner temptation; she is such, but is far more, she has reality and is not to be evaporated into a mere subjective condition. On the other hand we must not say that she is only an external spectacular scare-crow or stage-trick, gotten up to produce an effect, or to cater to the superstitions of the people; thus we lose her soul and our own too. Such is the grand mythical procedure of the poet, itself two-sided, and requiring the reader to be two-sided; he must have two eyes, and both open, yet one vision.

To lay stress upon the reality of the Weird Sisters, the poet has introduced two men beholding them at the same time, so that we cannot well assert the appearances to be a mere subjective delusion, as we might, if only one man saw them. Still we may ask, why did the poet employ such shapes in this drama, when he has portrayed in other dramas similar influences without resorting to the supernatural world? In *Lear*, for instance, Edmund certainly is placed in an environment of temptation, yet no Weird Sister or other specter voices it to him, but it is kept in its purely natural or unimaginative form. The answer must hit the center: it lies on the character of Banquo and Macbeth to see such specters. It is their form of soul without which they are not; in such way they figure the reality before them, by the deepest necessity of their natures; but Edmund's mind dealt otherwise with the same fact; the ethical principle is the same in the two sets of people, but the psychological form is wholly different. The

Weird Sisters are beheld by Macbeth and Banquo alone, and it must be considered as the strong distinctive phase of their spiritual being that they behold the appearances. Both have the same temptation; both are endowed with a strong imagination; both being in the same environment, witness the same apparition; in other words, the external influences which impel to evil, to ambitious thoughts, to future kingship are the same for both, and, in their excited minds, these influences take the form of the Weird Sisters. Such is the design of the poet; he shows us the soul-form of these characters, the tendency to cast the great spiritual facts of existence into the shapes of the imagination, which seem actual beings, and mislead men into following their fantastic suggestions.

That is, these two characters have in them the mythical spirit, their ways of thinking are mythical, evil and temptation take the mythical form; for them the world, indeed, has a tendency to become a Mythus. Their age, too, is a mythical one, also their nation in particular; hence Mythology is their final utterance, and this Mythology will be that of their age and nation. The prosaic Understanding is not their gift, rather the poetic Imagination, which figures realities. To our age, indeed, this mythical spirit is lost, is hardly comprehensible; the Weird Sisters are not real to us, as shapes, but their ethical meaning is as valid for us to-day, as it was for Macbeth and Banquo. Two different soul-forms of the same eternal fact, are ours and theirs; an unreal shape of a reality is what we call their vision of the Weird Sisters—the untrue appearance of a truth.

Another question is sometimes asked in this connection: Why has not the poet himself explained what he means by the strange appearances? He might have told the secret to his audience in a separate scene, or in a soliloquy. It is true that the reader who carefully weighs and compares the natural and supernatural Threads, in which both the reflective and the mythical conceptions find statement, will not have much difficulty in detecting the mystery. Still the poet has scrupulously guarded the reality of the Weird Sisters; whenever they appear they are treated as positive objective existences, in spite of Banquo's doubts. Mark the fact —that two persons behold them at the same time, address them and are addressed by them. Now, if they were seen by one person only, or by each person at different times, there would be no mystery, everybody would at once declare it to be a subjective phantom. Such is the case when the ghost of Banquo appears to Macbeth, but is seen by nobody else, though a number of guests with Lady Macbeth are present. The poet, then, is specially careful to preserve the air of reality in these shapes. For such a procedure he has a most excellent reason, one that lies at the very basis of Tragedy. He wishes to place his audience under the same influences as his hero, and involve them in the same doubts and conflicts. We, too, must look upon the Weird Sisters with the eyes of Macbeth and Banquo; we may not believe in them, or we may be able to explain them, still the great dramatic object is to portray characters which do behold them and believe in them, and for a time, to lend us the eyes and faith of such people. The audience must feel the same problem in all its depth and earnestness, and must be required to face the enigma of these appearances, for a character can be truly tragic to the spectators only when they are assailed by its difficulties and involved in its collision. The poet presents his work as life itself is presented to us; here is the fact, look at it, solve it. When the audience stand above the hero, and are at once made acquainted with all his complications, mistakes, and weaknesses, the realm of Comedy begins, the laugh is apt to be excited instead of the sympathetic tear. We make merry over men pursuing that which we know to be a disguise, or a shadow, or some delusion. To persons who can remain uninfluenced by their imagination, or to whom the soul-form of Macbeth and Banquo does not appeal, the present drama may seem absurd, and fit only to be laughed at. Few people, however, are so entirely free of the Dark Powers; a secret strand of faith in the influence of a demonic energy winds obscurely through every soul, and often needs but the occasion to rise into daylight. Smothered by education, ridiculed by the illuminated, even condemned to death as a witch, still the Weird Sister is alive.

Did Shakespeare believe in witches? It would be a rash man who could strongly affirm or deny the proposition. But we can know the more important matter that he employs these shapes for a genuine purpose, he seizes the Mythology of his time, and uses it just for what it is intended to express unto men. For Mythology is an honest and noble attempt of the human soul, at a certain stage of its culture, to utter its greatest truths, its profoundest problems; Mythology formulates, in its way, the struggles of the spirit for light, freedom, immortality; it is not an empty collection of sun-myths or dawn-myths, it seeks to show a providential world-order and man therein; the two wings on which it soars into its supernatural realm are good and evil. The mythologic age, it is true, has passed away, but the mythus remains as the work of the loftiest souls, Poets, Priests, Sages, in helping to construe the world, man, and Providence. The Weird Sisters are not introduced for mere theatrical effect, without any meaning; there is thought here, though it be mythologic thought, and we must think it over again in our own form, ere we can fully understand it, for our thought is no longer naturally mythical. Those who say that the poet merely employed an existing superstition for an external spectacular effect have indeed got rid of the difficulty, but it may be added, have got rid of Shakespeare too. Certainly the poet uses the popular Mythology of the time—he would not have been the true poet, if he had not—but what originated this Mythology in the hearts of the people? Just what originates it in Shakespeare, who goes back to the primitive mythical fountain, and makes it pour forth anew, filled with fresh life from his thought. Read Thomas Middleton's play "The Witch;" that is the machinery of witchcraft without its deep connection with the temptation and destiny; for this reason it lives only in a little glare of light from Shakespeare's work.

The play, very properly, opens with the witch-scene, wherein the primordial force is shown setting the whole drama in motion. The Weird Sisters wish to meet Macbeth, he is the one whom they mention by name, he is the one who is to be mainly influenced by their power, and he is the central character of the play. But they also meet Banquo, apparently not by their choice; through these two persons they impinge upon the Natural World, which is now to be introduced.

2. This is the Second Thread in the dramatic structure which we are now to follow out to the second appearance of the Weird Sisters, who will then give the drama a new direction. Already they have pointed to Macbeth as the chief figure of this Natural World; around him the other characters move. He has done the Great Deed, and is the Hero; he has put down treason and saved the King; he is, ideally though not actually, the supreme man of the State. So he is brought before us.

His starting point, then, in the drama, is the heroic Deed, which has in it two strands, or tendencies, both of which will pass into his character and determine it. The first strand in this Deed is the temptation which lurks in it, the evil side of the Great Action. Let us mark it sharply: he has conquered the traitor whom the weak King excited but did not conquer; this Deed makes him greater than the King, at least to his own imagination. But there is a second and opposite strand in this Deed; it shows him the penalty of treason in the fate of the Thane of Cawdor; in fact, he is just the man who has punished treason. Naturally, Macbeth will believe in retribution; it, too, springs out of the Deed, and enters into his character. Temptation to evil on the one hand, faith in the punishment of evil on the other, are seen to wind out of that primal act into his soul.

Macbeth is essentially the man of action; all his inner states, impulses, even emotions have a tendency of themselves to rush into performance; "the very firstlings of my heart shall be the firstlings of my hand." Particularly his imaginings are ever ready to make themselves deeds, and, on the contrary, it is the deed which gives material to his imagination. That is, Macbeth has no inner control, such as is furnished by thought; he has not that discipline by which the mind subdues its own rebellious subjects to its king—Reason; he shows the overbalancing of Will without the adequate supply of Thought, wherein he stands in striking contrast to Hamlet, who shows the overbalancing of Thought without the adequate supply of Will. His images fly into actions, and his actions give him images.

Accordingly, out of his Great Deed rises the

image of Temptation, over which he has little or no inner control; yet an image of Retribution also rises out of his Great Deed, exercising an outer control through fear. Between these two images he is tossed in a mighty tempest of the soul, without any spiritual mastery over them; he is tempted by the one, yet terrorized by the other. He sees only the outer punishment, as shown in the case of the Thane of Cawdor, for the wicked act; his scruple springs not from the love of the good, but from the fear of the evil. His is the untrained, superstitious, mythical spirit, in its weakness, yet heroic; the Mythus and the Hero grow together. Still, they pass away in the ripeness of time, the poet hints the process. The Will must be trained to the inner discipline, the Image must be held in account to Reason. The one thus becomes ethical, the other poetic.

Macbeth, then, has the burden of a Great Deed laid upon him, a Deed, which he is not to do, but which he has done; what is he going to make out of it for himself? A mighty responsibility is that of the Hero, who oftener breaks down under the weight of his Great Deed, after it is done, than before it is done. This is again a contrast to Hamlet, whose duty is to do the Deed, not to bear it after it is done. Macbeth, however, can do it, but cannot meet its consequences. Starting then from its Heroic Deed, we are to watch this character unfold before our eyes. It will reveal its temptation in the form of the image; it will reveal its faith in retribution also in the form of the image.

This process goes through three stages in the First Movement: the conflict with himself, the murder of the King, the murder of Banquo. Into this process all the other characters are drawn, and are to be looked at in connection with it.

(1.) The conflict of Macbeth with himself begins at once with his success in the outer action. There has been a terrific collision in the State, a great revolt has taken place, in which some of the King's subjects, aided by foreigners, have participated. But this revolt has been put down, mainly by the strong arm of Macbeth, assisted, however, by Banquo. The breach is healed, the throne is saved, peace again reigns. But now begins the internal struggle; that civil war, suppressed in the State, is transferred to the soul of Macbeth in the very act of suppression; he is the battle-ground, and is fighting with himself. What has he been doing? Putting down traitors to the King. But this act tempts him to become the traitor to the same King, to do that for which he has just punished a great nobleman, in whom he must see the consequences of treason. Such are the two sides of that war in his soul, Temptation and Retribution.

Just at this moment, with victory hardly yet beginning to shine out of the battle-clouds, the Weird Sisters in their horrid shapes rise up before him; "they met me in the day of success" he writes to his wife; that is just their time. Banquo is with him and sees them too; both are returning from the scene of their triumph, filled with the glory of their deeds. What honors are not now within their reach! Kingship—are they not greater than the King? Have they not saved his realm? Both have the same temptation and the same vision, as well as the same environment. Here the Supernatural World touches the Natural World; they coalesce in the words of Macbeth: "So foul and fair a day I have not seen," a contradictory designation, which the Weird Sisters had previously put together in their bodeful rune, and which also indicates the struggle already risen in the soul of Macbeth. Manifestly these shapes are in Macbeth, being born now; yet they are outside of him too.

Both Banquo and Macbeth question the spectral appearances, when the latter prophesy the future of the two warriors; especially the third Sister is prophetic, like the third Norse Valkyr, and hails him: "Macbeth that shalt be King hereafter." It strikes home to his secret thought, for he starts and seems "to fear things that do sound so fair;" well he may, as they have also their "foul" side for him. Banquo doubts: "Are ye fantastical, or that indeed which ye outwardly show?" Are ye in me or outside of me? No, they speak not to such a doubter; yet they will, if he rise to stronger demand and faith. "Speak, then, to me, who neither beg nor fear your favors nor your hate." Rather a defiant mood toward the temptresses; so they give him a very ambiguous prophecy compared to the definiteness of the answer to Macbeth; Loxias could not frame a more doubtful oracle:

"Lesser and greater than Macbeth;" "not so happy, yet much happier." But the third Valkyr will hit him; "Thou shalt get Kings, though thou be none." It would seem that such an answer would paralyze personal ambition for the throne; it does, and just therein reflects Banquo, and, moreover, laps him in the coils of destiny. He is, paralyzed in his action, and thus is caught in the sweep of the man who is not paralyzed in action.

Manifestly the fate of the two heroes is mysteriously wrapped up in these oracles, which in part foreshadow, and in part cause what they foreshadow. In the case of Macbeth, it is plain that the Weird Sister mirrors his inner thought back to him in a sudden startling sentence; kingship is that thought. But in the case of Banquo does she the same? Not so plainly, but none the less certainly; her first words to him, "greater and lesser" cancel each other, and so give his spiritual portrait. She paralyzes him, the moral man, though she cannot seduce him to the wicked act, as she can Macbeth; she says, can only say to him: "thou shalt be no King." Still she can tempt him with a little hope beyond: "thou shalt get Kings," wherein the thought of that son Fleance seems remotely to play. Success cannot mislead his moral nature, but may hamstring it, and prevent it from activity against the wrongful deed. Banquo has yielded just enough to the Weird Sister to palsy his arm from smiting Macbeth, who has yielded entirely. He does not the bad act, but he does not the good act, he the hero, the doer of great deeds; that is his fate, he is untrue to his heroic nature, for he is the successor of Macbeth, when the latter has fallen from duty. So the Great Deed, though it could not tempt him to do the wrong, could tempt him into not doing the right, and thus whirl him into the torrent of a tragic destiny.

It will be noticed that the moment the Weird Sisters are asked concerning their nature and origin, they vanish; such a response they cannot give, or, rather, their response to it is their disappearance. They are not to be investigated too closely, and Banquo still doubts in his way; yet a drop of their poison is in him and will remain. Now comes the sudden confirmation, Macbeth is saluted Thane of Cawdor by an embassy from the King, just as one of the witches saluted him; they are indeed prophetic. Banquo is stirred, and cries: "what, can the devil speak true?" wherein he recognizes the diabolic element in these shapes. Macbeth, however, has no such recognition, but coddles the thought: "The greatest is behind," and even tries to stir the hope in Banquo that "your children shall be Kings." Banquo at once catches the suspicion: "That trusted home, might yet enkindle you unto the crown;" for does he not feel a slight breath of the same demon in his own breast? Still Banquo's better nature has already put down the temptation, and he gives the moral solution of the Weird Sisters, though their psychological solution lies beyond his horizon. Listen to their moral meaning from his lips, as it lies deep in the soul of the entire play:

> And often times, to win us to our harm,
> The instruments of darkness tell us truths,
> Win us with honest trifles to betray us
> In deepest consequence.

But Macbeth cannot give the moral solution: ",This supernatural soliciting cannot be ill—cannot be good;" and so he fluctuates from side to side. Temptation comes, yet with a terrific fear of punishment, both being in the form of "horrible imaginings;" his murder of the King is "yet but fantastical," still the penality is upon him with its dire images, and

> Shakes so my single state of man that function
> Is smothered in surmise, and nothing is
> But what is not.

Banquo, however, has settled the question, is free of the moral conflict, quietly remarking: "Look how our partner's rapt." Upon this point their characters differentiate; in the same environment, with the same temptation in the same form psychslogically, morally they move in diverse directions. Again Macbeth's struggle is aroused, when the King appoints his own son as his successor; again we mark the impulse to the wicked deed, and yet the terror of it in the soul of Macbeth:

> The eye wink at the hand; yet let that be
> Which the eye fears, when it is done, to see.

At this point in the career of Macbeth, his wife is introduced. She, too, is connected with the Weird Sisters, a fact which must not be forgotten;

the first sentence of the letter which she is reading, and her own first sentence start from them. Their promises are just what she desired, and we at once hear their connection with her will in the strong resolve: "Thou shalt be what thou art promised." She makes herself the instrument of their prophecy. But she knows well the character of her husband, and fears that he will be irresolute, since the conflict between the good and the bad is so evenly poised in his mind. She utters a series of balanced antitheses about him, which exactly reproduce his spiritual picture, both in their form and in their meaning:

> Art not without ambition, but without
> The illness should attend it; what thou wouldst highly,
> That wouldst thou holily; wouldst not play false,
> And yet wouldst wrongly win.

But chiefly his fear of the evil rather than his love of the good she notes as the root of his vacillation: "Thou'dst have, great Glamis, that which rather thou dost fear to do, than wishest should be undone." This fear of retribution is what she must meet and overcome in him, and hereupon she states her place in the drama:

> Hie thee hither
> That I may pour my spirts in thine ear,
> And chastise with the valour of my tongue
> All that impedes thee from the golden round
> Which fate and metaphysical aid doth seem
> To have thee crowned withal.

Such is her function: to drive out of Macbeth, with her spirit and her tongue, the impediment now holding him back from the crown, which the

Supernatural World has promised him. Thus she makes herself the instrument of the Weird Sisters, yet of herself also; they are both outside of her, and in her too. She does not see them, like Banquo and Macbeth, but she feels them and addresses them. She is, indeed, the Weird Sister realized, not of the Supernatural, but of the Natural World. But this high strung condition is not her normal one, she forces herself into it by an act of will. When the servant announces the approach of the King toward her castle, she is momentarily thrown off her bent by the sudden emergency, and exclaims "Thou'rt mad to say it;" but she soon recovers herself. To be the instrument of the powers of evil, has required in her a prodigious effort of resolution; but she is ready, she will even abjure womanhood. She invokes the "spirits that tend on mortal thoughts" to unsex her; she will become herself a Weird Sister, a sexless woman, a monstrosity in nature and in soul. Such she has not been hitherto, manifestly. She will be all cruelty—no conscience, no pity; she is will wrought up to frenzy. Again she addresses the supernatural powers in the "murdering ministers" who are to transform her womanly attributes into those of the demon. She, too, is gifted with imagination, and is grandly poetic in these passages, being on this side also allied to Banquo and Macbeth.

Whence comes this colossal will-power in the woman? Critics have tried to trace it back to some source; enough, here it is. Doubtless, it has been called up by the circumstances; it is seemingly one of the outgrowths of that fertile Great Deed of the husband. For him, the man of action, that Deed has begotten inner irresolution, the halting between two courses; for her, the woman of home-life, it has roused the most intense inner resolution. She is the one of the pair who has the spirit's self-control; almost her first word to her husband is to reprove his lack of self-suppression: "Your face, my Thame, is as a book where men may read strange matters." Then she gives an example of her own power in this way when she receives the King. Did she have an inner training which her husband never had? Perchance the woman, in her emotional, nay, in her conventional life, gets the discipline which the active man lacks. At least her nature now suddenly burst forth into an enormous energy of will, directed inwardly, as well as outwardly. Still Macbeth cannot catch resolution from his wife, he gives the matter a final consideration in his first long soliloquy, and concludes not to kill Duncan. He has no religious scruples; he would risk the world to come, if he were sure he would escape in this world. But he has the profoundest conviction that there is always on earth a retribution for the wicked deed. Thrice in succession he declares this doctrine:

> But in these cases
> We still have judgment here; that we but teach
> Bloody instructions, which, being taught, return
> To plague the inventor; this even-handed justice
> Commends the ingredients of our poisoned chalice
> To our own lips.

In fact, the whole soliloquy is a grand homily on retribution, and winds up with a train of gorgeous imagery, gotten up by the poet Macbeth, to give a spectacular display of punishment. Imagination still rules him, though he also speaks abstractly of his temptation as "vaulting ambition," which may be taken as his own interpretation of the Weird Sister. But this ambition "overleaps itself and falls on the other" side, which calls up the penalty. It is clear that Macbeth has no true moral groundwork of character; he shows no positive love of the good, but merely the negative fear of the evil. Not even the religious terror of Hell reaches him, but the cowardly fear of personal ill.

Such a man will not be hard to shake, and no sooner has he resolved, from the danger of punishment, not to kill the King, than his wife appears, and, after a short resistance on his part, sweeps him from his moorings, for really he has no anchor against her will. She appeals to his love: "From this time such I account thy love," if thou wilt not do this deed, which will "give solely sovereign sway and masterdom." Surely love, then, cannot be her supreme end. But, chiefly, she assails that fear of punishment which is the single restraint in him, with a blasting derision:

> Art thou afeard
> To be the same in thine own act and valor
> As thou art in desire?

To be sure, her argument is that of immorality: thou art a coward not to be that which thou desirest to be. Now morality bids us do quite the opposite, namely, suppress desire when inconsistent with what is right. Macbeth's first answer is the true one: "I dare do all that may become a man; who dares do more, is none;" but this answer springs not from his inmost being, but is rehearsed like a moral saw. But her argument is good against Macbeth, for whom it is intended; he has simply the fear of punishment, not the love of virtue, he is a moral coward, as his wife declares. So she shames him, the brave soldier, with poltroonery—a charge which he endures from the lips of her whom he loves. But what about her in this proceeding? She has already unsexed herself; she goes further now, she unmothers herself—

>   I have given suck and know
> How tender 'tis to love the babe that milks me:
> I would, while it was smiling in my face
> Have plucked my nipple from his boneless gums
> And dashed the brains out, had I so sworn as you
> Have done, to this.

No limit to her ambitious will, not motherhood, and, we must think, not wifehood. It is to be noticed that the pair have already talked the matter over before these late events, and Macbeth seems to have been the originator. He has long caressed the thought, has even proposed once to execute it, but she seems to have held him back: "Nor time nor place did then adhere, and yet you would make both." But now she is resolved and cannot be unstrung from her tension; in the grip of her own will she is held fixed like fate, and also holds her husband.

We can feel his slow giving way in his question: "If we should fail;" wherein his fear of punishment again hovers before his mind, and gives him a momentary shudder in his descent. But he is yielding; his wife furnishes the plan which seems to obviate all danger of detection; it sweeps away, momentarily, his fear of punishment; he falls in with it, and even completes its details, and we hear his word of resolve:

> I am settled, and bend up
> Each corporal agent to this terrible feat.

(2.) The second crisis of Macbeth's career is embraced in the Second Act, which exhibits the murder of the King and its revelation to the outer world. We shall witness Macbeth's struggles just before and just after the bloody action; again he will be harrassed by those terrible images, Temptation and Retribution, though they now take new shapes. Thus from the supreme Deed against treason has been born, in direct descent, the supreme Deed of treason.

Again in the beginning of the Act the poet touches his first chord—the similarity and the difference in the characters of Macbeth and Banquo. Both have the same strong imagination; both the same temptation. Banquo is disturbed during the day by bad fancies; but particularly he is worried by wicked dreams during the night, when he cannot control the fantastic play of his mind. He wishes not to sleep, and prays to be kept free from "the cursed thoughts that nature gives way to in repose." The moral restraint continues in him; still he cannot keep from telling Macbeth: "I dreamt last night of the three Weird Sisters;" surely their virus is working within him in spite of himself. "To you they have showed some truth"—and why not to me, the mind adds. That son Fleance at his side falls within the prophecy, if he himself does not; truly his dearest object, his very love, has in it the danger of temptation. But Macbeth is already beyond that first stage of the Weird Sisters: "I think not of them;" he hints some dark plan or conspiracy to Banquo, which "shall make honor for you." But listen to Banquo's answer:

> So I lose none
> In seeking to augment it, but still keep
> My bosom franchised and my allegiance clear,
> I shall be counselled.

Which again marks strongly the contrast between the two men, and seems to hint the suspicion of Banquo.

But now we are to see Macbeth alone and hear what he is thinking about. He beholds the image of a dagger hovering in the air and marshalling "me the way that I was going," when he has resolved upon the murder. So real is this dagger that he clutches for it, and wonders that it is not as "sensible to feeling as to sight." He even draws his own dagger from his side and compares the two: "I see thee yet, in form as palpable as this which now I draw." Surely the poet tells us here that Macbeth is not fully able to distinguish the images of his fancy from real things. The dagger even changes before his eyes: "On thy blade and dudgeon gouts of blood, which was not so before." A terrible image of Temptation, employing the very instrument of murder, lures him on; it is as if the Weird Sister held that dagger toward his hand and marshalled him forward. So he struggles, dashed between image and reality till he seems to decide against his imagination:

> There's no such thing,
> It is the bloody business which informs
> Thus to mine eyes.

But this decision is momentary; he gets rid of the dagger, only to be roused by another still more terrible image of murder which connects directly with the Weird Sisters by the mention of Hecate:

> Now witchcraft celebrates
> Pale Hecate's offerings, and withered murder,
> Alarumed by his sentinel the wolf,
> Whose howl's his watch, thus with his stealthy pace,
> With Tarquin's ravishing strides, towards his design
> Moves like a ghost.

Which is a spectral night-picture of himself as he moves to the murder. Again he seizes upon the witch-world, the dark side of his people's Mythology, to image temptation in its success, and this ghost-like shape is himself. His terror too, darts up with an image, but he suppresses it and his poetical speech stops in the man of action: "Words to the heat of deeds too cool breath gives."

The deed is done, the King is murdered. What now? This same imagination rise up in tenfold power and becomes the instrument of punishment—the mighty weapon of his own soul. We have seen all along how Macbeth believed in retribution; now it appears in those fearful voices which he hears from the sleepers, because he is murdering sleep, "the innocent sleep;" religious fear, too, plays in, he cannot say "amen" to the cry "God bless us." But the culmination is the very voice of retribution, crying

> Glamis hath murdered sleep and therefore Cawdor
> Shall sleep no more, Macbeth shall sleep no more.

He has slain repose in the sleeping Duncan. The prophecy of that voice will be fulfiled to the letter. Macbeth will be harassed from now on; he gets rest no more; in very truth he has murdered it. Every noise appals him, hands come and seem to "pluck out mine eyes," the great ocean will not "wash this blood clean from my hand." In the last Act, Lady Macbeth, when her will-power is relaxed, will be given over to the same image of washing her bloody hand, whereby the common trait of imagination in husband and wife is indicated. Macbeth is now what she will be hereafter.

Still, even in the present scene we notice that she has no small difficulty in suppressing her imagination, particularly when she is alone. She always observes the external prognostications, the croak of the raven, the shriek of the owl, the cry of the cricket. She could not do the deed of murder because she saw the semblance of her father in the sleeping Duncan. Then in the very crisis of the discovery of the murder she faints, her tension of will could hold out no longer. But, at present, that will is keyed up to its highest pitch in suppressing the imagination of her husband. She pleads with him, shames him, uses her former argument of cowardice; it is all to no purpose in his overwhelming images of retribution. He will not carry the dagger back: "I am afraid to think what I have done; look on it again I dare not." In an hysterical effort of will, she seizes the daggers, and will carry them back herself, frantically denying the very thing which she is feeling most strongly: "the sleeping and the dead are but as pictures," yet most terrible pictures to her now, as she has just shown in regard to the sleeping Duncan. Then that last utterance with its ghastly pun:

If he do bleed,
I'll gild the faces of the grooms withal,
For it must seem their guilt.

In her frenzy of will-tension she has now become the demon with a scoffing jest in the midst of hellish work. Unsexed, unmothered, she now is diabolic, yet the supreme effort of her volition is spent, henceforward she will show it, but not at such a strain.

Thus that castle has been turned into a Hell with fiends in it; here enters the porter who imagines himself to be the porter of Hell-gate. He too, has imagination in accord with the spirit of the whole play, and he has all to himself a small Last Judgment for sinners of the time. It is an humble comic reflection of the monstrous deed within and of the judgment coming, its most external manifestation just at the gate of the castle, which lets in the outer world. But here is that outer world, knocking, knocking, with its fearful echo through the halls, reaching to the very hearts of the guilty master and mistress; it cannot be kept out, it must come upon murder and collide with it. This, then, is the second strand of the Natural World which the poet now interweaves into the action.

Yet even this Natural World, in its most external manifestation, is trying to tell the guilty act. Lennox, one of the new-comers, speaks of the unruly night, as if the elements had been thrown into convulsion by some hidden wickedness; "Lamentings heard in the air, strange screams of death," as if the secret must be told by Nature; "prophesyings with accents terrible" were heard, and some said "the earth was feverous and did shake." Such are the premonitions of the great crime whose possibility, it seems, has already been felt abroad, and finds expression in the imagination of the people. After such a prelude, we are prepared to hear the announcement; Macduff brings the news of the murder to the awakened house.

Macbeth and Lady Macbeth have now to exercise their arts of dissimulation, and both break down. The wife, after two or three exclamations, is carried out in a swoon; the husband, by his extravagant and superfluous declamation, reveals himself as the feigner in the company; he is clearly seen to be acting an assumed part:

> Here lay Duncan,
> His silver skin laced with his golden blood,
> And his gashed stabs looked like a breach in Nature
> For ruin's wasteful entrance.

That he was more ready to slay the King's servants, than to hear their evidence, also turns suspicion upon him. The King's sons note the contrast between themselves, genuine mourners, and the noisy excess of Macbeth, and at once take to flight. But what will Banquo do now? He undoubtedly suspects the right person of the murder, and swears

> In the great hand of God I stand, and thence
> Against the undivulged pretence I fight
> Of treasonous malice.

But he will not keep his oath, he will delay, and be caught by the man of action. Macduff also makes the same oath, and the rest of the noblemen, but they will flee the country or make peace with the murderer, whereby they become involved, more or less, in the net of fate.

Thus has the dire deed passed into the world, and become a part of its history. Nevermore can it be concealed in that castle of Hell; the world must now proceed to purify itself of this stain. For the mark is upon it, and it shows that mark everywhere; a reflection of the dark deed we have already seen twice; first in the porter who deems himself gate-keeper of the infernal regions; secondly, in the wild convulsions of Nature as recorded by Lennox. But the poet is going to cast a third image on the face of Nature—an image of the guilty deed after it is done. This takes place in the last scene of the Second Act, in the talk of Ross and the old man, who are faint copies of Banquo and Macbeth, on their imaginative side, seeing, if not the Weird Sisters, at least the deeds of man pictured in the occurrences of Nature. "The heavens, as troubled with man's act, threaten his bloody stage;" darkness in daytime, the falcon killed by the mousing owl, Duncan's horses contending against obedience and eating each other, are some of the fearful portents which the time has brought forth. Nature not only pictures the moral confusion, but is herself confused and thrown into strife; a bad deed sets the whole universe ajar, which must re-act and rid itself of the discord. In such manner these imaginative people find utterance, and indicate their faith in the ethical world-order.

(3). We are now brought to the third crisis in the career of Macbeth, which is shown in the Third Act, and moves quite on the same lines as the two preceeding crises. First, Banquo is again touched upon, he is deeply aroused by the fulfilment of the prophecy in the case of Macbeth, though he suspects "thou play'dst most foully for it." More strong than ever is that fatal paralysis of his, the temptation stays his hand from taking part against guilt, he prefers to think of his posterity as Kings, he hugs the thought: "May they (the Weird Sisters) not be my oracles as well, and set me up in hope?" They have indeed; "but hush! no more!" for here comes the new King who is his fate, ready to entrap him and his son in the very toils of his temptation and inaction, though he has sworn, in the presence of the murderer, to avenge the murdered King.

As in both the previous crises, we see Macbeth again turning over the new state of things in a soliloquy. We have noticed how the fear of retribution was generated even out of his good deed, the suppression of treason, to such a degree that he feared to kill the King; so now the fear of retribution in a new shape is generated out of his bad deed, the murder of Duncan. He has himself taught the "bloody instructions which return to plague the inventor;" he must believe that he will be punished. But by whom? Banquo is the man; was he not the first to swear to fight against "treasonous malice?" But still further, he, with the same environment and the same imagination as Macbeth, has not turned traitor, has resisted all the attempts which have been made to draw him into conspiracy. No wonder, then, that "our fears in Banquo stick deep;" no wonder that "under him my Genius is rebuked;" for Banquo is a perpetual picture held up before Macbeth's guilty conscience, a continual reminder of that which he ought to have done, a rebuke to his character. Banquo rightly refrained then from doing, but now such refraining is his doom.

From the murder of the King is born, also, the counter belief, that the penalty may be escaped.

Macbeth has successfully made way with Duncan; he is not yet punished but rather rewarded for his murder. Hence he will try to set aside the penalty; he will try to prevent anybody from doing what he has done, namely, from killing a king; he will attempt to stop his own deed from getting back to himself. Such is the mill in which he is now ground: he believes in retribution, yet is going to forestall it. Thus his murder creates about him a new world of guilt and punishment, necessitates another murder and its penalty. He seeks to circumvent his conviction, yet his very act creates anew the conviction. The wicked deed begets his belief in punishment, and this belief begets in turn the wicked deed.

But this new temptation reaches out not alone to the second but to the third murder. The Weird Sisters—the primal source—hailed Banquo father to a line of Kings, though he should be no King himself. So the death of the father might merely hasten the fulfilment of the prophecy. This is the second fear of Macbeth, that his sceptre would be "wrenched from his gripe with an unlineal hand," namely the son of Banquo, "no son of mine succeeding," for though Macbeth appears to have no children, still he seems to think he may have an heir yet. So Fleance, Banquo's son, is to be included in the deed of blood.

This throws Macbeth into opposition to the Weird Sisters, and still more deeply into a conflict with himself. He has followed their promises hitherto, but now he is going to fight their decree.

He believes them to be true prophets, yet he will nullify them. It is a prophecy of theirs which has turned out true in his own case, and which has declared that Banquo's posterity also will be kings. Acting upon the belief that the event is certain to take place, still he proposes to forestall it. With faith in the prophecy, he will prevent its fulfilment. Thus the Weird Sisters furnish him the new temptation to circumvent their own decree, and drive him to attempt a double murder, that of Banquo and his son. He deems them to be fate, still he will defy them: "Come fate into the list and champion me to the utterance!" Such is the double drive of murder in this soliloquy: first, against Banquo in person, whose "royalty of nature" he fears; secondly, against Fleance upon whom the promise of the Weird Sisters falls.

But after the resolution, as in the case of the King, he finds no peace till the deed be done. He is scourged with his imagination, he keeps alone, "of sorriest fancies his companions making," he eats his "meal in fear," and sleeps "in the affliction of these terrible dreams;" he prefers death to lying "on the torture of the mind," and envies "Duncan in his grave." Driven by his fear of retribution, which is now his temptation also, he cries: "O full of scorpions is my mind; Banquo and his Fleance lives." He thinks that he can get peace by murdering them, that in them he will slay the images of his own brain. Again, as just before the death of the King, he calls up the murder about to take place, in a dark picture of the imagination; the night-side of his people's Mythology will again furnish him the image of the wicked deed; Hecate, too, is mentioned, who connects with the Weird Sisters, and is queen of night. In such dark bodeful imagery is the crime enveloped; the bat, the shard-borne beetle, the crow, and seeling Night are the environment; light thickens, and

> Good things of day begin to droop and drowse
> Whiles night's black agents to their preys do rouse.

Banquo is murdered by hired assassins, who talk with Macbeth in a long scene, quite out of proportion with the brevity and hurry of the general course of this play. But in them the methods of Macbeth are seen, he has gathered the desperate and wicked for his instruments; hear them speak—

> I am one, my liege,
> Whom the vile blows and buffets of the world
> Have so incensed that I am reckless what
> I do to spite the world.

The second murderer says the same thing in substance; no wonder that Banquo has been the enemy to such men; truly all the destructive elements of society are clustering round Macbeth. But Fleance escapes their blow, and Macbeth has not yet succeeded in forestalling the Weird Sisters; fate is still outside of him.

After the death of Banquo, imagination will again punish Macbeth as it punished him after the death of Duncan, only with greater intensity. Then he heard the imagined voice of retribution, now the murdered man appears in person with "gory locks," and with "twenty mortal murders" on his crown, and takes his seat at the table of the guests. Imagination now has all the force of reality; it controls Macbeth, even in the presence of company, and makes him reveal the dreadful secret. Through it, Banquo himself returns to earth, points out his murderer, and to the guilty soul accomplishes his revenge. Macbeth cannot banish this image as he did the air-drawn dagger, with which Lady Macbeth identifies it. Moreover "it is the very painting of your fear," the terror of the penalty working through the imagination. Nobody present sees the ghost but him, whereby it is shown to be his mental one alone.

It will be noticed that this ghost of Banquo appears twice. Both times his name is spoken by Macbeth, which seems to be the cue for his appearance; Macbeth, in feigning speech, wishes him to be present, when lo! here he is. Hypocrisy cannot hide; the very attempt to conceal the deed, reveals it; stronger than all artifice is nature. The specter seems to disappear both times when Macbeth thinks of it as a ghost and not as a reality; he banishes it so that it does not return when he can say: "Hence, horrible shadow! unreal mockery hence!" His own explanation of the appearance of Banquo's ghost turns back again to that faith in retribution: "It will have blood, they say; blood will have blood;" all nature conspires to bring out the guilty man: "Stones have been known to speak and trees to move;" such is his belief.

Lady Macbeth again preforms her previous function, that of suppressing the imagination of her husband, but it goes quite beyond her control. Again she shames him with cowardice: "Are you a man?" She excuses his conduct to the excited and suspicious guests; in fact, the two have revealed in their present behavior the secret of Banquo's murder, as they previously revealed that of the King. Again, too, we see that Lady Macbeth is exercising upon herself a more violent suppression than she is upon her husband; she has the same tortures of imagination as he, and has found no happiness, as she intimates to herself; in fact, when alone, she utters just what Macbeth utters, hinting the enviable lot of the dead Duncan.

> 'Tis safer to be that which we destroy
> Than by destruction dwell in doubtful joy.

But when she is in her husband's presence, she claps the breaks both upon him and herself. In the ghost-scene she has had to exercise a triple control, over her husband, over the guests, and what is not the least, over herself. The strain was prodigious, at its end she seems to droop, utters no comments upon what has just transpired; with a quiet remark or two, she tells her husband, " you lack the season of all natures, sleep," which is her last waking sentence, and is, indeed, her own condition. That mighty tension of will now relaxes, never again to recover its power; never again will she be seen controlling Macbeth, never again controlling herself; she is henceforth to be given over to her own "thick-coming fancies." One may almost hear the chord of her will snap in this last strain.

But how about Macbeth? We can see that the power of the imagination has quite reached its climax; we behold it completely controlling the individual by its phantoms in the case of the ghost; this control is now to be fixed and made permanent in the Weird Sister, to whom he is to go next. Macbeth has been wrestling with these phantoms all along, he has sought to destroy them by crime, but this has only aroused them the more. Just that belief in retribution creates them afresh, yet also brings the attempt to forestall the penalty; now it pushes him against a new object of suspicion, Macduff. He will not return, he will not repent:

> I am in blood
> Stepp'd in so far that, should I wade no more,
> Returning were as tedious as to go o'er.

Nay, there is to be no reflecting upon his plans, they must be at once performed, he cannot endure any thought:

> Strange things I have in head that will to hand,
> Which must be acted ere they may be scanned.

This process of murder begetting terror and of terror begetting murder is to go on, he cannot get out of its maelstrom. We have now carried down the action, with its two threads, through the First

Movement, which shows the guilt of Macbeth He passes from being the savior of the realm into just the opposite—its destroyer; he moves from putting down the traitor to being the traitor. This transition has been shown in its three crises, namely, the struggle with himself, with the King, and with Banquo, the loyal supporter of the King. Both royalty and loyalty he has swept out of existence by his deed; yet he is King and has subjects. Will he escape his own law? Can he "trammel up the consequence" and not have his own "bloody instructions" read to him? That is now the question of the rest of the play.

At this critical turning-point, both Macbeth and Lady Macbeth refuse to go back and undo their deeds. The matter is distinctly before the mind of Macbeth, but he declines: "Returning were as tedious as to go o'er." That terror of his he ascribes to the want of "hard use;" the most awful shapes are scourging both of them back from their course, but they persist. They refuse mediation and defy conscience, hence for them the outcome can be only tragic. They reject repentance at the last opportunity; there will be no return out of their perverse life, no restoration. This will, therefore, not be a mediated drama, which turns upon the repentance of the guilty soul, and the undoing of the wicked deed.

Along with this guilty career of Macbeth, the institutions of society have been perverted; the head of the State is an usurper, justice is exercised by a criminal, authority is in the hands of him who has defied and destroyed it, obedience becomes a crime, and loyalty to the King is treason. What is the honest man to do when his very virtue turns to wrong? Such is the perversion of the world's order now before us; not simply Macbeth is involved as an individual, but the whole social fabric; it is a world turned upside down through guilt.

II.

The ethical world has been thrown into confusion by the guilt of Macbeth; now the movement sets in toward the restoration of its harmony. He who put down the traitor has himself become the successful traitor, and has secured his position by removing Banquo, who was next to him in greatness and in prospective power. But his own action is to be brought back to him; as he served traitors, so will he be served himself, and the circle of his deed will be made complete. The State and the social system which he has perverted by crime are to be purified; the ethical order of the world is to be vindicated; the man who introduces disturbance into it is to be eliminated. The process of this elimination will be shown in the Second Movement.

The turning point of the drama is emphatically marked by the second appearance of the Weird Sisters. Temptation has culminated, now retribution sets in strongly, not however so much the inner retribution through the imagination, which has been already portrayed, but the external retribution, which brings home to the guilty man the true equivalent of his deeds, and at the same time cleanses the institutional world, which the great criminal has polluted at its very fountain head.

Here, also, we shall find in the structure the same two Threads that we found in the First Movement. The supernatural realm of the Weird Sisters again makes its appearance, retaining its former character, but changing, to a certain degree, its purpose. The natural realm has still its two groups or strands; first, the guilty pair, Macbeth and his wife, for each of whom retribution is prepared, though in different ways; second, those composing the grand reaction at home and abroad, who, with the aid of foreigners, sweep out the criminal, and restore the order of society.

Doubtless the reader has already queried: Why should Macbeth wish now to go to the Weird Sisters? Previously he met them, in the present case he wills to meet them; what are the grounds for this second interview? Their former prophecy has come to an end in fulfilment, he is on the throne. He naturally asks himself: What has the future in store for me now? Moreover, two doubts must disturb him. First, will the promise of the Weird Sisters to Banquo concerning the latter's posterity be fulfilled? In other words, he must question his soul: Have I forestalled in his case the oracle which has told the truth in my own case? That same oracle he will consult concerning the truth of itself. But his second doubt is the most imperious one to be allayed: Is there any punishment for my deeds? Still his faith in retribution is driving him, in the present case driving him to interrogate Destiny itself concerning his future. Thus to his imagination rises the Weird Sister; what will she say to him?

We have already seen that her voice is the voice of the environment to the man. Now this environment says to Macbeth: You have murdered, and you have escaped; do not be afraid of that goblin of retribution in your fancy. That is, she inculcates security, Macbeth can do what he pleases, regardless of consequences. Such is again the progeny of his deed, it begets the Weird Sister, the temptress, who says to the soul trembling at brink of guilt: Fear not, do it, you will escape the penalty, as you have escaped in the past. So Macbeth's world without speaks to his world within.

Already we have sought to penetrate the realm of witchery in the preceding Movement; now we need only repeat its four essential facts. 1st. It is the voice of the circumstances to the individual who is placed in them as in his reality; for around every human being is an environment speaking to him, and he must consult it. 2nd. This voice speaks to what is already in the man, and so he hears it; but if he be not prepared within, he cannot hear it, though it still speak. The individual gets out of his circumstances good or ill, wealth or poverty, presidency or gallows. The union of the man within and the world without makes life, action; what of the environment is not for him, passes by him unheard. 3rd. This voice of the environment speaking to man must have some image or utterance; he has to express for himself in some way the great fact of his life. 4th. Such an image is at hand in the case of Macbeth; his age, nation, race has elaborated it, and he finds it ready made. The Mythus is such an image, and Macbeth is essentially mythical in spirit, and he falls at once into its creation, as it sets forth this evil principle, which lurks in every man's environment and in himself. The Poets, Artists, Sages too, seize such mythologic forms of the people, and mould them into an expression; Shakespeare takes the Weird Sister for his poetic utterance and at the same time shows Macbeth naturally dropping into her image for his expression.

1. Accordingly we pick up at this point our first Thread again—the Supernatural World. We catch a new hint of its organization; it has a queen, Hecate, taken from Classic Mythology, and placed over Teutonic witches, in the true spirit of the Renascence. Her function is particularly marked, she is to change the previous course of the poem. Hence she reproves the Weird Sisters for the favors to Macbeth, who is "but a wayward son," and selfish; manifestly a case of Satan reproving sin. Her authority has not been recognized, now she will show what it means, both for the witches and for Macbeth.

Well, what does it mean? Hecate is, indeed, a phase of this diabolic process; she is evil, but that evil which punishes evil. That is, the wicked act has now reached the point at which it becomes self-destructive. The first witches led into crime, they were the temptresses; the second and supreme one, Hecate, is the punisher, mainly; hence she undoes the work of the first, and thus brings forth the good. In the universal order evil is a self-canceling process, it turns upon itself and wipes itself out. Accordingly, if the first witchery was temptation, the second is retribution; and if the first witches were subjects, the second witch is a queen, rules, and over-rules the first.

This is quite the position of Mephistopheles in the poem of "Faust," the fiend defining himself there as

> Part of that power
> Which always wills the Bad, and always works the Good.

Such is the mythical presentation of evil, though usually the two sides are united in one being. Thus Satan, in the Christian conception, is both tempter and punisher; first he entices to sin, but the person who yields and follows him is just the person whom he punishes. The Devil, traitor that he is, always bears hardest upon his best friends; the greater their fidelity to him, the more he scorches them in his hell-fire. So the mythus of the demons rests upon that profoundest truth that evil is forever destroying itself in the long run, and Macbeth obeying the witches, is scourged by the witch, whose highest function is to do just this scourging; hence Hecate is queen and supreme. Thus it must be, the wicked Hecate punishes the wicked Macbeth.

But how will she do it? She tells plainly:

> By magic sleights
> Shall raise such artificial sprites,
> As by the strength of their illusion
> Shall draw him on to his confusion.
> He shall spurn fate, scorn death, and bear
> His hopes 'bove wisdom, grace and fear,
> And you all know security
> Is mortals' chiefest enemy.

So Hecate too is a temptress, but for the immediate purpose of hastening the penalty. Macbeth will be trapped into "security," that regardlessness of consequences, which springs from successful crime; he will violate all dictates of wisdom, despise religion, even will cast off his former fear of retribution; nay, he will defy fate, try to overslaugh the prediction of the Weird Sister, in fact he has done so already. Truly Hecate voices the inner condition of Macbeth, who now deems himself above the penalty, and dares act without any thought of consequences:

> Strange things I have in head that will to hand,
> Which must be acted ere they may be scanned.

Such is the voice which Macbeth hears out of his environment, but this environment has another voice, which he does not hear, not the magic words of illusion, but the threatening speech of reality—that ironical talk of Lennox. (Act III. Sc. 6.) As in the beginning of the play we pass from the fantastic world of the Weird Sisters to the real world, so it is here at this second beginning of the action; all of Macbeth's guilt is known, and his future purposes are suspected. We see, too, the start of the grand re-action, and the manner of it; Scotland is to be purified from England, which has, in contrast, the good King, "the most pious Edward." So Macbeth lives in his own witch-world, which he has made; he cannot hear or cannot regard that true voice of his environment which utter Scotia's prayer through the lips of Lennox:

> Some holy angel
> Fly to the court of England, that a swift blessing
> May soon return to this our suffering country
> Under a hand accursed.

If we have heard the voice of Hecate, the queen of the witches, we are now (Fourth Act) to see what the subordinate witches are doing. They are brought before us in their kitchen, boiling in their cauldron a "gruel thick and slab," into which the hateful and destructive things of Nature are thrown; this hell-broth we may call Macbeth's world, or an image thereof, all of whose elements combine to torture such a man and finally to put him out of the way. He has, indeed, transformed his environment and all society into a seething cauldron of hellish properties, and we catch the ominous chorus which is the key-note of the time:

> Double double toil and trouble,
> Fire burn and cauldron bubble.

Into this witch-realm Macbeth enters, and we find his disposition in accord with the song of the hags; he is willing to see the whole world, physical and spiritual "tumble all together," that he may get an answer—"even till destruction sicken." In such a man they will encourage defiance, "security," to drive him on to his punishment.

Even a third set of magic shapes, the artificial sprites of Hecate rise—apparitions, whom the witches call "our masters." There are three of them, and they set forth in magic reflection the future of Macbeth in the various stages of his punishment which now determines the witches. The first is his own head severed from the body; hence "he knows thy thought." Then the warning, "beware Macduff," is one with his own mind: "Thou has harped my fear aright." Clearly the phantom and himself are one. But behold another apparition; a bloody child, "more potent than the first." It is Macduff his slayer, yet urging him:

> Be bloody bold and resolute; laugh to scorn
> The power of man, for none of woman born
> Shall harm Macbeth.

Thus his chief enemy urges upon him a blind confidence in his own destiny—his foe is really his "security." The third apparition is a child crowned, with a tree in his hand, manifestly a fatal shoot from Birnam Wood; this is Malcolm, also his enemy, yet he says

> Be lion-mettled, proud, and take no care
> Who chafes, who frets or where conspirers are;
> Macbeth shall never vanquished be until
> Great Birnam Wood to high Dunsinane hill
> Shall come against him.

This is just what Hecate proposed in making him "spurn fate and bear his hopes 'bove wisdom grace and fear;" through the illusion of phantasms, he is brought to believe that he is beyond responsibility and out of the reach of retribution; he is led to rely on destiny without regard to the ethical nature of the deed. He has, therefore, lost his fear of punishment, he no longer has faith in the moral order of the world, but relies upon an external prophecy, which always must be an equivocation of the fiend.

Again we must consider these prophecies as in him, a part of his own evil nature, hardened by crime, and audacious from success. Yet they are outside of him too, they are his world now, the oracular voice which he hears everywhere out of his environment, which tells him "to bear his hopes 'bove wisdom, grace and fear," as there is no penalty. It is the insolence begotten of successful wrong, yet is the swift means of its own punishment. In this state of soul the man will hear such predictions out of his surroundings, for they are in himself. It is true that Macbeth could not know beforehand the special details about Macduff's birth, and about the moving of Birnam Wood; but he could know that any promise or prophecy of immunity from the penalty of the wicked act is a juggle of the demons. If you listen to such a prophecy, you are lost.

We should notice another significant fact about these apparitions rising up before Macbeth. One is the crowned Malcolm, who will take away his kingdom; another is Macduff, who will slay him; the third is his own head severed from his body. They prognosticate the destiny of Macbeth in its three stages—dethronement, death, decapitation. Yet these phantoms give him advice and determine his conduct; that is, his own destroyers tell him that he cannot be destroyed; this becomes just the cause of his destruction. It strengthens his insolent reliance upon his destiny, without his paying any regard to the ethical character of his deed. Hence these apparitions, though tempting him to "security," are really leading him to execution. In murdering Banquo, he has murdered, both in himself and in the world, the moral scruple, for Banquo represents it, and Macbeth has gotten rid of it; by that deed he is another man, and it is another world. In this spirit he coddles the thought that rebellion cannot touch him, he is above any death through violence:

> Our high-placed Macbeth
> Shall live the lease of Nature, pay his breath
> To time and mortal custom.

Being secure about himself, he will next seek to know concerning the future inheritance of the throne, as that was one of his motives in the murder of Banquo. But he learns that Banquo's children and not his own are to be successors in the kingdom. He has, therefore, not succeeded in forestalling the first prophecy of the Weird Sisters; on this side, the death of Banquo has been for nothing. Nor ought he to have looked for any thing else. The Weird Sisters could not be expected, even by him, to predict truly in his own case, but falsely in another similar case. Moreover, this thought lives in him too; he knows that

Fleance has escaped and is alive, and that, therefore, Banquo's posterity may succeed to the crown. In a general way, this show of eight Kings, Banquo's descendants, lies in him at the time, though the special manner is for the future to reveal. But he may well see that "the blood-boltered Banquo smiles upon me and points at them for his."

His failure, however, leads him to curse these prophetic shapes, he is now done with them forever. From this time forward Macbeth seeks no more the Weird Sisters, nor is he longer harrassed with the specters of the imagination. "And damned all those that trust them," wherein his curse includes himself. "No more sights," he sternly says; he will drown in a whirl of activity all his mental phantoms; he will fight till every suspected man as well as the kindred of the same be swept away—evidently a large undertaking. Up and off: "the flighty purpose never is o'ertook, unless the deed go with it:" Macduff has fled, but wife and children remain:

"This deed I'll do, before this purpose cool."

Such is the Supernatural World of the Second Movement, and its influence upon Macbeth. He alone beholds it now, he has no Banquo for a companion in his vision; Lennox, though apparently in his presence, cannot see anything of it, having no gift for such a sight. It is shown in three phases: Hecate, the queen, who deludes into security; the Witches, who cook the diabolic gruel for Macbeth; the Apparitions, who, while showing him the very process of his death, flatter him into a defiance of it. All have one thing in common: they lead him swiftly toward the penalty by having him suppress the fear of it; they are the voices of Destiny bringing on punishment through a disbelief in punishment.

But thus the witch-world has destroyed itself; we remember that it sprang from the fear of retribution; when that fear is quenched, it is quenched. Macbeth will still cling to the two ambiguous prophecies, but the terror which called up in so much vigor the imaginary world, is gone; the specters have, as far as he is concerned, ended themselves. Macbeth is the man who has only the fear of evil, and not the positive love of the good; when the fear of evil is removed, he falls utterly to the bad, and even loses his imagination, through which his conscience works upon his life.

What will henceforth be the condition of Macbeth? The world is empty, when man no longer has a terror of the consequences of evil. If he can do wrong, and yet believe that he is exempt from the penalty, his inner life is dead; no terror of conscience is the wilderness of the soul. Remorse is a blessing, its stings are full of hope to the evil-doer who has them, compared to the evil-doer who has them not; they are scourging him to undo his wicked deed, they belong to the process of purification. We may even declare it to be to the advantage of Lady Macbeth, in this last part of the play, that she shows herself capable of remorse, though she be unable to carry it forward to its fruition in repentance. But Macbeth violently sweeps it out of his soul, and there is left desolation; still this desolation he will find the most terrible punishment.

2. We shall next consider the Second Thread, the Natural World, as it appears in this Second Movement. Its general scope and outcome has been already reflected in the Supernatural World, which is now to reveal itself in the form of reality. This Thread divides itself into two distinct, in fact, opposing strands: the first is the guilty pair for whom punishment is being prepared; the second is the re-action against them, the great uprising, native and foreign, which is the means of the punishment of Macbeth, as well as of the purification of the State.

(*a.*) The career of Macbeth and his wife in the First Movement was a continued descent till they reached the turning-point, the very limit of their characters, which now show a great change, yet a true development out of their former selves. This development is what we must specially note, and, if possible, justify. Lady Macbeth in person is introduced but once—in the famous night-walking scene. The objection is often made that this scene is not motived with sufficient plainness; that the leap into it is not at all accounted for by her preceding conduct. But a careful survey of her previous actions and sayings will refute the charge. It has been above noted that she cites, and seems to believe in, the prognostications of nature; that she calls up the image of her father, when about to murder the grooms, and is, thereby, deterred from the act; that once she gives way to her suppressed emotional character and faints. But the most striking instance of her belief in the Supernatural World is found in the passage where she invokes the "spirits that tend on mortal thoughts," and the "murdering ministers" of the air. The predominance of her imagination is most emphatically brought out in these places; in this respect she was, no doubt, intended by the poet to rank in quite the same category with Macbeth and Banquo. Her self-command, however, is sufficient to suppress her own tendency to fantastic creation, as well as that of her husband. This is just her function in the first part of the drama. In the presence of Macbeth the stern, cool understanding always seems to control her actions, except the one time. But when she is alone she cannot help manifesting the deepest trait of her nature.

Therefore, in her waking moments, Lady Macbeth can temporarily crush the workings of her imagination by her colossal strength of will. But the hour comes when this fierce grip is relaxed—when the mind is freed from its central controlling power, and its activities rush out in all directions like the released winds of Æolus. Then we may expect that the suppressed imagination will exhibit itself in its native might, or, indeed, will burst forth with tenfold fury, as the fires of the pent-up volcano. The poet simply gives the fact; he brings before us Lady Macbeth awake when this trait is smothered, and Lady Macbeth asleep when it must be manifested in its highest potence. There would seem to be no very great necessity for delineating any intervening stage of her mind—in fact, there is none.

But what now will be the subject which her imagination will seize upon in sleep? Note its power over the physical system; she rises out of bed, walks about, writes upon a piece of paper, speaks aloud—indeed, quite equals her waking state. Its theme, however, will be that which has made the strongest impression upon it, namely, the scenes of that eventful night when Duncan was murdered, together with their consequences. It will reproduce with striking fidelity the two sides of her nature, which have before been noticed. For, in the first place, her self-command appears here adumbrated in her dreams; she quiets her husband, reproves his fear, suppresses the phantoms of his mind, and directs his actions after the murder. But, in the second place, the great and important element of this representation is the imagination portraying, not her assumed, but her actual, mental condition. The rubbing of her hands to wash out the gory spot, and her inability to get them clean, the smell of blood upon them, the sigh when she finds her attempts ineffectual, are the most terrific symbols of remorse. The culmination is, "the Thame of Fife had a wife: where is she now?" Lady Macbeth, too, is a wife; her own domestic relation has been murdered—here is the punishment. Again we behold conscience working through the imagination. The doctor, who is the interpreter for the audience in this scene, tells the secret: "More needs she the divine than the physician;" her ailment is not bodily, but spiritual. Also her fluctuation between the two above-mentioned elements of her character is to be observed; for it is, to a certain extent, a picture of what she actually was in her waking state.

Her attempt to wash her hands clean of the blood-spots upon them is her own answer to that former expression of hers: "A little water clears us of this deed." So she said to her husband in her strong self-suppression, when he declared that his blood-stained hands would "the multitudinous seas incarnadine;" now we see what must have been going on within her even then. She has a lighted taper beside her continually at present, she is afraid of darkness; she too "fears a painted devil," painted by her imagination on Night. The three great murders of the play, those of Duncan, Lady Macduff, and Banquo she images in this scene, with her double self in the center of the picture; thrice she tries to cleanse "this little hand," thrice the allusion to blood on them is made, and throws a red flash of infernal lightning upon Stygian blackness. Thus she shows the outburst of her imagination; but with the outburst, also the suppression of it in her dream. This is one of the strongest instances of Shakespeare's symbolism; what an image of the inner world is cast in this act of washing the hands! Yet the scene has the most vivid realism too; it is not even written in verse but in prose; as if in her dreams

Lady Macbeth could not be expected to speak in the measured speech of poetry, which demands something of a waking skill and purpose. The doctor, who is awake, drops back to verse in his final comment upon the case. But we see that Lady Macbeth too feels the retribution which her husband felt; she also has "murdered sleep," and, therefore, she will "sleep no more."

In the case of Lady Macbeth, as well as in the case of her husband, we behold the internal retribution accomplished through the imagination. But her it destroys; she cannot withstand its attacks, nor avoid them by outward activity. We must consider her to have been left alone some length of time—"since his majesty went into the field." She thus was handed over to her own thoughts—no doubt her most terrible enemies. She began with unsexing herself, in which step is contained the germ of her fate; for to unsex the woman is to destroy the woman as woman. Abjuring her emotional nature she proceded to cruelty and crime. At last we see her in the process of being eaten up by the Furies of her own creation. The exact manner of her death is not given, nor need it be. The motive, however, is most ample; imagination, with its "thick-coming fancies," is her executioner.

The somewhat prevalent notion of making love the mainspring of Lady Macbeth's actions, and of seeing in her the tender, devoted wife, who committed the most horrible crimes merely out of affection for her husband, is ridiculous, and is, one may well assert, contradicted by the whole tenor of the play. The very point emphasized in her characterization at the beginning is that she abjured womanhood, with its tenderness and love, and prayed to be filled, "from the crown to the toe, top full of direst cruelty," and her woman's breasts to be milked for gall! To be the wife is clearly not her highest ambition—that she is already; but it is to be the queen. There is no consistency or unity in her character if love be its leading principle. To this passion the husband may justly lay some claim, but not the wife, who suppresses her emotional nature.

The second person of this group is Macbeth, whose career we shall now take up again and trace to its close. Macduff had excited suspicion by absenting himself from the royal feast, and previously he had sworn with Banquo to avenge the murder of Duncan. But he discovers his danger and flees. His wife and children are left behind, and are destroyed in his stead. This is the third great crime of Macbeth. He has quite run through the scale of human guilt; he has destroyed the foundation of the State in the murder of the rightful king; he has destroyed loyalty to just authority in the murder of Banquo; now he destroys the Family in the murder of its innocent members. Logically his criminal career is now complete; consequently the poet has given no other special case of his cruel acts. Still, the process continues, and must continue, as is indicated in a general way by the statements that every morn "new widows howl, new orphans cry," and "the dead man's knell is there scarce asked, for whom?" Every human being is now the object of his suspicion; the existence of any individual is conceived to be an act of hostility by the jealous tyrant; for, having slain man wantonly, he very truly infers that man is his enemy. He is becoming in reality what he is logically in the first murder—the destroyer of the human race. His act involves the annihilation of the species. In order to escape the monster a general flight from Scotland must take place, which flight will collect the instruments for his destruction.

It is not to be affirmed that all are guilty who have to suffer in this grand perversion of social order. Still there is a general paralysis in Scotland, like that of Banquo; her people, especially her noblemen, do not rise and throw off the usurper in their own might. The sin of omission, of refusal, is universal; it is most striking in the case of Lady Macduff. She complains of her husband who has had to flee, and who is the chosen slayer of Macbeth; she will not endure her lot, she spurns patience, which Ross urges; at last she refuses to follow the warning to flee with her children, in sullen pride saying: "I have done no harm." She is not guiltless; but even innocence, in this grand cataclysm of the moral world, is not always respected; it must, at least, use intelligence to take care of itself. Lady Macduff has lost her faith in the providential order, though it has just done its part in trying to save her by a timely warning; she has lost her moral fixity:

> I do remember now
> I am in this earthly world, where to do harm
> Is often laudable, to do good sometimes
> Accounted dangerous folly.

But her little son is the opposite, he has the natural belief of the child, he can live "as birds do, with what I get;" moreover he sees through the untruthfulness of his mother: "My father is not dead, for all your saying." It is curious that both the mother and the murderer agree in saying of Macduff, "He's a traitor;" but the boy disagrees in emphatically responding to the murderer, "Thou liest." So Lady Macduff is swept into the maelstrom by not acting up to her light; hers is the refusal to do when Providence plainly calls; she, as mother, involves her innocent children in her fate.

The main fact now to be noticed in the character of Macbeth is that he is no longer swayed by his imagination. This change was indicated at the end of his interview with the Weird Sisters; he is now able to dismiss such "sights" altogether. His outward activity must help to absorb his mind, for his foes are marching against him; the reality before him is quite as terrible as any image can be. But Macbeth himself states clearly the main ground of this remarkable change. Previously he had declared that his dire phantasms were merely the result of his inexperience in crime:

> — My strange and self-abuse
> Is the initiate fear that wants hard use;
> We are but young in deed.

But now he contrasts his present with his former condition in this respect:

> I have almost forgot the taste of fear.
> The time has been my senses would have quail'd
> To hear a night-shriek; and my fell of hair
> Would at a dismal treatise rouse, and stir
> As life were in't; I have supp'd full with horrors;
> Direness, familiar to my slaughterous thoughts,
> Cannot once start me.

Here is exactly stated the difference between his two mental states and its cause. Familiarity with crime has hardened his thoughts; repetition of guilt has seared his conscience. Hence no retributive ghosts appear after the murder of Macduff's family. But his whole mind is seared too—it is a desolation; "life is but a walking shadow;" "I have lived long enough;" "life is fall'n into the sear, the yellow leaf;" "I 'gin to be a-weary of the sun," etc. That is, since the cessation of his imagination his spirit is dead—an inward desert—because his imagination was the center of his spiritual activity. There, is, however, one object to which he still shows attachment—it is his wife. She dies—the victim of "thick-coming fancies;" there remains only his dependence upon the two prophecies; these also break down, for, though their reality is carefully maintained, they are merely symbols of his external reliance upon his imagined destiny, to the disregard of all ethical conduct. He tries to believe that he will not perish, no matter what he does. Hence the prophecies are a delusion—in fact, his own delusion. It will thus be seen that both Macbeth and his wife have their common psychological principle in the imagination, though its development in each is just the opposite. In the first Movement of the drama Lady Macbeth suppresses her imagination, while Macbeth yields to his; in the second the reverse takes place.

Macbeth, in his grand collapse, goes through a series of external losses, each of which is followed by a wail of despair that gives a look into his soul. First is the loss of friends and adherents; still he continues his insolence and relies upon his two prophecies. But we hear also the inner cry: "I am sick at heart." Second is the loss of his most loved object, the queen, of whose death he knows the cause, and feels the shadow in himself. Life is now but an empty monotony, whose echo is heard in his very words:

> To-morrow, and to-morrow, and to-morrow,
> Creeps in this petty pace from day to day
> To the last syllable of recorded time.

Third is the loss of one of the prophecies, when Birnam Wood starts to move toward Dunsinane. Now doubt begins to enter his soul along with desolation: "I pull in resolution and begin to doubt." Fourth is the loss of the second prophecy; doubt becomes certainty, and he dies after beholding the grand disillusion of his life:

> And be these juggling fiends no more believed,
> That palter with us in a double sense,
> That keep the word of promise to our ear,
> And break it to our hope.

The element of physical courage remains when

all else is gone; Macbeth perishes fighting bravely. The invading army fulfils the prophecies, performs the seeming impossibilities. Whatever miracles protect such a man as Macbeth knows himself to be, must rest on some delusion; they are really the concealed instruments which are employed for his destruction. Fate is fond of irony. That Birnam Wood should move and hide in it an army for Macbeth's overthrow, is a prophecy setting forth, not victory, but the actual manner of his defeat. Then the expression, "no man of woman born," does not exclude, but hides the slayer; the prophecy really points out the very person who is to kill him. This is truly an "equivocation of the fiend that lies like truth," suggesting that the transgressor will escape the ethical law of the world yet just therein leading him to punishment. Prophecy has two sides, one of ignorance and one of knowledge; the particular side we cannot know, it is in the future; but the universal side, the law, we can know, for it is eternal, present as well as future and past. We cannot know beforehand how Birnam Wood will move; but we know that it will move sooner than that the Law will move, and give to transgression immunity from the penalty.

(*b.*) The second group of the Natural World —the avengers from abroad—now becomes prominent and active. Hitherto, under Duncan, this element was simply passive; but under his son, Malcolm, it is beginning the grand re-action which will restore the shattered social order and again give peace to the nation. Malcolm reveals his regal traits in a talk with Macduff, whom he tests severely before accepting; he has not the fatal confidence of his father, Duncan; he is, too, a man of action; already he has enlisted an army in England on behalf of his cause. His array of moral qualities we may accept on his own statement; he is not lustful, false or avaricious:

> Scarcely have coveted what was mine own,
> At no time broke my faith, would not betray
> The devil to his fellow, and delight
> No less in truth than life.

A right royal character, we say, around whom the fugitive Scotchmen may well gather, to bring about the great restoration. But the chief agent in this restoration is England, who is to help and to heal her sick neighbor. Her substantial contribution for this purpose is the old war-horse Siward, "with 10,000 warlike men." But the best gift that England furnishes is the example of her monarch, the "good king"—a contrast to the bad King Macbeth, and a pattern to the future King Malcolm, who here speaks his praise. This King has the power to cure "strangely-visited people," and "to succeeding royalty he leaves the healing benediction." Thus he is able to transfer his gift. But now he will aid in curing, not individuals, but a whole nation; "he hath a heavenly gift of prophesy" also, the divine foresight very needful in a king. Evidently, Malcolm has been much impressed by the "good king;" he has found his ideal. If this passage be a compliment to King

James, under it is the far deeper compliment to England.

The attack is made, the castle "is gently rendered," the tyrant is slain. The avengers are present—Malcolm, son of the murdered king, and Macduff, father of the murdered family; but somehow we miss Fleance, son of Banquo, who ought to be present, to make the list complete. Malcolm gives us a glimpse of the new order; he will restore justice, punishing "the cruel ministers of this dead butcher," and "calling home our exiled friends." His allusion to Lady Macbeth's suicide is evidently based on a popular rumor. Thus the restoration is complete, we behold the re-adjustment of that world of Scotch confusion; those who have been tried and have endured the trial, are now the restorers and rulers.

One of the peculiarities of the present drama is the fate that overtakes a series of characters, whose sole guilt is the refusal to act at the providential moment—the sin of omission. These are especially Duncan, Banquo, and Lady Macduff, but their trait seems common at the time to all Scotland. They are not shown committing any ethical violation worthy of death; they appear innocent beings overwhelmed in a catastrophe from the outside; and this treatment is deeply consistent with the form and movement of the play, which exhibits Destiny. The Weird Sisters, instruments of Destiny, give to Macbeth his impulse; he is driven upon these victims, apparently guiltless, who fall because they stand in the way of a mighty force. Still, in their case, also, Destiny is internal as well as external; it is their refusal to act when the call comes—that dire paralysis of duty. In this drama, inaction is Fate, quite as much as bad action.

We must notice, too, that the ethical elements, which are usually the most prominent matter, and are given in their native form in other plays, are here somewhat withdrawn into the background, and are clothed in an alien mythical shape. To be sure the ethical world is the main thing, and cannot be absent; it has been pointed out in the career of Macbeth. But the psychological interest equals, possibly surpasses, the ethical; the activities of mind, as well as the world's moral forces, appear to spring at once into independent forms of the imagination. Life with its inner and outer influences is sporting in the mask of fantasy. Macbeth knows abstractly of his own ambition, but his chief temptation seems to be held out to him by the phantoms of the air; and, though an external punishment is brought home to him, still his inner retribution, as well as that of his wife, is mainly found in the fantastic workings of the brain. Judging by its treatment, its theme, its language, and its characters, we may call this play, distinctively, the Tragedy of the Imagination.

Nor should we pass by the gleam of the world-historical spirit which seems to be hovering over this drama. Scotland, not through her own effort, has been able to free herself, but aided by England; if the single nation cannot, then the world must rid itself of the great disturber and the great disturbance. For the nations, too, are in a system; a displacement of one disorders all, and the universal current sets in to rectify the trouble. Macbeth has introduced such a disorder into his own country, and through it into the world, which will at last have to make the correction, if his own people do not.

It will be seen that the play runs in the same general groove as *King Lear;* there is a great social disturbance and perversion, with final restoration. But in *King Lear* the outer interference, coming from France, is defeated; England is to correct her own troubles from within, though she may set Scotland in order. The poet is an Englishman, patriotically so. At first we think that this difference of treatment results from national prejudice; but we reflect and find that the poet is true to the historic fact. England's relation to Scotland has been, in general, a healing, peace-bringing one; but Shakespeare has not sung of his country's interference in Ireland, which has certainly produced some discords. Still he is, in the main, right in the character which he here gives to his people.

HAMLET.

Chapter First.—Preliminary Topics.

Hamlet is the Sphinx of modern literature. The difference of opinion concerning its purport and character is quite as general as the study of the work. Persons of the same grade of culture and ability hold the most contradictory theories respecting its signification; even the same persons change their notions about it at different periods of life. To others, again, it remains an unsolved mystery. Yet, curious to say, everybody recurs to this play as if it possessed some strange fascination over the mind—as if it had some secret nourishment for the spirit of man which always drew him back to take repeated draughts. A work to which intelligence thus clings must be something more than an idle riddle—in fact, it must lay open some of the profoundest problems of life. Even to appreciate and comprehend such a problem when stated requires no ordinary degree of culture and thought. Every individual brings his own intellectual capacity to the comprehension of the play, and it is no wonder that people differ so much, since they have so many different mental measuring-rods. If one man has a deeper or shallower insight than another, there must be a corresponding difference of opinion. Also, advancing years bring along great spiritual mutations; new views of life and broader experience must reveal different phases in *Hamlet*, if it be that absolute work which enlightened mankind generally believe it to be. Hence we may account for the frequent occurrence of a change of opinion respecting it in the same person at the several periods of life. Indeed, a man ought, perhaps, to change his opinion concerning this drama once every decade during the first forty years of existence: it would, in most cases, be a good sign of increased culture and maturer intellect. According to our own premises, therefore, we can hardly expect to satisfy all, or the majority, or even ourselves after the lapse of years; when we have done, it is expected that the theories will still be conflicting. But we intend to grapple honestly with its difficulties, which are both many and great, and attempt to state the thought which gives unity to its widely diversified parts.

The play is a series of problems, of perplexing questions, concerning which opinions in every way contradictory have been held. The most important, as well as the most disputed, of these problems is the insanity of Hamlet. But, after taking away this question of insanity, there still remains a very great difference of opinion. In regard to the character of Hamlet, one man considers him to be courageous—another, cowardly; one, that he is moral in the highest degree—another, that he is wicked; one, that he possesses vast energy of will—another, that he has little or no power of action. The same diversity of judgment exists in regard to the play as a Whole. It has been condemned as the wild work of a barbarian; it has been praised as the highest product of modern Art. Between these two extremes almost every shade of opinion has had its representative. Even Goethe, speaking through one of his characters, denies its unity; he declares that they are many things—such as the story of Fortinbras, the journey of Laertes to France, the sending of Hamlet to England—which have no justification in the thought of the work. That is, if it be a true totality, we must find some higher solution, and some more adequate and comprehensive statement, than that of Goethe. In fact, most of these conflicting opinions may, in this way, be harmonized; they are not absolutely false, but only partial, views, which become erroneous by laying claim to universality.

Hamlet is, indeed, a sort of universal man; in him every individual sees on some side a picture of himself; each one bears away what he comprehends, and often thinks it is all. If Goethe—whose criticism of this play in *Wilhelm Meister* is undoubtedly the best that has yet been given—complained of the many external and unnecessary incidents, our difficulty, be it said with all the respect due to so great a genius, is quite of the opposite kind—we are compelled to supply so much. The poet has left so many faint outlines, and even wide gaps, to be filled up by the thought and imagination, that we would find here, if anywhere, a blemish in the construction of the drama. He ought rather to have taken a whole volume and a whole life for his work, as Goethe himself did in his *Faust.* But the defense of Shakespeare is at hand. He wrote for representation, which is an essential side of the drama; hence the limits which it imposed upon his Art must be respected. In the space of a few hours he develops what might be the theme of the grandest epic. He has been forced to drop much that would otherwise be necessary, and the missing links must be supplied if one wishes to grasp the connecting thought of the piece. It will be seen that, for this reason, we shall often have to go outside of the poem and bridge over the chasms—for which work, however, the poet always furnishes the hint. But let it not be understood by this that we are correcting the defects of the play, or even completing what was before imperfect; besides the presumptuousness of the attempt, such a proceeding is destructive of all true criticism, whose duty cannot be to supply the deficiencies of a work of Art, or to see in it things which do not exist. Still what the latent, yet necessary thought of the piece, requires, is to be unfolded into vision by the expositor.

I. *Hamlet's Insanity.* At the very threshold stands the question of Hamlet's insanity. Was it real or feigned? If he is insane, and so intended by the poet, let us shut the book and say no more; for, certainly, there is nothing more to be said. But even on general principles we cannot grant that such is the case. Art is the expression of Reason, and that, too, of the Reason of a nation, of an age, of an epoch; eliminate this principle—pray what is left? Criticism, if it be true to its highest end, points out and unfolds the rational element in a drama or other work of Art; but here it could only say, this poem professedly depicts the Irrational—hence the Ugly. A work which has as its theme the Ugly cannot well possess much beauty. Moreover, what delight or instruction can there be in the portraiture of the Irrational? Think of the choicest spirits of this and former generations finding spiritual nourishment in the capricious oddities of a madman! In fact, this play would thus become repugnant alike to the intellectual and the moral nature of man; repugnant to his intellectual nature, for it would be stripped of all true intelligence in the dethronement of Reason; repugnant to his moral nature, for insanity destroys responsibility, and thus Hamlet could in nowise be held accountable for his acts.

Here lies the greatest objection to the above-mentioned view: it takes away the notion of responsibility, and, thereby, blasts the very germ of the play. That the poet intends no such thing seems very evident. Shakespeare has shown us characters passing into insanity on ethical grounds, in consequence of some violation; but to write a book on insanity is not his purpose. Hamlet has the profoundest feeling of duty—the most sensitive moral nature. Moreover, the termination of his career at the end of the play shows how Shakespeare would have us regard the matter. To destroy an insane man for his deeds would be, not merely an absurdity, but a moral horror.

The view that Hamlet is mad has lately been promulgated with much emphasis by several physicians who have had large experience in the treatment of the insane. Their method of procedure is curious—resting upon a wholly physical basis, though they are judging a work of Art. They carefully reckon up the symptoms, and show the various stages—evidently regarding the unfortunate Prince as one of their own patients, and the whole play as a treatise on insanity. One is at first inclined to think that these doctors ought to take the place of their patients, and be incarcerated for a while in an insane asylum. Yet we should not, perhaps, blame them; for does not everybody read into *Hamlet* his own life-experience and culture? Why not let these men read into it their own insanity in peace? In fact, more insanity has been shown by certain writers on Hamlet's insanity, than was ever shown by Hamlet himself. Cellullar pathology has been called in to explain it; Hamlet's brain has been actually dissected, and the very brain-cell pointed out, whose collapse produced his mental aberration. In defining his madness, the words of Polonius have been literally verified:

> For, to define true madness,
> What is it but to be nothing else but mad?

But such a writer is exceptional, and only worthy of notice as showing the physical method in its excess. Most of the doctors who support the theory of Hamlet's insanity are very careful and moderate in their statements, coolly scientific, we may say; but we cannot help thinking their procedure inapposite. The experts, however, do not agree among themselves; some would put Hamlet into the insane asylum, some would not; so the authority of science can be cited on both sides, and leaves us just where we were, to help ourselves out by other means. After all, the best method is to take the whole play into our vision, and let its complete light shine upon the parts. And the whole play, holding Hamlet responsible for his deeds, especially for what may be considered his insanest deed—the killing of Polonius—moves in a direction opposite to that of insanity. Still, it must be granted that Hamlet is not altogether healthy; he shows a disordered state of feeling, but no unhinging of the mind, in spite of what Ophelia and others say in the course of the drama.

A modification of this medical opinion is that Hamlet is deranged in some of his faculties, though not in all—is mad at times, with lucid intervals, etc. These views are hardly worthy of a detailed examination; in them all definiteness fades away; their supporters are evidently on both sides, and on neither. But a true criterion may be laid down to guide our wandering steps in this trackless waste of uncertainty. *Hamlet is never so mad as not to be responsible.* Hence, with any ordinary definition of insanity, he is not mad at all. He has, undoubtedly, weaknesses—so has every mortal. He possesses finite sides to his character and intelligence; otherwise, he could hardly perish as the hero of a tragedy. A definition of insanity which includes Hamlet would sweep at least three-fourths of mankind into the mad-house. That he is lacking in the element of will, that he is melancholy in his feelings, that his reasoning is often unsound and, in fact, so intended by himself, is all very true, but does not make out a case of insanity. He assumes madness for a special purpose, and says so when he speaks of his antic disposition; nothing can be plainer than this purpose throughout the entire play. He took a mask to conceal his own designs, to discover the secrets of the King and to deceive the court, and, particularly, Polonius, the sharp-scented detective, who was sure to be placed upon his track.

It is manifest that Hamlet wishes to produce the impression of an insane man—a thing which a really insane man would hardly seek to do. Mad people are not so eager to play mad, but rather to play sane. At this point there seems to be a great hitch in the argument of the doctors. They say that when Hamlet speaks of putting on "an antic disposition," it shows, not a disguised but a real, madness, inasmuch as insane people are very subtle in excusing their eccentric conduct, even when they cannot help it, and in hiding their insanity. Very true; but this is just the opposite of the case of Hamlet, who wishes to conceal his sanity rather, and to make the world believe he is insane. An insane man trying to feign an insanity which he already has without feigning, is, then, Hamlet; if this be his condition, there can be no further doubt, not only of Hamlet's, but of Shakespeare's madness.

Hamlet's treatment of Ophelia is often held to be a mark of an unsettled mind. It is harsh, but we must see the provocation. She who ought to love him and cling to him, has believed the dishonoring suspicions of her father and brother, and sent back his tokens. Then she has allowed herself to become the instrument of his enemies, whereat a sane man might be led to exclaim: "Get thee to a nunnery."

His ultimate object was to find out the guilt of the King; for this purpose he deemed it necessary to divert the attention of the court—headed and guided in its opinions by Polonius—as far as possible from the design of which he might otherwise be suspected. But why should he take the special form of insanity to hide his plans? This was determined by the character of Polonius, who was no fool, but very astute in his particular calling—who had, therefore, to be caught in his own net. That trait of his character in which all others were resumed was cunning. Now, Hamlet was known to the court as a man of profound candor and earnestness, and disinclined to all trickery and deceit; hence, to meet Polonius, he had to reverse his entire nature and reputation. But how would everybody regard this sudden transformation? Either in its true light as a disguise, in which case the whole design of it would fail, or that the man had lost his wits. Hence Hamlet, in order to conceal his plans and thoughts, had to counterfeit madness; such was the impression that he was compelled to make upon the world. Thus he had a veil, beneath which he could be cunning, too, and indulge in all sorts of vagaries without exciting suspicion, and could thwart Polonius and the other court spies on all sides. Such was his great and sudden change, which has so mystified both King and court.

Yet Hamlet, once started in his disguise, begins to take pleasure in it; he seems to find a certain relief in playing an assumed part—a relief from his internal struggles; though not insane, he takes an insane delight in feigning insanity. He is fond of plotting, sporting, mocking, masking, loves the theatre, and is often a most theatrical sort of a person. What an actor! we have to cry out at times; truly a hypocrite, in the old sense of the word, we have to call him. Yet this is but the outside of him; he is also deeply in earnest, has the most sensitive moral nature, and a conscience responsive to every whisper of duty. Under his mask he is bearing up the burden of a world. No doubt he takes delight in disguise; though he has the profoundest motive for feigning insanity, he feigns it sometimes without motive. The twofold element of his nature—sincerity and dissimulation—is to be grasped together into one character.

Moreover, Hamlet was intimate with Ophelia, the daughter of Polonius, and had been dismissed by the father's orders; here was just what was wanted, namely, a ground to give Polonius for the theory of Hamlet's madness—love for Ophelia. This ground Hamlet furnishes him; the self-conceit of the old courtier, mixed with paternal pride, quite led him astray; besides, he did not, and could not, comprehend the profound ethical nature of Hamlet, who had a deep, underlying motive for the disguise. Still, Polonius sometimes half suspects the truth, for he cannot but observe that there is method in Hamlet's madness.

Such are the reasons why Hamlet had to feign insanity. He was the self-chosen instrument of a mighty design, which, however, for a time, required concealment; concealment demanded cunning; cunning was the reversal of his entire rational nature; still, to carry out his end, he had to submit to the circumstances, and to assume the garb of the Irrational. How perfectly our poet has succeeded in portraying this disguise is shown by the fact that quite a number of modern critics have been deceived as badly as Polonius. They maintain that Hamlet is mad; that his profound intelligence, and his deep, conscious planning, mean nothing, or, to cite the expression of one of them, that "madness is compatible with *some* of the ripest and richest manifestations of intellect;" whereof Hamlet is an example. Just the thought of old Polonius. Hear him: "How pregnant, *sometimes*, his replies are! a happiness that often madness hits on, which reason and sanity could not so prosperously be delivered of." We cannot but regard those persons who believe in the madness of Hamlet as in the condition of Polonius in the play—most completely befooled by Hamlet's disguise, and laughed at by the poet himself. If, too, the leading characters of the play are considered, but little will be found to justify the hypothesis of Hamlet's madness. Besides Polonius, only the two women—the Queen and Ophelia—neither of whom was strong enough to have an independent opinion, take Hamlet to be mad. The King, though a little doubtful at first, soon knows better, and acts upon his conviction to the end; moreover, Horatio, the most intimate friend and chosen vindicator of Hamlet, does not seem to have the remotest notion of the insanity of Hamlet.

The people of the play, however, like the readers of it, divide into two main parties on the question of Hamlet's madness. It is a great problem at court; there the two theories were held which have been held ever since, and will be held forever. The poet takes into his play the audience of centuries and its doubt; each person must see the solution for himself, or leave it unseen. Indeed, Hamlet himself divides on his own question; he calls himself mad and not mad, even argues that he is and is not mad, in different places. Still further, when he speaks of the same act—his wild conduct at the grave of Ophelia—he calls it madness at one time, and something else at another time. Speaking of it to Horatio, his bosom friend (Act V. Sc. 2), he says, "I forgot myself," and that he was put "into a towering passion." But speaking of it to Laertes a little later, in the presence of the court, by way of apology he calls it madness, and proceeds to give a mad account of himself. Here it is manifest that the difference of occasion produces the difference of statement. His disguise is not for Horatio, but for the court. But such an adjustment to the situation is not the work of a madman.

Still another theory on this subject is possible, and has been maintained. It is that Hamlet is neither mad nor feigns madness. To most readers, doubtless, such a view contradicts the whole tenor of the play. Hamlet has certainly made the impression of an insane man upon the members of the court generally, except the King; are they, then, the mad people? Also, he has endeavored to produce just that impression; both his intention and its effect can hardly be explained away. It may be said that Hamlet is only acting his own nature in his wild freaks; that this is the permanent element of his character—to play the madman. But this, too, is simulation; besides, if there is one thing emphasized, it is the great change which has come over him—our much-changed son he is called. Certainly his present conduct is so different from what it has been that the whole court are trying to find the cause of the transformation. But, if it were Hamlet's nature from youth to act as he now acts, it certainly would not be such a matter of surprise and sharp inquiry.

The theories concerning Hamlet's madness may be classed under three heads: First, that his madness is real; second, that it is feigned; third, that it is neither real nor feigned. Even a fourth theory may be distinguished—that it is both real and feigned. These shade into each other, forming almost every variety of opinion; indeed, they are sometimes combined into a startling contradiction, as, for example, in the statement that Hamlet is both mad and is feigning madness. It is hard, assuredly, to draw the line; the sole anchor in this ocean of opinion would seem to be the insight—*Hamlet is never so mad as not to be responsible.*

But the theory of feigned insanity has a very grave difficulty which the other theories do not have, and which, probably, compelled them into being. What is the motive of the man? What good is to be gained by such a pretense? Nay, does not this simulated madness add new difficulties to his situation? He would seem of himself to have given to the King the very best pretext for putting him out of the way by incarcerating him in a mad-house. Even his great popularity could not help him, for the people would say, a madman can not be allowed to run loose. It has even been brought forward as an argument that the best proof of real insanity is to feign insanity under such circumstances. Hardly any two writers agree about the purpose of this strange simulation, and the poet here, as on so many other points, gives no decisive clew. So the apple of discord is thrown among the supporters of the doctrine of feigned insanity, after having valiantly defended their cause against its enemies. It is said that Hamlet's object was to conceal his own thoughts, to assassinate secretly the King, to escape without responsibility, to amuse himself by confounding others—there is no end to the various motives assigned. Some have held that the disguise was not necessary to effect Hamlet's purpose; others have even thought that it was in the way of his success. Hence it was a mistake, his first great mistake, from which all the tragic consequences flowed. But we have already traveled too far in this primeval chaos of conjecture. So much may be finally said: Hamlet's insanity is feigned, his immediate object being to deceive Polonius and the court, in order that he might more surely pursue his greater and more ultimate object—the discovery and punishment of the King's guilt.

II. *The Question of Time in the Drama.*—Time has introduced an element of discord; the action seems, to one person, to last ten days; to another, ten years. Neither period can be sustained by precise facts and figures; the essential links are always made of conjectures—usually a very weak material. The poet, however, wants to avoid the arithmetical, and to excite the imaginative, faculty; accordingly it may be confessed that the action seems long—indeed, a good life-time. *Hamlet* is a grand development, which cannot shoot up in twenty-four hours — the sufficient limit of many a good French play. You must appear to live with it—develop with it; it should, make Time long instead of short; and, on the other hand, we must not infer that it drags, causing weariness; a great deal of movement is here, and rapid movement—no stagnation. The action is both rapid and long; the two qualities are not inconsistent— as a long and busy life, for instance. The longer it seems the more the reader is likely to be obtaining from it; let him not hurry to the end of it any more than to the end of his own life. So it will continue, no doubt, to seem short to some, and long to others; two such classes of readers do, indeed, exist for every good book. Both acceleration and retardation have been skillfully pointed out in *Hamlet* and elsewhere in Shakespeare; but the deeper fact is, not this difference of dramatic time, but the unity underlying it, wherein fast and slow become one.

The same trouble exists with the age of Hamlet. A youth at the beginning, and thirty or more years old at the end, of the play—strange inconsistency! Whereat still stranger proposals of compromise—let us add the extremes and divide the sum by two, which gets, say, twenty-four years as the fixed and unchangeable age of Hamlet in the future. "O horrible! O horrible! most horrible!" May the writer say that, for him, instead of having ten or a dozen years of Hamlet's life-picture from Shakespeare's hand, he would have been glad to have started with the Danish Prince as a baby, and had his life prolonged to four-score, like the aged Faust. Yes, Hamlet is a growth—must be seized as a growth; but of growth the outer setting is time. Hamlet as merely young, and Hamlet as merely old, are equally absurd.

When shall it be comprehended that the real forms of Time and Place are ruthlessly sacrificed by Shakespeare? Time-Probability, Place-Probability—all external probabilities are employed by him to express his thought; to it everything must yield as the supreme object. Why must we continue to hear that wretched category, Probability, applied to the creative Imagination; to the author of specters, ghosts, fairies, witches; to the creator of ideal worlds, with their own Space and Time?

III. *The Dramatic Collision.*—First of all, in importance, is the collision, which constitutes the basis of the action of the entire play, and which lies between Hamlet and the King. They form the most wonderful contrast, yet both exhibit sides of the same great thought. Hamlet has morality without action, the King has action without morality. Hamlet cannot do his deed at the behest of duty, nor can the King undo—that is, repent of—his deed at the command of conscience. Hamlet represents the undone which should be done, the King represents the done which should be undone. Neither reaches the goal which reason so clearly sets before them, and both perish by the inherent contradiction of their lives. Each seeks the death of the other, and, by the most rigid poetic justice, they die by the retribution of their deeds.

Hamlet has the most powerful motives which can urge the human breast; his struggle is with one who has murdered his father, debauched his mother, and usurped, if not his throne, at least his chance of the succession. These facts are not revealed to him of a sudden in all their fullness— it is the course of the poem to unfold them gradually before his mind; but even at the beginning his prophetic soul surmised the whole truth. It is a curious psychological fact that sensitive natures often feel that of which they have no information; instinct and presentiment seem to supply the place of knowledge. The melancholy of Hamlet, at the very outset, shows his morbid activity of feeling, though there is a partial motive in the conduct of his mother, which is known to him. But when the guilt of the King is as clear as day, he does not act. Why? The answer to this question must give the first necessary insight into his character.

Let us make, once more, the oft-repeated comparison with the Greek view, for there is an excellent opportunity. In the legend of Orestes, who has been so frequently contrasted with Hamlet, notably by Herder and Gervinus, we see the same content—father murdered, mother debauched, throne usurped. But Orestes, true to the tragic instinct of Greece, is one with his end; he marches directly to it by the deepest necessity of his nature. He never stops to reflect on the character of his act; he never for a moment doubts what he is to do; nothing can possibly interpose itself between him and his deed. To be sure, if that deed were wrong, the dreadful Furies might pursue him with their terrors; but they were something external to him, with which he, in the main, had nothing to do. In other words, he never asked, never could ask, himself, in a moral sense, the question: Is this act right or wrong? There was his dead father; his only duty was revenge. He might thereby commit another crime equally great, but this reflection he did not make. He did not possess what is now called a moral consciousness; nor was it possessed, except in an embryonic state, by the Grecian world, for it is the special product of the modern spirit of Christendom.

Now, if we add this moral element to Orestes, we shall in all essential features have Hamlet. Its leading characteristic is to react against the end proposed—to call it into question, and to test the same by its own criteria. Hamlet is impelled by the strongest incentives to kill the King—such is one side; but the other side comes up before him with appalling strength—have I the right to kill him? And here it is important to inquire into the nature of this right which has such authority with Hamlet. It is not law, it is not custom, nor even public opinion—indeed, it would defy all these if it came into conflict with them; it is, therefore, nothing established and possessing objective validity. Moreover, mankind would, for the most part, justify him if he slew the King Hence it is *himself*, his own subjectivity, which he sets up as the absolute umpire of his actions. He cannot satisfy *himself* that he should do the deed, however great the other considerations may be which impel him to do it. Here we see the moral consciousness in its extreme expression; it is the assertion of the right of the individual to determine the nature of his act. That the modern world gives validity to this right need not be told to the reader. It is commonly called conscience in the wider, and not strictly religious, use of the word; by it the individual claims the privilege of determining his own action *through himself*, against all demands of objective institutions, as State, Law, or any established authority.

In Hamlet these two sides are in the most direct contradiction. He acknowledges both principles; he thinks it to be his sacred duty to avenge his father—at the same time he feels the unspeakable iniquity and misery of murder. The difficulty is he cannot subordinate these two principles of action; at one moment the one is uppermost, but the next moment the other is stronger. Such is the terrible struggle which rends his heart asunder and destroys his peace of mind. It should be observed that in his language he dwells more upon his revenge, and he tries to goad himself onward to it, but there is always the moral scruple which stays his hand. The presupposition of the entire play is the moral nature of Hamlet; hence it is not brought into prominence directly, but is always implied as the element which he is trying to overcome; it is the native stock, which he is attempting to inoculate with a new resolution.

Nor are his scruples without foundation. He is seeking revenge, which means that he is taking justice into his own hands. But thus he commits a new wrong, which, in its turn, begets another wrong—the result of which conduct, as exhibited in history, is the feud which transmits itself from generation to generation. It is the annulment of law for the individual to administer the law in his own case. There is, therefore, an institution of society—the court of justice—before which the criminal is to be cited to receive the penalty due to his crimes. But, in the present instance, the criminal happens to be the King himself—the very fountain of justice and authority. His trial would, in consequence, be a mockery—a contradiction in terms. What remains? Only this: That, if the King is to be punished at all, it must be by the individual—by Hamlet. Thus the deed is thrown back upon him, single and alone, with all its consequences and responsibilities. Here we see the internal conflict, which always palsied the arm of Hamlet; it was a fearful struggle, which may well excite our pity and terror—he would not, yet he could; he could not, yet he would.

It is just at this point that we must seek for the tragic element in Hamlet's character. Tragedy is not merely stage-slaughter. In its true significance it exhibits a collision of duties, which duties may have equal validity in the breast of the hero; he perishes beneath their strife, because he knows not how to subordinate them. Here also may be noticed an essential distinction between ancient and modern tragedy. In the former, the character is the bearer of one end alone—each individual has his single object to accomplish, in the execution of which he lays his whole existence; hence the collision is more external, and between the different individuals who have different ends. But modern tragedy, while it has this element, too, possesses in its most complete manifestations an additional principle; it makes the collision internal as well as external. The same individual has two different and contradictory ends, both of which demand realization; thus there is a double collision—with himself on the one hand, and with the external individual on the other.

Here the poet might stop, basing his characterization of Hamlet wholly upon this moral element; here some critics very positively state that he does stop. They declare that Hamlet's unwillingness to act proceeds from his doubt concerning the King's guilt; that his conscience alone keeps him from sweeping to the deed. Unquestionably he hates murder from the bottom of his soul—especially murder for an unproved crime. Still, when the crime is proved, and he says and believes that it is proved, he does not act. Something else, therefore, belongs to his character; a higher synthesis of it must be made, not neglecting its moral side. The hesitation of Hamlet springs, not merely from his conscience, but also from his intellect; it lies in his mental, as well as in his moral, composition.

IV. *Psychology of Hamlet.*—We are now ready for the complete statement of the conflict in Hamlet's mind. It involves in its sweep, not only the moral, but also the entire intellectual, nature of man. Conscience being also a phase of mind, the whole may be summed up in the expression—subjective Intelligence versus Will. We shall revert for a moment to our former illustration taken from the Greeks. They lacked, not only the moral consciousness above mentioned, but the whole realm of which it is only a part—the absolute mediation of spirit with itself; in other words, subjectivity in its highest form, or, to employ still another expression, the complete thought of Freedom. On the theoretical side this is seen in their doctrine of Fate, which at last ruled the King of Gods and Men—the mighty Jupiter. An external power thus controls even the Absolute; the highest, after all, has over itself a higher. But it is most plainly observed, in the practical affairs of the Greeks, every important action was determined by omens, by oracles, by prophetic utterances; the greatest generals never gave battle without consulting the sacrifices. This custom, so strange to our ways of thinking, was founded upon an essential limitation of the Grecian spirit. It demanded this external impulse, and no Greek could, as we say, make up his mind—that is, have his mind determine out of its own activity, from its own infinite depths, what was to be done. This element, which will, perhaps, be better understood by the contrast with the Greeks, who did not have it, must be also added to Hamlet, in order to embrace all the elements of his character.

Hence between Hamlet and his deed is interposed what may be called the entire world of subjectivity. It is, moreover, this world in its onesideness, without the objectifying element of Will. We have dwelt upon one phase of this principle—moral consciousness; but it has many phases, and, indeed, includes the whole sphere of Intelligence as distinguished from Will. The fact is, therefore, to be emphasized that Hamlet represents the entire range of subjective spirit. This has three leading forms, each of which we shall find in excessive development in Hamlet.

The first and lowest of these forms is the emotional principle of man's nature, which includes the feelings, presentiments, impulses—all of which are important elements in Hamlet's character, and sometimes are found in morbid activity. It is the dark realm of the Unconscious, in which the guiding light of reason may be dimmed or quite extinguished. So, it will be seen, when Hamlet follows impulse, not only all rational action is destroyed, but he becomes a criminal. The excess of emotion and passion, in which Hamlet is generally portrayed by the poet, is highly characteristic of a subjective nature, which must always lack that calmness and steadiness which result from a conscious mastery over the objective world.

The second form is what may be termed the phenomenal principle of mind, in which the subject become conscious of itself on the one hand, and of an external world of reality on the other. Upon this world of reality the mind now imposes its own subjective forms—applies its own one-sided predicates to all the manifold phases of existence. Thus the whole objective world, from the realm of nature upwards, may be completely transformed by being passed through a peculiar mental medium. To its glance this world only appears to be—is phenomenal, and often phenomenally bad. Now, Hamlet exhibits many characteristics of such a state of mind. He cannot see the rationality of the world; it is a dire, horrible phantasm, which he would be glad to leave in a hurry.

>   —Tis an unweeded garden
> That grows to seed; things rank and gross in nature
> Possess it merely.

Thus he did not look at the moral order of the universe in its true reality, but as transmuted in its passage through his own discolored mind. Indeed, sometimes even his sensations and perceptions of external objects seem to be affected in the same way, as Coleridge has observed. There is an expression of his, which, though it probably has a different shade of meaning in the connection where it is found, may, nevertheless be applied here— "there is nothing good or bad, but thinking makes it so." The predominance of this phenomenal principle has its culmination in the unreal ghostly element of the play—a side which will be considered more fully in another place, when we come to treat of the Ghost.

The third form of subjective spirit is the reflective, which is the most important of all, in the consideration of Hamlet. In the first sphere—the emotional—mental operations were unconscious and instinctive; in the second—the phenomenal—we see the realm of consciousness begin, and the mind busied with the objective world; but now, in third, it goes back to itself and grasps its own doings. The mind turns from the contemplation of external reality, which trait it showed in the last phase—the phenomenal—and looks at itself, feeds upon its own operations. This is the extreme of subjectivity; the intellect is pushed to the very limit of its own negation, and, unless it can make the logical transition to the Will, it must remain forever entangled in its own meshes. Consider its condition. The mind retires in upon itself, and looks at its own operations; this process, however, is a mental process, and, in its turn must be scanned; this step, too, being like the preceeding, demands examination as well as they; the result is, an infinite series in which the mind is hopelessly caught, and in which all action must perish. Such is what we call Reflection—an interminable passing from one subjective notion to another, which, in its fundamental nature, is mere repetition. Here is the point where we must seize the character of Hamlet in its concentration; here we must place the limit beyond which he cannot finally stir. This finitude, which he cannot overcome, is the ultimate cause of his ruin.

If we examine the above-mentioned principles with care, we think that from them can be deduced the main peculiarities of Hamlet's character, and its seeming contradictions can be understood. We can thus account for the tendency of his mind to play with itself—to seek out hidden relations in every direction. We can thus comprehend how he is so perfectly conscious of all his states, and even of his weaknesses; for Hamlet knows what is the matter with himself, and declares it in the bitterest language of self-denunciation. His fondness for quibbling, which seeks the hidden relations of words, is one phase of this same element; his tendency to spin out a notion into all its relations is another—the one finding its material in language, the other in thought. His intellectual keenness in deceiving, in feigning madness, in discovering the plans of his enemies, in reading the thoughts and intentions of others who are sent to pump him or ensnare him, and in many other similar cases, shows him the master of every form of subjective intelligence. He could cast himself into these infinite Protean shapes—could even carry them out as individual acts, but the ultimate purpose of them all was a fruit which he could never reach. Finally, the moral consciousness before spoken of must be referred to this head; for it is only the subjective element claiming the right to determine the deed, demanding that therein it be satisfied, and, in the case of Hamlet, refusing to be satisfied.

Moreover, many of the weak elements of Hamlet's character spring from the same source. Hence his procrastination; for his mind cannot free itself from the net of its own working so as to translate itself into objectivity. He resolves on the death of the King, even with passion; he places his end before himself, even with violence; but that end is subjective, and, hence, exposed to the endless twistings and curvetings of Reflection, so that it at last is buried beneath the confusion. His sporting with possibilities also finds its basis here; for the mind is the world of possibilities; they only exist in it, and are hardly to be found in the world of actuality. Here, then, is a glorious field for the exercise of his peculiar faculty; what may be is ever before his mind, and has quite as much validity as what is—nay, sometimes more. Again, how perfect are the excuses which he can frame for not acting, as in the case when he refuses to strike the fatal blow while the King is at prayer, lest the latter might go to heaven! Nobody knew better than Hamlet the absurdity of such a proposition, yet it is good enough for a pretext. But all these psychological peculiarities, of which the play is full, need not be stated, for they have the same logical basis.

Such is the most general form of the internal collision in Hamlet. He is the grand representative of the entire realm of subjectivity, and he exhibits its finitude and its negation in his own fate; for subjective spirit—mere intelligence without activity—cannot save a human being. Man must be able, not merely to understand the world, but to create it anew in a certain degree; not merely to translate it into the forms of his own mind, but to impose his own forms upon it—to make it the bearer of his own ends. Thus only can he assert his universality. Hamlet knows of action in its highest sense, since he is master of the world of thought, yet he cannot attain to it, though perpetually striving after it. He cannot realize his plan; he cannot make himself valid in the objective world but to a limited degree, and, so far as he falls short of this, he can hardly be called an actual being, since he—his mind, his thought—has no existence in the world of reality. How, then, can he continue to live? It must be found in the end that he has not strength of individuality sufficient to maintain life. He complains of the external world, which is always intruding upon his privacy and disturbing his quiet intercourse with himself; he even meditates to end this "sea of troubles" by ending his own existence. It is a troublesome world, indeed, which, if it be not controlled, must necessarily control.

V. *Hamlet's Action and Non-Action.*—But it is not the purpose herein to maintain that Hamlet is excluded from every species of action. On the contrary, there is only one kind of action from which he is wholly excluded, though a tendency to procrastination is not infrequently apparent. Just here occurs, perhaps, the greatest difficulty in comprehending Hamlet's character. He is wonderfully ready to do certain things; other things he will not do, and cannot bring himself to do—in fine, he acts, and does not act. Hence different critics have given exactly opposite opinions of him; one class say he possesses no power of action; another class declare that he possesses a vast energy of Will. How can this contradiction be reconciled? Only by distinguishing the different kinds of action of which men are capable. Undoubtedly Hamlet can do some things, but the great deed he cannot reach. We shall attempt a classification of the different forms of action, and point out what lies in the power of Hamlet.

1. Impulse has sway over Hamlet at times, as over every human being. This is the first and lowest form of action—unconscious, unreflecting—and belongs to the emotional nature of man, in which, as we have before seen, Hamlet is by no means wanting. Under its influence people act upon the spur of the moment, without thinking of consequences. Hence Hamlet's drawback—reflection—is not now present, and there is nothing to restrain him from action. But the instant there is delay sufficient to let his thoughts get a start, then farewell deed; impulse possesses him no longer. This is most strikingly shown when he sees the King at prayer; his first impulse is to slay him, but a reflection steps between, and the accomplishment of his plan is again deferred. Moreover, impulse may lead to immoral action, even to crime, since it acts regardless of content; it cannot inquire of itself, What is the nature of this deed which I am doing? but blindly carries itself into execution. Hamlet, therefore, as a sentient being, is capable of this kind of action; and here is where we must seek the source of all his positive acts. He slays Polonius under the influence of a momentary im-

pulse, and finally, even in the catastrophe, it requires the goading of a sudden passion to bring him to kill the King.

2. Hamlet possesses what may be called negative action—the power of frustrating the designs of his enemies. He exhibits an infinite acuteness in seeing through their plans; in fact, this seems an exercise of intellectual subtlety, in which he takes special delight; he also possesses the practical strength to render futile all the attempts of the King against his person. He is prepared for everything; his confidence in himself, in this direction, is unlimited; he knows that he can "delve one yard below their mines and blow them at the moon." But here his power of action ends; it has only this negative result—the defeat of the schemes against him. It is undeniable that this requires speedy resolution and quick execution, and, hence, may appear contradictory to what has been before stated; still, it is not inconsistent with the character of Hamlet. For this sort of action, though it is no doubt a deed, ends with negating some other deed, and not with any truly positive act. Moreover, it is a condition of the drama itself that Hamlet possess so much action, at least, as to maintain himself for a while; otherwise, he must fall a victim to the first conspiracy, and the play abruptly terminate. It is only the great substantial deed, which includes all other deeds in its end, that Hamlet cannot perform. This brings us to the next kind of action.

3. It is what we term Rational Action from

which Hamlet is excluded. Here the individual seizes a true and justifiable end, and carries it into execution. This end Intelligence knows as rational, for it alone can recognize the worth and validity of an end, and the Will brings it to realization. Thus we have the highest union of Intelligence and Will, which gives the most exalted form of action. This unity Hamlet cannot reach; he grasps the end, and comprehends it in its fullest significance; but there it remains, caught in its own toils. But what would true action demand? There may be doubts and difficulties in the way, but these are ultimately brushed aside; there may even be moral scruples which rear their front—and this is actually the case with Hamlet—but these, too, must finally be subordinated—the higher to the lower. Thus the rational man acts; having seized the highest end, he casts aside all doubts, reflections, also moral misgivings; for the true morality must be contained in his end, if it be really the highest.

Now, what is this end? Hamlet is invoked to vindicate both the Family and State, together with his own individual rights; it is his father, the King, who is slain; his mother, the Queen, who is debauched; himself who is deprived of a throne. The order of the world is thus turned upside down; he knows that he is born to set it right; that this is the highest duty, to which every inferior duty must yield; he repeatedly makes his resolution in the strongest terms, yet, after all, he allows his purpose to be first clouded and then defeated by his moral feelings and interminable reflections. The objective world of Spirit,—State, Family, Society, Right—which Hamlet, by station and culture, is called upon to maintain as the highest end which man can place before himself—since upon them depend his very existence as a rational being—is lost in the inextricable mazes of subjectivity.

But it is not intended to affirm that the true way of setting the time in order was to kill the King. Revenge may be wrong and conscience right; then Rational Action demands that conscience be followed. But Hamlet will neither renounce nor obey one or the other. His deed is caught in the antithesis of two principles of his character; he will not act from revenge on account of conscience, and he will not act from conscience on account of revenge.

By this distinction between the kinds of deeds it would seem that the striking contradiction in the character of Hamlet—his action and his non-action—can be reconciled. We are to consider what he can perform and what he cannot. Certain kinds of action lie in his power, but the one great act is beyond his ability. In like manner the difference of opinion among critics upon this subject would meet with a satisfactory solution.

Moreover, this distinction will assist us in dispelling a confusion which very often haunts the reader of this drama. When it is said that Hamlet's reflection destroys his action, is it meant that we should never think before we act? Many have taken such to be the poet's meaning, and have even accepted the doctrine that we must go back to impulse, and cut loose from our intellect; in other words, they declare that instinctive is higher and truer than conscious activity. They do this because they think that nothing remains but to take the lower form of action—impulse. But we have seen above that there is another more exalted kind—Rational Action—which demands thought, for its content can be seized only by thought, and, indeed, that content itself is thought in its objective form. Thus Intelligence passes over into reality—becomes a principle of action. Man now grasps a substantial end by mind, and then carries it into execution. That the poet does not regard impulse as the true basis of action is shown by the fact that he gives it to Hamlet, who, by this very means, is first made a criminal, and then brought to destruction. Hence the lesson is that we are to reflect before acting, but not to stop there.

Rational Action is the great object, and that always includes Intelligence. Having grasped a true end (of course through Intelligence), we should proceed to realize it without thinking on all possible relations and consequences; for subjective reflection looks at the deed, and summons up every imaginable possibility. As these are simply infinite the action is infinitely deferred. Consider, for a moment, what *may* take place, if you merely go to your daily occupation—a team may run over you, a house may fall on you, a stray bullet may hit you—and it will be evident what possibilities lie in the most ordinary act, what excuses a lively fancy can rouse up to shirk the performance of any duty. Hamlet clearly recognizes this rational end, yet will not translate it into reality, because of "thinking too precisely on the event," to use his own expression.

VI. *The death of Polonius.*—This has given great difficulty, and even offense; its object should be fully comprehended, for it not only illustrates the character of Hamlet, but also is one of the leading motives of the play. No other incident shows so deep a design, or is so appropriate for its purpose. Hamlet, acting blindly through impulse, slays the wrong one; the result is—guilt. This warning, therefore, speaks from the rash act: Let no rational being give up control to impulse which cannot see, cannot distinguish, the nature of a deed. Man must, therefore, reflect before proceeding to action. But, through reflection, Hamlet is unable to do the deed; thus he cannot perform the great injunction laid upon his soul. Such is his dilemma; if he acts, it is through impulse, and he falls into guilt; if he reflects, he cannot act—that is, he cannot do the Great Deed of his life, and so commits, at least, a sin of omission. What will be Hamlet's solution? He tells it himself in the latter part of the play: Throw yourself back into impulse, and abandon control through Intelligence. But what will be the result of such a doctrine? Death—the thinking being who cannot act from thought must perish.

Through the killing of Polonius, Hamlet has committed the very crime which he was seeking to punish; the son of a father murdered has himself murdered a father. Retribution will call up against him a son, at whose hands he will meet his fate. Hamlet recognizes this fact in full; he beholds in the person of Laertes not only his own cause, but his own deed coming back:

> For by the image of my cause, I see
> The portraiture of his; I'll court his favors.

So this incident offers the profoundest illustration of Hamlet's character, and, at the same time, furnishes the motive of his death. Polonius may have deserved to die for his offenses, but Hamlet had no right to slay him. Thus Hamlet does himself the primal deed of guilt.

VII. *The Primal Deed.*—A deed has been done, a deed of horror and guilt, the murder of a King; this deed is the Fate which works through the play till the end, and entangles in its serpentine coils all the leading characters. Yet we must regard these characters as free in action, though they manifest weakness and limitation, whereby they become tragic. That wicked deed we may picture to ourselves as an enormous boa constrictor, which winds through the drama, and laps and crushes passing human victims in its sudden sinuosities. Yet these victims, by the very fact of possessing life and reason, have always in themselves the danger of such a monster. This horrible deed is a new Laocoon group, much larger and more intricate than the old one, revealing afresh the double texture, in which Fate is the warp and Freedom the woof, of the garment of life.

The characters of the play range themselves in some relation to this deed. First is the present King, the guilty doer, to whom we may add the Queen, mother of Hamlet, a guilty participant; if not a murderess, at least faithless. The second set is the family of Polonius, father, son, daughter, but no mother; all of them together we may name the conscienceless set, the ever-ready tools of the King. The third and more remote group is that of the courtiers, of whom Rosencrantz and Guildenstern, the hypocritical friends of Hamlet, yet slavish instruments of the King, are swept into the fateful net. The fourth is Hamlet, a group of characters almost to himself, the great enemy of the murderous deed and its allotted avenger; still he, too, becomes entangled in it, and perishes along with the guilty doer. Thus the sweep of the deed involves the two opposites, Hamlet and the King, its doer and its avenger, in one common destiny.

This wicked deed has been thrown, as it were, into the Ethical World, which has to purify itself of the same, if this Ethical World continue to exist. The process of such purification is given variously by the poet in his different dramas; here all the chief characters are eliminated from society, or eliminate themselves; there remains as ruler an outsider, Fortinbras of Norway. Mark him well, he belongs most profoundly to the poet's economy; he hovers over the beginning, middle, and end of the play; we see him at the start as the man of action, who is seeking to make his own State whole, to be truly the healer of his country. Such a function he is to perform for Denmark also; he stands in striking contrast to the Danish Royal House with its internal plottings, crimes, and inactivities. He represents the purification which overarches all this scene of crime and death; he is the catharsis, which is indeed the true tragic outcome—not the negative, but the positive result of tragedy. In *Lear* and in *Macbeth* this process of purification is woven into the inner movement of the play; but here it rather envelops the whole action, from first to last, like the providential order above us.

Another characteristic of this guilty deed in the present drama must never be left out of mind. It is veiled in mystery; it is revealed to Hamlet and to us not by living evidence, but by dead, which yet speaks. No human eye, but the doer's, has seen the deed, still it is made known, must be made known. A voice comes and tells, a secret voice to us, still we know it to be the voice of the moral order of the world, which has been so deeply violated, it tells the truth and commands the expiation. Thus its word profoundly accords with our reason, though its shape transcend our understanding.

In some way, we must feel the necessity of this voice from beyond. The present King has simply murdered his brother, but is that all? No; in that act is involved another act—his death. He does the first, the second is brought about by the world over him, which he has defied. A world supplementing and completing the cycle of the human deed is our strongest faith and deepest want; in this drama that world has its personal representative, sent from beyond, and speaking "with most miraculous organ."

VIII. *The Ghost's Act.*—The First Act is poetically the best Act of the play, and gives the motives which unfold into the whole work. It is, moreover, the Ghost's Act, and contains the grand revelation as well as the grand mystery. In it the Supernatural and Natural Worlds are brought together, the one impinging upon and driving the other. The Ghost starts the play, as the Weird Sisters start *Macbeth*. We shall, accordingly, take a survey of this Act, scene by scene, and seek to penetrate its economy.

In the First Scene we find that the Ghost had already appeared twice to the soldiers on guard at the castle, when the matter is investigated by Horatio, a scholar, who did not believe in ghosts. He sees it also, sees it twice, and has to confess that his disbelief is confuted. He addresses it, asks it to speak, but it vanishes at any attempt to hold communication with itself. Horatio, though in particular non-plused, has in general a theory of the appearance: "This bodes some strange eruption to our State;" and the eruption is connected with young Fortinbras, not without significance. Horatio, being a learned man from the University, cites a classic instance of ghosts, "a little ere the mightiest Julius fell;" so this Ghost indicates "the like precurse of fierce events." To his mind it is a political omen, unfavorable also, which is to be told to young Hamlet, to whom it may possibly speak. The great fact of this scene is that the Ghost must be taken as objective; it is seen twice by two soldiers at least, before Horatio sees it, and he sees it twice in the presence of two soldiers, who also see it along with him. There is no explaining the Ghost away as a subjective phantasm.

In the Second Scene we pass, as it were, from the Supernatural into the Natural World, yet the first line, which tells of "our dear brother's death,", connects with the Ghost. The new King reveals his outer grief and his inner joy, and so he declares

> That we with wisest sorrow think on him
> Together with remembrance of ourselves.

Observe, too, how this King meets Fortinbras, not with arms as the elder Hamlet did, but with diplomacy; to which procedure we cannot object, though in it we must read the sign. Then he permits Laertes to return to Paris, but will not suffer Hamlet to return to Wittenberg, wherein again there is no little significance. Wittenberg and Paris are two tendencies of the soul, two tendencies of that age, and of this age. Here is one of Shakespeare's passing glimpses, still it is but a glimpse, so we must not delay too long upon it. But the main fact of this scene is the appearance of Hamlet. His very first words reflect the commingled light and darkness of the character:

> A little more than kin and less than kind.

We stop to think to ourselves, what does he mean?

We see a sense, yet the sense darts behind a cloud. We catch the sarcasm, and yet there is something which we do not catch. Many explanations are given, still there remains the inexplicable. Let us hear his second speech:

> *King.* How is it that the clouds still hang on you?
> *Hamlet.* Not so, my lord; I am too much in the sun.

Again we stop and wonder; meaning is here, but there is also mystery; indeed that must be Hamlet, a mingling of meaning and mystery. He quite defines himself in his next response.

> Seems, madman! nay, it is; I know not "seems."

There is an outer side which "a man might play," and later on Hamlet will play it, nay, just now he is playing it, and cannot help himself; still he can also truly say:

> But I have that within which passeth show.

And he has it even here, it is his mystery. Hamlet finds himself in a world from which he would gladly escape by suicide—a world made by the wicked deed, whose environment is crushing him, though he is not yet fully conscious of it; but it oppresses him, and hence comes his melancholy. In his soliloquy he dwells upon two things; first, the hasty marriage of his mother; second, her marriage with such a man as Claudius, who, we see, is the real center of his suspicion, being so emphatically contrasted with his father.

Next, we notice that Hamlet is internally ready

to see the Ghost, wherein the poet's art may well be thought upon:

> *Hamlet.* My father! methinks I see my father.
> *Horatio.* O where, my lord?
> *Hamlet.* In my mind's eye, Horatio.
> *Horatio.* I saw him once; he was a goodly King.
> *Hamlet.* He was a man, take him for all in all
> I shall not look upon his like again.
> *Horatio.* My lord, I think I saw him yesternight.
> *Hamlet.* Saw! who?
> *Horatio.* My lord, the King your father.
> *Hamlet.* The King my father!

Whereupon the whole story of the apparition is told. Hamlet may well be surprised that his inner vision so suddenly changes to an outer reality. "I see my father in my mind's eye;" the image within and the specter without are directly connected. In the First Scene we noted how careful the poet was to make the Ghost objective; in the present scene he is careful to make it subjective also; it exists both in the man and in the world. Further on, Hamlet gives his interpretation of the appearance: "all is not well;" moreover he fears "some foul play," wherein his suspicion crops out; then he declares his emphatic faith that

> Fouls deeds will rise,
> Though all the earth overwhelm them to men's eyes.

This spirit means to him some foul deed, and such it is; when it gets a voice, it will tell that deed. It cannot speak to Horatio, he has not the inner preparation; Hamlet alone is the man to hear it. The mutual attitude of the King and Hamlet is now settled, and will continue to unfold into many forms through the play; each is concealing what the other is trying to find out, and each strongly suspects the other in that concealment.

The Third Scene introduces another phase of this decaying life in Denmark, which supplements what we have just beheld in the highest functionaries of the State, the King and the Queen. It is the family of Polonius, father, son, daughter—pliant instruments of the monarch, who are to be included in the sweep of the grand revenge. Here they deny truth and morality to Hamlet, because they have none themselves, in the high sense of conscience. But the main fact of the scene for us at present is, that Hamlet's love is also destroyed in this Danish atmosphere. He has wooed the daughter Ophelia, but father and son brand his love as lust, and bid her break the bond, which she does. She apparently believes them, but such a belief is crushing to her; when a woman comes to think that love is lust, her life is already unbalanced, and if she reach the unrestraint of lunacy, she will sing the songs of Ophelia. In this scene her father and brother laid in her the tragic germ which time will develop. But Hamlet is now alone, indeed; his own mother is corrupted and lost to him; even the more tender relation is stained, broken and cast away. It is no wonder that to him Denmark is a prison and one of the worst, and he may well say: "Man delights not me; no, nor woman neither;" for he has as tough experience with women as with men.

In the Fourth Scene, while the company is waiting for the Ghost, the noise of revel comes from the King's palace, and stirs Hamlet to a curious tissue of reflections, which shows another trait in his character, the reflective:

> So oft it chances in particular men,
> That for some vicious mole of nature in them,
> As, in their birth—wherein they are not guilty,
> Since nature cannot choose his origin—
> By the overgrowth of some complexion,
> Oft breaking down the pales and forts of reason, etc.

Here we see Hamlet caught in an infinite series of reflections, from which he is unable to extricate himself. Nor can he rescue his sentence and bring it to an end, though he repeatedly resolves to do so; the very grammar of it becomes a picture of Hamlet's mind. Moreover he is really portraying himself; "that vicious mole" is his own, not only described but shown in the structure of the passage, which also has a "mole" in it. Critics complain of its style, but Shakespeare is not thinking of style, but character. The last sentence turns to haze:

> The dram of eale
> Doth all the noble substance of a dout
> To his own scandal.

What does this mean? Commentators cry corruption, and try to mend the passage; but it has meaning in its very uncertainty. Hamlet seems unable to close his sentence, caught in that treadmill of eternally self-begetting reflection; language itself grows dim and indefinite, begins to be shadowy, ghostly, when lo! the Ghost in person appears and forces the sentence to a sudden end. Here the intellectual tendency of Hamlet is indicated; his thought gets lost in its own intricacies, and his speech wanders off into an unreal, dubious realm, whither we cannot follow. The transition from Hamlet's mind to that specter is, we think, cunningly prepared; the reflective man lapses into the Ghost-seer. But the Ghost will not speak to him in the presence of others, though it shows itself to them all; manifestly Hamlet alone is ready for its utterance. Only the inner and outer specter can communicate. The connection between his imagination and the Ghost is made by Hamlet himself:

> If his occulted guilt
> Do not itself unkennel in one speech,
> It is a damned Ghost that we have seen,
> And my imaginations are as foul
> As Vulcan's stithy.

In the Fifth Scene it speaks and tells the story of the father's murder and the mother's infidelity. It is an unhappy Ghost, evidently in process of discipline, being "doomed for a certain term to walk the night," for the good spirit returns not as a specter; also being "confined to fast in fires" during the day, on account of "the foul crimes done in my days of nature." Hamlet, in spite of admiration of his father, thinks "'tis heavy with him" in that future state, and the reader must think so too.

For listen to its injunction—revenge. Such is the essence of the Ghost—revenge. A command is laid upon the son which makes him a murderer, the murderer of his uncle, just as the latter was guilty of a brother's murder. It seeks to make the son what the uncle is. Thrice it utters the bodeful command; further on we shall hear it speak a second time that word—revenge. No wonder the Ghost is yet to burn for its sins; it is really in its own Hell-fire, those "sulphurous and tormenting flames" kindled by itself in that one word—revenge. Moreover it flings the son living into the same flames, though the son doubts, hesitates, resists to the last.

It is this command of revenge which whelms Hamlet into his most bitter conflict, that with his conscience. The guilty King, Claudius, ought to be punished, yet there is no institution to which he is accountable, and his punishment falls to the lot of some person. This person is the next of kin, according to ancient Teutonic usage; Hamlet is thus the appointed avenger. But he is the moral man, to him the slaying of his uncle is murder. He is the child of the Reformation with its moral conscience; yet his political conscience, or at least that of his age, still cries out for revenge. He is placed in an epoch of transition; the old and the new order clash in him, and make him tragic. The political problem of Hamlet is solved by making the Supreme Ruler of the State responsible for his action—a solution which time has wrought out in government, especially in Anglo-Saxon countries. But in the present drama, the duty of revenge has still an institutional sanction, as it were, and thus collides with another duty, that of not revenging.

The origin of the Ghost is not given, it remains the mystery to Hamlet and to us. Hamlet is the Ghost-seer, and specially the Ghost-hearer; yet we may not affirm that the Ghost has no reality whatever. Hamlet is in a condition to see it and to hear it, as Homer's heroes must be in a condition to see and to hear the Gods, before the Gods can show themselves. Hamlet does not make the fact announced, he does not make even the form; he can see and hear it, this is just his nature. The inner Hamlet and the outer Ghost meet and converse.

We must think, too, that this ghostly form is the appropriate one for the communication, being the form for a voice of the spirit disembodied: "I am thy father's spirit." When the dead man speaks, it cannot be his body, but the bodiless form which is called his ghost. Though the form be unreal, it states the fact, it is the voice of the deed, it is the murdered man himself returning to tell his story, not as a material but a spiritual entity. The very air, imprinted with the Deed, takes his shape and speaks his voice. The world-order being violated cries out, must cry out in some way, that it may be purged of that wicked act.

Such is the faith of men, a faith often alluded to by Shakespeare. The spiritual universe has some method of voicing the unseen crime, of pointing out "the secretest man of blood." This faith is expressed in a mythical form in the Ghost, now voicing the ethical order, which cannot exist with the guilty deed lurking in its bosom. Such a faith we all have in some form, perhaps not in the ghostly. But even this belief in ghosts has its truth; it is man's assertion of the soul's persistance after death, it is the people's conception of immortality, the race's faith that the person endures. In this respect, too, the Ghost is but an image of Hamlet's inner state and belief:

> I do not set my life at a pin's fee,
> And for my soul, what can it do to that,
> Being a thing immortal as itself?

But after all is told, there remains an unknown factor of mystery in the Ghost? Is there actually such a form? Does the spirit return and speak? So the Mythus holds, from Homer down; but the Mythus is not yet science in this case. Our age demands that the appearance be subjected to the laws of the Understanding, and such subjection of the Ghost has not yet taken place. Science may yet demonstrate the law of such appearances, it may yet be able to call them forth, but then the Ghost will be no Ghost. It still belongs to the Supernatural World, along with the Weird Sisters, from whom, however, it is quite distinct. But like the Weird Sister, the poet makes it, in the first place, objective, visible to others besides Hamlet; truly it exists in the world. Secondly, it is subjective also, it is in Hamlet, and he alone hears its voice. Thirdly, this voice takes the form of the Ghost for utterance, being the voice of the murdered man telling the unwitnessed deed of guilt. Fourthly, this form of the Ghost was furnished to the poet by the faith of his race, which declares even under this mythical garb, its belief in immortality, and its belief in an ethical order of the world which brings to light and punishes the hidden crime. So Hamlet, too, believes:

> For murder, though it have no tongue, will speak
> With most miraculous organ.

These two beliefs, implied by the Ghost, are, accordingly, the expressed beliefs of Hamlet. He has already spoken of the soul as immortal, and he further declares, in substance, that murder will out. We see how careful the poet has been to show the correspondences between the internal Hamlet and the external Ghost; the one says what the other says, though in a different manner. We must follow Shakespeare in preserving the complete validity of both sides; this is his art, his truth. We must not permit the Ghost to vanish into a mere internal condition of Hamlet, nor, on the other hand, must we consider it as a purely external phantasm, wholly outside of him, gotten up for spectacular effect, and catering to the superstition of the age of the poet.

IX. *Structural Lines of Hamlet's Character.*— The character of Hamlet takes a wide range and embraces the most contradictory traits, those of rationality and irrationality, as well as those of activity and inactivity, all of which have been previously discussed. To obtain a complete survey of this character is almost like going through a whole science of mind; the drama is a psychology. We discern from the very first an outward and an inward Hamlet; in fact he makes such a distinction himself quite at the start, when he says that he knows not "seems," but has "that within which passeth show." We must consider this external side, though with him it be the less important.

1. The outward Hamlet is as he appears in the world, his address, his courtly manners; he is "the glass of fashion and the mould of form," he has all the externals of his princely estate, which are so extolled by Ophelia, and which we notice in his reception of the players and elsewhere. Then comes his ready wit and passing jest, capable of turning to bitter satire; he has sportfulness, even waggishness, he delights in playing hide-and-go-seek with others, and even with himself. He sports with both word and thought, hence his verbal and mental puns, which the reader cannot always catch; he loves to mystify his fellow-speakers, even to play with mystery itself. Such is the surface of his conduct, on which, as he floats along, he is perpetually diving out of sight and coming up again. We see sportive ripples, but they often break into hot tears; then we behold the inner Hamlet with intense soul-struggles hidden under an outward demeanor, which, after all, casts a shadow of what is going on inside. This play, this disguise which he seems so fond of, we find to be a relief from the internal tragedy of his life, as well as a concealment. Herein he recalls that American President who found in humorous anecdote and story a refuge from the civil war of his own heart, as well as from the civil war of his country.

2. Of this inner Hamlet we observe four phases in deepening order; we may call them the four Hamlets.

1st. There is the instinctive, impulsive Hamlet, a man of presentiment, of oppressive melancholy, of boding instinct, who feels the guilty deed before it is told him, a dweller in the dark unconscious realm of emotion and passion; he is the man who acts through impulse, and thereby slays Polonius, and at last the King. This is quite opposite to the reflective side of his nature.

2nd. Hamlet as Ghost-seer, or rather as Ghost-hearer, in whom the unconscious presentiment rises to an image, with a voice which utters the Deed, and lays upon him the hard command of revenge. An imaginative man he is now, who can see his father both "in his mind's eye," and as Ghost.

3rd. The moral Hamlet, the man with an inner law, conscience, which commands against the command of the Ghost, forbids revenge, forbids both murder and suicide. Yet the duty to avenge his father's blood remains too; fiercely the conflict rages within, but conscience overawes him, and he has to confess:

> Thus conscience doth make cowards of us all.

4th. The intellectual Hamlet, the man in whom thought undermines action, who has in his soul that deepest of all chasms—Intellect divorcing itself from Will. As a reflective man he must know himself, and so he describes this tendency in himself:

> And thus the native hue of resolution
> Is sicklied o'er with the pale cast of thought,
> And enterprises of great pith and moment
> With this regard their currents turn away,
> And lose the name of action.

Thus the conscience-conflict and the thought-conflict are placed beside each other in the soliloquy on suicide, as they are also in the soliloquy on Fortinbras, where the one is hinted as a "craven scruple," and the other spoken of as "large discourse looking before and after," and as "godlike reason," which is not given "to fust in us unused," that is, without being realized in action.

So we behold the four Hamlets, the instinctive, imaginative, moral, intellectual—yet one Hamlet. He conflicts with himself, since he is so many Hamlets, and cannot subordinate them all. He talks with himself in apparent soliloquy, yet it is one Hamlet talking with another Hamlet. His drama is essentially an inner or soul-drama, of which the main characters are himself.

X. *Lines of Hamlet Criticism.*—The lines of Hamlet criticism follow quite on the lines which we have just seen to be those of Hamlet's character. Some phase of it makes a strong impression upon the critic, who then proceeds to look at the whole man from the one trait. The Hamlet literature, hardly more than a century old, is getting to have a history like that of a national literature. It has its fashions, its excesses; all sorts of topics are drawn into it from every side. Some centuries hence, the history of the opinions on *Hamlet*, with all their fluctuations, will make a most curious chapter in the book of the Human Intellect. Even at present, it is a great psychological discipline to study how this play has affected different minds and different periods. Mr. Furness has given much material for such a study in that magnificent monument to the poet and to himself, the Variorum *Hamlet*, to which we owe many obligations.

The views of Hamlet's character have moved in three main lines. The first view is that of Goethe, who felt strongly Hamlet's paralysis of will, and accounts for it by saying that "Shakespeare sought to depict a great deed laid upon a soul unequal to the performance of it. * * * Here is an oak tree planted in a costly vase, which should have received into its bosom only lovely flowers; the roots spread out, the vase is shivered to pieces. * * * A beautiful, pure, noble, moral nature, without the strength of nerve which makes the hero, sinks beneath a burden which it can neither bear nor throw off." That is, Goethe sees the moral conflict, and seems to think that this is the sole essential matter. But it is not all, and his opinion, in consequence, must be supplemented by that of Schlegel, who strongly marks the thought-conflict in Hamlet, calling the play "a Tragedy of Thought." Schlegel further declares: "The Whole is intended to show that a consideration, which would exhaust all the relations and possible consequences of a deed to the very limits of human foresight, cripples the power of acting." This is the second line of opinion, which was also maintained, substantially, by Coleridge, quite as soon as it was by Schlegel.

Both these opinions seek to account for Hamlet's want of action. Goethe sees it as the result of the moral conflict (Revenge *vs.* Conscience;) but

Schlegel sees it as the result of the psychological conflict (Will *vs.* Thought.) Both opinions are right, if they are not made exclusive; both conflicts, as we have seen, are in Hamlet. But not only inactivity he shows; he has also activity; hence there arises a third line of opinion which lays stress upon Hamlet's power of will.

This trait has, perhaps, been most strongly set forth by Ulrici, who claims to have been the first to vindicate Hamlet's ability to act, though before him Herder had pointedly said that Hamlet was not wanting in will. This view is also correct, if it be not made exclusive; Hamlet is certainly capable of action, especially the impulsive Hamlet, and the counterplotting Hamlet. Thus all three views are right, and indicate valid traits; but all three may become wrong by making too great claims.

On these three lines, mainly, Hamlet criticism has run, with indefinite repetition; it is destined, probably, to move in these grooves, to a greater or less extent. Brilliant attempts, like that of Werder, have been made to throw it into other directions, but with doubtful success; they are but little eddies in the great stream. A synthesis of all the fundamental traits which analysis has found in the character of Hamlet, is a task which criticism has yet to perform.

XI. *Historic Features in the Drama.*—Hamlet we may conceive of as a man about thirty years of age, who has spent some time at the University of Wittenberg. It is to be observed that this is a German University and the home of the Reformation—hints which the poet has not given without a far-reaching purpose. For it is indicated that the culture of Hamlet is German, in contrast to the French culture of Laertes, who goes to Paris, which is not known as the home of any reformation, particularly not of a moral one. Also, the German is now and always has been, speculative rather than practical, and, for this reason, he is to-day the teacher of the world in thought and philosophy. In Germany, too, began that rebellion against the external forms of the Church, in favor of subjective freedom, which rebellion was nourished in this very Wittenberg. In contrast to Paris it laid stress upon the internal and spiritual nature of man rather than upon the outward show and conventionalities of life. So, by a happy stroke, the poet has identified Hamlet with the great historical movement of modern times—a movement which sought to free the human mind from an excessive servitude to external forms, and to bring it to a profounder self-consciousness. Hamlet is true to his education in the highest degree; he represents an historic epoch, whose inner struggles he has taken into his own bosom.

Thus both the Teutonic and Romanic worlds are woven into the play, yet everywhere with the tinge of the Renascence. The names of the characters form a curious study. There are the Italian or Italianized names—Horatio, Bernardo, Francisco, Reynaldo, the last three being Italianized from the old Teutonic; one sometimes wonders at these Italian soldiers keeping guard in Denmark.

Then come the Latin and Latinized names—Claudius, Cornelius, Marcellus are the veriest old Romans, while Polonius seems a Latinized modern of the Renascence. But his children have Greek names—Laertes and Ophelia—as if the Hellenizing influence must be represented too. Then the genuine Teutonic names—Rosencrantz, Guildenstern, Gertrude, with one in French or Norman-French, Fortinbras. Hamlet's name, is, doubtless, Teutonic, but like the man himself, somewhat veiled in mystery. These Greek, Latin and Italian names must have been added by the poet (or, possibly, in part by some dramatic predecessor,) as the legend employs Teutonic names.

We are not to seek any etymological allegory under the cover of these names; we are not to hunt in their meanings an interpretation of the play. The signification of the word Ophelia or Gertrude will not reveal the character of the women so called. But there is a meaning in this commingling of the names belonging to Northern and Southern Europe; we may see in it faintly the great revival and intellectual intercourse of nations after the Middle Ages; we may catch in it a tinge of the Italian Renascence going back to Greece and Rome for its humane studies and imparting them to the rest of Europe, especially to the Teutonic portion; we may feel in it, perchance, a slight throb of the German Reformation, reaching through these humane studies of the South after the inner light, that of the soul and conscience. The mere names, however, cannot bring us very far; they are but the faintest, fleetest shadows, which are to be filled with the flesh and blood and breath of life from another source.

Nor are we to consider this drama as an historical allegory, putting under a veiled form events and persons of Elizabethan history. Doubtless Shakespeare was profoundly influenced by the great actions and important individuals of his time; he must have often thought of both in writing his plays. Still we cannot be satisfied to think, in spite of the striking similarities, that Gertrude is Mary Queen of Scots, that the murdered King is her former husband Lord Darnley, that the present King, Claudius, is the murderer Bothwell, whose "o'er hasty marriage" with Queen Mary occurred three months after the death of Darnley, that Hamlet is her son King James. Still less successful seems the attempt to consider Hamlet as Sir Philip Sidney, and from this standpoint to re-construct the play out of the members of Queen Elizabeth's court. (See Furness, Variorum *Hamlet*, Vol II. p 236-40). Shakespeare's dramas are not allegories; they exist in their own right, and do not put one particular person or thing for another. They have meaning, the profoundest, but this meaning lies in them, not outside of them in something else. Shakespeare's son was called Hamnet, who died under twelve years of age, possibly during some phase of the composition of this drama; at any rate the father must often have thought of his dead boy in writing or speaking the name of Hamlet. But who can trace the influence of this personal experience in the play?

XII. *History of the Hamlet Legend.*—Saxo Grammaticus, who, toward the end of the twelfth century, wrote a Danish History, is the primitive source of the legend of Hamlet, as far as it has yet been traced. But it probably obtained European currency through Belleforest's collection of "Tragic Stories," in a volume printed in French at Paris in 1570, from which, doubtless, it passed to England. Finally an English book called the "Hystorie of Hamblet," bearing the date of 1608, tells the story of the Danish Prince, and emphatically suggests the work of Shakespeare. These are the three books in which the mythical form of the legend had been preserved for more than four centuries.

In the shape in which these three books give it, we observe it to be a grim Teutonic legend springing out of a distant heathen age, which rests upon the rudest form of justice, namely, personal revenge. The King (or Governor,) is murdered by his brother, who has corrupted his wife, and then usurps his throne. There is a son of the murdered King, who counterfeits madness, yet is suspected and watched by courtiers set upon his track, till he slays one, as Hamlet does Polonius. Then he is sent to England, whence he returns, wreaks his revenge upon his uncle, and is himself made King. The old legend, however, does not stop here, but repeats the deeds of blood and infidelity; for Hamlet, after his return and coronation, is assailed by another uncle, Wiglerus, and being betrayed by his wife Hermetrude, is slain; after his death she marries his uncle and murderer, Wiglerus. Thus the legend ends quite as it began, with the murder of kindred and the faithlessness of the wife; revenge follows murder and murder follows revenge, and there is no solution of the difficulty.

Now upon this ancient Teutonic revenge the poet is going to engraft a new spirit, which hesitates to do the vengeful deed. Hamlet is deeply dissatisfied with that world of murder and revenge into which he has been born, hence his melancholy, his reaction against it. There is no Ghost in the old legend with its message from beyond; there needs no Ghost to command vengeance, it is already active. Nor is Hamlet turned back by accident ere he reaches England; just as little does he suffer the penalty for slaying the old courtier behind the arras. But a new world has arisen; upon the old Teuton with his hot revenge and quick action are superposed conscience and thought—a Christian, we might say, a Prostestant questioning and introspection. The inner law of duty and the outer law of retaliation collide in him, and he cannot master their collision; he becomes tragic, and falls between "the fell and incensed points of mighty opposites;" for we must observe that, if he refuses to follow revenge, just as much does he refuse to follow conscience.

The man who simulates insanity with cunning purpose is a veritable possession of the race; he is found East and West, in Semitic scripture, and in

Celtic legend; especially he has become a world-character through Roman Brutus, with whom old Saxo Grammaticus already compares Hamlet. Shakespeare thus seized a type which had become fixed in the imaginations of men, and was as old as Literature. But to this ancient type, which is general, he gives new life, which endows it with a fresh and vivid individuality. If Hamlet, however, be actually insane, the poet has been anticipated by legend in this field also, especially in the case of Greek Orestes.

The first great Teutonic poem is *Hamlet*, revealing distinctively the Northern spirit, as well as moving in a Northern environment. The second great Teutonic poem is Goethe's *Faust*, which has a deep kinship with *Hamlet*. Each touches a problem of thought; in the case of the Danish Prince thought has a tendency to blast action, while the companion of Mephisto reveals the destructive side of thought, which in its negative, skeptical outcome begets the Devil. Hamlet's fiend is passive rather, a paralysis; Faust's fiend is decidedly active, a propulsion. Both poems reach down to a heathen foundation, upon which a new order is built; both go back to a Teutonic aforetime, which is impinging upon an era of change; both belong essentially to the Reformation, and both, to attain their highest development, rise out of a legendary into a dramatic form. The Hamlet legend is next to nothing, till, by the touch of the poet, it becomes the Hamlet drama.

XIII. *History of the Hamlet Drama.*—The

Hamlet legend, accordingly, cannot be said to have impressed itself deeply upon the Teutonic consciousness, till it took the shape of the Hamlet drama. This transition indicates not merely a great change of form, but a greater change of meaning; the old legend with its passion and revenge, being filled with conscience and thought, becomes the new drama. The same change essentially takes place in England at the same time, and to a degree in Northern Europe; conscience and thought, with their strange prohibitions and deep probings, at first palsy the hand and "puzzle the will" of the people in whose soul they begin to work. Such a soul in its struggling from one side to the other, not the legend, but the drama will present in Hamlet, though the legend often shows the dramatic kernel sprouting within.

The first allusion in English Literature to a Hamlet drama is found in an Epistle by Thomas Nash prefixed to Greene's *Menaphon*, a book bearing the date of 1589, when Shakespeare was twenty-five years old, and when he had been in London about four years. Was this earliest Hamlet drama the production of Shakespeare? The best judges divide upon the question, but it seems probable that he may then have first put his hand to *Hamlet*. Other allusions have been discovered, extending to the year 1603, which is the date of the First Quarto, with Shakespeare's name upon its title page. Next year (1604) the Second Quarto appeared, with numerous additions, "enlarged to almost as much again as it was, according to the true and perfect copy," as the statement runs upon its title page.

This is not the place to discuss the many conjectures which have been spun around these two Quartos. Both have the same vignette; the same initials of the name of the publisher appear in both. But the Second Quarto claims to be printed after "the true and perfect copy," a claim which the First Quarto does not make, and which seems to account for the difference in size and character between the two. A careful study and comparison of each with the other is one of the best introductions into the workshop of the poet. The First Quarto is less mature, yet more dramatic externally; it has the action, but not the deepened characterization, especially in the part of Hamlet. The conscience-conflict of the Danish Prince it recognizes, though not so fully as the Second Quarto; but the thought-conflict it leaves out almost wholly. It knows the line:

> Thus conscience doth make cowards of us all.

But it has not the lines which follow:

> And thus the native hue of resolution
> Is sicklied o'er with the pale cast of thought.

Other omissions of the same kind can be traced in it throughout. The transition from the First to the Second Quarto is from a dramatic to an epical fullness, which fits the work better for reading than for acting. The poet, by giving into the hands of the publisher a "true and perfect copy" seems to have recognized another public than that of the play-house, namely, the vast army of readers who are still the chief public of this drama. And Shakespeare's reading public appears to have responded nobly, as in the next few years no less than three new editions were issued. A still different text is that of the Folio of 1623, inasmuch as it bears a relation both to the First and Second Quartos.

If then the Hamlet drama of 1589 belonged wholly or in part to Shakespeare, he was at least fifteen years in bringing the work to its present perfection. One thinks that the poet must have been always filling in and transforming his plays; they grew, they developed gradually; doubtless they were written largely from the green-room, with the poet's eye both upon his theme and his audience. His best plays, in fact, were written by the English people quite as much as by himself. His audience demanded not so much a new subject as an old subject treated in a new way; an old play wrought over and furnished with fresh and deeper motives seems to have been preferred. In like manner the Greek dramatists took the old legend and gave it a new turn; so we have still remaining to us the three plays of Electra and Orestes by the three Greek tragic poets.

Shakespeare, then, did not write Hamlet at one gush; rather, he wrote his life into it, from manhood to middle-age. So the Danish Prince may well seem both young and old; he is both. The composition of *Hamlet* has its parallel in the composition of *Faust*, which extends over quite sixty years of Goethe's life. Like *Faust*, too, it bursts the limits of the old theater, and rises to a new dramatic art; the action has to show a paralysis of action, which is not so much for the stage as for our private study. The First Quarto with its 2143 lines is the acting play, which, in the Second Quarto with its 3719 lines, is expanded beyond the bounds of the scenic drama into a great epical drama.

XIV. *Structure of the Hamlet Drama.*—The ethical element in which the drama moves is the Family, of which there has been a double violation—against both father and mother. Thus the son rises up for revenge, which, however, demands the murder of the uncle—a deed which the son refuses to perform, through moral scruples and intellectual hesitation. But, acting through impulse, he slays a father, and thereby becomes guilty of the very crime against the Family which he is seeking to punish. Thus he calls up against himself another son, who applies to him the logic of his own deed. Also, the State is always standing in the background as a minor factor of the collision. Hamlet's father was King, and Hamlet believed himself to have been wrongfully deprived of the throne. Some maintain that Claudius was not a usurper, as Denmark was an elective monarchy; such could hardly have been Hamlet's view of the succession, and probably it was not the poet's. The political violation is repeatedly dwelt upon, though it is by no means so strongly emphasized as the domestic violation. Thus Family and State are both present; but these ethical elements become almost latent in the overwhelming prominence given to the psychological elements.

Let us now grasp fully the organization of the play. There are two main movements, of which the first portrays the conflict between Hamlet and the King; each is seeking to find out the plans of his opponent, and, when they are found out, to destroy him. At the same time, each has an internal conflict with himself—Hamlet with his will and conscience; the King with his conscience. Both are foiled doubly. In the external conflict neither gets rid of the other—Hamlet does not slay the King, nor does the King succeed in sending Hamlet to England; in the internal conflict neither can heal the breach of own soul—Hamlet will not act, the King will not repent. Here then is the turning-point of the tragedy, the grand refusal of both Hamlet and the King to transform their lives, and to put them into harmony with the ethical order of the world. The First Movement, in general, shows guilt—the King has murdered the old Hamlet, and the young Hamlet murders Polonius, while others are getting involved in the guilty deed.

The Second Movement portrays the final retribution, along with the great changes in the minds and in the circumstances of the various persons. Ophelia goes mad; Hamlet, not acting, comes to believe in fate, and surrenders himself to the guidance of external accident; the King, not repenting, is hardened by transgression, and plunges readily into a new crime. Still, the external conflict between Hamlet and the King continues after Hamlet's return from his short voyage; the King has now, as his chief instrument, Laertes, who, undertaking to avenge the murder of a father, suffers himself to be perverted into the instrument of the murderer of a father. All these perish by the logic of their deeds, together with the Queen, who, not repenting but continuing to share in her husband's perverse life, shares in his death.

Thus we behold the guilty deed in two mighty sweeps, enveloping, then destroying a whole court, a little world. The culmination is the refusal to repent, to change the wicked conduct of life; the guilty ones are driven to strong self-reproach, even to remorse, but they relapse into the old way when this remorse (really their good angel) passes on. Then they rapidly descend to their tragic fate, for they have refused the saving offer; they cannot be mediated. Conscience makes a last appeal, when its voice seems to grow silent. The question of conscience is thus the culminating point of the action.

The present division into Acts is inept, and does not proceed from Shakespeare, but from a later hand. The Third Act should end with Scene Fourth, Act Fourth, where the soliloquy of Hamlet upon Fortinbras is given. Thus the First Movement would occupy three Acts, and the Second Movement two Acts. In this structural point the tragedy would then quite correspond with *Lear* and *Macbeth*, its mighty brothers. All three are alike in another point of construction: the First Movement is full, rapid, intense, while the Second Movement is less completely developed, and shows a falling-off in spirit and style somewhat. The poet employs his power in unfolding his characters out of their germinal principle; when they are unfolded he seems to have less interest in carrying them out to the conclusion, which already lies in their conduct. Hence the sudden leaps and omissions in the last two Acts of all these plays, as compared with the first three. Indeed, we may note the same fact in some of Shakespeare's historical dramas.

Besides these Movements, there are two Threads running through the whole play; these we shall call the Hamlet-Thread and the King's Thread, as Hamlet and the King are the central forces, around which the other characters group themselves, and which make the collision. A short abstract of each Thread in each Movement will be given in order to reveal the joints of the dramatic organism.

The First Thread of the First Movement is that of Hamlet, and it has two phases, the external and the internal. On the one hand, it exhibits the influences which come upon him from without, one set of which drives him to do the deed, the other set of which conflicts with him in his purpose; on the other hand, it exhibits the counteraction of these influences through his moral and intellectual hesitation. Thus the blood is taken out of all external forces, and the deed becomes, as it were, a ghost; transmuted through his peculiar mental medium, the objective world turns to an unreality. Still, he believes that intelligence can control human action, and hopes for this result in his own case. His sole instrument is his friend, Horatio; but there must also be grouped around him those influences which work upon him externally—as the Ghost, together with the soldiers who see it, the players, Fortinbras and the Captain, the gravediggers. These are the groups of the Hamlet Thread.

The Second Thread of the First Movement is that of the King surrounded by his instruments. He, too, has a double conflict—an external one with Hamlet, and an internal one with himself. His first object is to discover Hamlet's secret, and then to get rid of him when found to be dangerous. His instruments may be classed in three groups. The first is for the general purpose of State, they have little or nothing to do with Hamlet, as Voltimand and Cornelius; the second is composed of courtiers—the servile tools of the monarch—as Rosencrantz and Guildenstern, to whom Osrick may be added; the third is the family of Polonius —father, son, and daughter—most intimately bound up in the destiny of the House of Denmark—all of whom are used as instruments by the King against Hamlet, and are ground to death in the conflict. The King, therefore, sets influences to work, while Hamlet lets influences come upon him; Hamlet possesses action to the extent of nullifying these influences, but he cannot do the great positive deed.

The First Thread of the Second Movement continues the development of Hamlet. He had been sent off to England to be murdered, when, by accident, he is once more brought back to Denmark. The conflict with the King is opened anew, but under wholly different circumstances. Hamlet no longer has faith in intelligence as the controlling power in the world; it is chance; it is destiny. Thus he throws himself into the arms of fate; previously he believed in action, though not acting; now he does not even believe in action. The man who would not do the deed has come to deny the very possibility of the deed as the product of rational foresight. This psychological change is the most important feature of Hamlet's characterization, and constitutes the essential difference between the First and Second Movements. But, when he thinks for a moment of proceeding to action, there stands Laertes opposed to him—the real embodiment of his own destiny—for Laertes must slay him if he slay the King; both have the same ground of revenge. At this appearance his arms falls palsied by his side, and he quietly lets himself be caught in a plot which he knew of, or strongly suspected.

The Second Thread of the Second Movement is that of the King, whose chief instrument against Hamlet is now Laertes. The death of the parent, Polonius, furnishes a strong motive to the son, which is further intensified by the condition of his sister, Ophelia, whose madness and death are here given. But Laertes ruins his cause by allowing himself to be made an instrument of the diabolical plans of the King—that King who is himself the murderer of a father, and who is now seeking to destroy the son. Thus Laertes is whirled into the tragic circle of retribution, and becomes the author of his own fate. He aids the destroyer of the parent to destroy the avenger of the parent, which avenger is, logically himself. He thus assails his own principle, and, as it were, passes the sentence of death upon himself.

The method of the following developement will be a little different from the usual manner. The two Threads—that of Hamlet and that of the King will be carried separately through the two Movements; thus a survey of the total development of each side is given without interruption. But the reader has the means of following the action by Movements instead of Threads, if he so chooses, as all these divisions of the play are carefully designated at the proper places.

CHAPTER SECOND.

The Hamlet Thread.

Our task is now to unfold the part of Hamlet through the whole play, and note its intricacies of thought and structure, as they wind through the action. Two sets of circumstances are brought to bear upon Hamlet, who reacts against both, and thus shows two phases of reaction against his environment.

The first set of circumstances is what we may call the Incalculable, they are what happens without purpose or foreknowledge—the realm of accident. In the First Movement four such occurences come upon Hamlet: the conduct of his mother, the Ghost, the actors, and Fortinbras. These spring from that great reservoir of Chance, drops from which fall every day upon the individual, or peradventure a stream, which he has to swallow, else it will swallow him. Still, in this Chance, there is a plan, we note; these four occurrences are directed upon Hamlet to drive him forward to the deed, and they increase in power till the culmination. Hamlet himself sees and states the fact of them:

> How all occasions do inform against me
> And spur my dull revenge!

These so-called occasions, then, are the spur to action; but against them he reacts inwardly, and the deed collapses in his internal struggles. He has enough conscience to paralyze revenge, and enough revenge to paralyze conscience.

The second set of influences which come upon Hamlet, and interweave with the first set, spring from the Court—the King and his instruments, who are trying to discover the secret of Hamlet, and find the task as difficult as the reader of the play does. They are put to work upon Hamlet, but he knows what they are about, he meets plot with plot, he not only thwarts the whole Court, but brings home to its various members the penalty of their deeds. Here Hamlet both knows and acts. If the first set of circumstances were incalculable, and paralyzed his activity, this second set are calculable, and arouse his activity. He foils the schemes against him—which is the sphere of what has been already called his negative action.

I.

Out of these two sets of external influences, and the corresponding reaction against each, the Hamlet Thread is spun by the poet. With all these elements in mind, we shall now follow it to the turning-point of the dramatic action, that is, through the First Movement.

1. The first set of external influences upon Hamlet begin with the conduct of his mother. Her marriage, especially with such a man as Claudius, so soon after her husband's death, has touched to the core the profound ethical nature of Hamlet, who feels that therein the family relation is essentially annihilated. He has to deny to his own mother all true womanhood; hence the moral world seems to him, the son, to be falling into chaos. Denmark has become a hell to him; "things rank and gross in nature possess it merely;" the success of villainy and the power of sensuality would drive him out of existence, if "the Everlasting had not fixed his canon against self-slaughter." So the moral law holds him fast at the start, and causes him to react inwardly against the external pressure of the world. But the burden of the conflict weighs him down with melancholy; moreover, a great wrong in his environment is crushing him, though he does not know what it is. Still he has an instinct of what has happened, a dumb presentiment, which is now to rise into a vivid image gifted with a voice.

The second of these external influences which come upon Hamlet is the Ghost, for which preparation is made in the very first scene of the play. It tells the terrible tale of his father's murder, and enjoins the still more terrible revenge. The motives for action are now complete; presentiment has become knowledge. The Ghost has been already discussed, but a few remarks upon its dramatic relations may be added. The easiest way of getting rid of the difficulty is, no doubt, to take the apparition just as it is, without further troubling ourselves about the matter. We may say that the poet merely employed an existing superstition for theatrical effect. It may be held that it is used as a species of poetical machinery, somewhat as Virgil used the Grecian Mythology. Still, this will not do. Nearly all close readers of Shakespeare have the firmest faith that he never introduces supernatural forms without a profound spiritual signification. Another theory is that the Ghost was gotten up by somebody—say Horatio, or the soldiers, or persons not mentioned in the play; and there are several passages which, being read with such an opinion in view, are sufficient to excite an impression to this effect. Again, it is supposed by some, that the Ghost is a typical representation of Hamlet's suspicion, or possibly, that of the people —an objectification of the vague and ghost-like doubts, hintings, rumors of the time. Besides special objections against each of these views, there lies the general objection against all of them— there is no adequate ground stated for the employment of the Ghost. The poet has himself given us no solution of the difficulty, when a mere hint would have been sufficient. We may suppose, therefore, that he intended to leave his audience in the dark about the matter; that he designed to have them see just what Hamlet sees, and no more. He simply represents the Ghost as one of those external influences which are to spur Hamlet on to action. This is its function in the play, but the secret of its origin must remain forever untold.

Its reality must be carefully observed; it speaks the truth; it tells what is nowhere else told in the drama; it gives the pathos to Hamlet, and furnishes the basis of his action; it acts quite the same, in this respect, as if it were no Ghost. There is no hint that it has falsified, and, in fact, the entire course and purport of the drama rest upon its statements in reference to the murder of the King and the faithlessness of his wife. We have seen how close was the relation between the character of Hamlet and the form of the Ghost; the latter is an external picture of what the man is inside. It has already been stated how he melts all reality into his own subjective shapes; how he conjures up all sorts of relations, doubts, possibilities, excuses— which may be called the ghosts of Reflection. Now, Hamlet mostly lived in this unreal, subjective world, where true existence turns to a shadow. The Ghost here means just this—an unreal form of a reality. It is the way in which a fact has a tendency to reveal itself to such a mind—a fact whose actual nature is entirely changed and colored by the mental medium through which it passes, and its real character is transformed into the unreal, ghostly.

There are, therefore, two elements in the Ghost, both of which must be kept distinctly before the mind—the real and the unreal; or, it is both objective and subjective, it exists in the world externally, and in the man internally. On the one hand, it represents occurrences which actually took place;

its utterences are true, and are taken throughout the play just as if they had been spoken by an ordinary character. Hamlet, to be sure, hesitates in one place to accept its statements, but that is only an excuse for deferring action. On the other hand, its form is unreal, ghostly, subjective—which form, is, as it were, the shadow cast from Hamlet's mind.

But how does the opinion here presented consist with the fact that others see the Ghost besides Hamlet? It is again to be noted with what care the poet guards the objectivity of the Ghost as one of its essential elements; for it is not only seen by others, but it is seen by others before it is seen by Hamlet himself. Not the least hint is given of its secret in the whole play, and its objective nature is most rigorously preserved. So great and so striking is the precaution of the poet, in this respect, that we cannot help attributing it to the most careful design. But what dramatic ground is there for such a procedure? A most excellent ground, and one that exhibits the profoundest conception of Tragic Art. *The poet wishes to involve his audience in the same doubts and conflicts as his hero.* He designs the apparition for us, too; we are to look upon it, as it were, with Hamlet's eyes, and, hence, must not know anything more about it than Hamlet himself. To be sure, we may not regard it with his trust; we may disbelieve entirely in ghosts; but thus the nature of his mind is revealed, and the chasm between his consciousness and our own is made manifest. Still further, the audience must have the same problem before them as Hamlet; they must be assailed by the same difficulty—must be required to solve the enigma of the Ghost. Thus a character becomes tragic to the spectators when they are rent by the same contradiction which destroys the hero. If the audience stand above the hero, and comprehend all his complications and mistakes, we begin to enter the realm of Comedy.

Suppose the subject were treated otherwise. The poet might have dispensed with the Ghost, and had the news of the murder told to Hamlet, in a separate scene, by some spy who had secreted himself in the garden; but then we would lose the objective form which exhibits Hamlet's mind, though he might still be portrayed as vacillating. Again, the poet might have let the spectators into the mystery of the Ghost, while he kept it a secret to Hamlet; then the whole pathos of the character would be destroyed, for this depends upon the audience sharing in the same struggle as the hero. Such are the grounds upon which rests the justification of the poet in giving strong dramatic validity to the Ghost; for these reasons so many people in the play see it besides Hamlet; his mental characteristics are thus shown as they could be by no other means; finally, in this way the tragic element is brought out in its fullest significance, since the audience must solve the same problem, and is involved in the same difficulties as Hamlet.

We must also note his inner reaction against

this external influence. The Ghost commands revenge, which at first Hamlet accepts, and he will sweep to it "with wings as swift as meditation or the thoughts of love." But next we see him doubting: "the spirit I have seen may be the devil;" again his conscience has risen with its scruple. He doubts the morality of the Ghost with its revenge, and he doubts its reality; it may both tell a lie and be a lie. He even connects it with his own subjective condition: "out of my weakness and my melancholy" that spirit perhaps "abuses me to damn me." Clearly conscience is up in arms against the Ghost. Meantime another occurrence from the realm of Chance has wound itself into his existence—the actors have come. He drops the Ghost, and seizes the new incident:

> The play's the thing
> In which I'll catch the conscience of the King.

The third external influence is the company of actors. The connection of this part with the preceding is by no means remote. For the drama which they act is also not the reality, but only the representation of the reality. The Ghost is the dim, uncertain shadowy representation of the deed—the primitive conception; the drama is the clear objective representation of the deed in an ideal form, yet is not the real action itself. Now, the whole course of the play is to show the influences which spur Hamlet on to do the deed first enjoined by the Ghost, namely, to revenge his father's murder. Revenge means like for like;

Hamlet is to do to the King what the King did to his father. But he will first represent it on the stage, and then, he thinks, act it himself. Hence this play within the play is an intermediate link between the Ghost and the ultimate deed. It is also very characteristic of Hamlet that he is fond of the Drama; it pictures action, but requires none from him; so, in his mind, he loves to contemplate action, but hates to act.

These players are described quite fully in the drama, they are of Shakespeare's own profession, of which he takes occasion to unfold his ideas. In the histrionic art, Hamlet lays stress upon moderation, is averse to the strong effects demanded by the populace. Then in dramatic art he speaks of the excellent play which "pleased not the million;" that is the one from which he wishes to hear an extract. Such is the contrast between what is good and what is superficially popular. Do we not catch the poet here, breathing in an undertone concerning his own works? Moreover these actors have been compelled to wander by a stroke of fate, in which Hamlet finds an analogy to his father and his uncle. They drop into the action by chance, but Hamlet utilizes them in a scheme which goes to the soul of dramatic art, making it image the wicked deed, and thus elevating it into a kind of conscience which holds up before the guilty man his act.

Hamlet's changed demeanor has already excited the suspicion of the court, and all the characters of the play who are employed as instruments of the King are set to work in order to worm out his secret. But the players have arrived; Hamlet calls for his favorite speech, entitled "The Slaughter of Priam." But why is this lengthy, and apparently irrelevant, declamation brought in here? Its point lies in the inconsolable grief of Hecuba, wife of Priam, who has just beheld the murder of her husband. Hamlet calls for it as furnishing an ideal contrast to the conduct of his faithless mother; contemplating it, he can get rid, for a moment, of the disagreeable reality around him, and of the pressing duty. Thus it is seen that this long insertion is in the deepest harmony with the subject of the tragedy, and bears, as a motive, directly upon Hamlet. But that which sets him on fire is the action of the player, who seems to be more influenced by a mere fiction than he himself by the most fearful actual occurrence. Bitter self-reproach follows, with apparently a new resolution. But a doubt rises; a reflection enters— the Ghost *may* be a deception; hence there is another deferment till he can catch the conscience of the King in a play. Nor can he do otherwise; for what is the deed told by the Ghost to Hamlet but a shadowy specter? So he doubts the deed which has been done, and doubts the deed which he is to do.

But the matter cannot rest here. The keen reflective Hamlet must know his own state. Already he has shown misgivings in respect to his ability to accomplish his work. Hence, when we next meet him—it is in the far-famed soliloquy on suicide—he is perfectly aware of his mental condition, and seems to regard it as final, as something which cannot be helped. We have already pointed out the motive for self-murder which was frequently hovering before his mind. The subject again comes up in this connection, as he has now become conscious of his irresolution, and is still pressed on by the most fearful injunctions. What is he to do? Kill himself—let us first cast up the credit and the debit side of death. Death relieves us from all the natural shocks that flesh is heir to, from all wrongs—in general, from the whips and scorns of time; so much is clear gain. But hold! there is a dream-world beyond; there's the rub:

> For, in that sleep of death, what dreams *may* come,
> When we have shuffled off this mortal coil,
> Must give us pause.

Upon this bare possibility we shall forego all the acknowledged advantages of death. Hamlet has already declared that the external world was too strong for his frail individuality; he cannot resist the slings and arrows of outrageous fortune, but is prone to passively suffer all which collides with him. He sees that death is the only destiny of such a person. But what deters him from the act of suicide? The future state, which, whatever else may be said about it, is the land of shadows, of unrealities to the living man, for the simple reason that he has not yet realized that state, and cannot do so till after death. This realm, being so perfectly void, is a fine field for the imagination, since there is absolutely nothing in the way. Let no one think that by these remarks we are doubting or denying the great doctrine of immortality; but this rests upon quite other grounds, namely, the rationality of man, and cannot be given by imagination. Hamlet, true to his character, assigns the greater validity to this specter of unreality. Whatever the future state may be to others, to him it is, and can only be, the land of possibilities. But the principal thing to be observed is that he is now aware of his own condition, and gives it expression:

> And thus the native hue of resolution
> Is sicklied o'er with the pale cast of thought.

Moreover, his moral nature also rebels at the idea of suicide, as it did at the idea of murder:

> Thus conscience does make cowards of us all.

The struggle of Hamlet against the King has thus become internal—against himself. The destruction of Claudius was enjoined upon him as the most sacred duty, yet he cannot bring himself to its performance, and is now conscious of the fact. What does he think of himself? "If I have not strength of individuality enough to do such a duty, then I have not strength enough to live; I am too weak to assert myself in this world of rude, buffeting tempests." Such is his conclusion. But he can no more kill himself than he can kill the King, and for the same reason. It would be a contradiction if he could. Hence we see the same unreality, the same spectral excuses, coming up to forestall action in the latter case as in the former. So Hamlet remains still a living being, with the same conflicts as before, which are now renewed with increased fury.

The play within the play succeeds perfectly, but has also had another result not so favorable to Hamlet. If the latter has now perfect evidence, the King also has become aware of the fact that Hamlet is apprised of his guilt. Consequently, more decisive measures must be taken to get rid of the dangerous dissembler. Preparations are accordingly made to dispatch him to England and there murder him. But this play has struck another chord in the King's character, which, on one or two occasions hitherto has shown some signs of life—conscience. The attempt at prayer, by the King, forms the counterpart to Hamlet's soliloquy on suicide. The King here has done the deed; his desire is that it should be undone. Note the steps; for we have in this passage the most complete exposition of the noblest Christian doctrine, and it is worth more than many volumes of Theology. He attempts prayer, which means he tries to place himself in harmony with the Divine Being—the rational principle of the Universe. But that Being he has offended, to the last degree, by his conduct, and there seems to be no reconciliation. But is there no hope? Yes, there is mercy for even the greatest criminal. How? First, by a complete repentance in spirit for the act; second, by surrendering all its advantages—that is, *you must make that undone which you have done, as far as lies in your power.* You cannot restore the dead, it is true, nor call back the past, but you can do justice to the living by ample restitution. The spirit of man has this power: It can heal its own wounds; the Will can withdraw itself from its deed and say, "it is no longer mine." Such is subjective repentance. But this is not enough. There must be an objective correspondence, else it is not complete; the deed must be reversed; all gains and advantages must be unconditionally surrendered. Hence the King feels that he cannot be forgiven as long as he is still possessed

> Of those effects for which I did the murder—
> My crown, mine own ambition, and my queen.

Verily, there is no way out but to make a clean breast of the matter, as we say with true metaphor; and, furthermore, he cannot buy off his own conscience—"there is no shuffling." What remains? Only the bitter demands of repentance. This he tries, and, moreover, essays formal prayer, but without success; he cannot repent. His crimes are too monstrous for him to retrace his steps. Can he give up his queen, his throne, confess the murder of his brother, renounce his plans against young Hamlet? It were to demand too much of poor human nature to expect it—yet such is the only way of salvation. Here we see the contrast between the two: Conscience keeping back Hamlet, yet spurring on the King; the one seeks to do, the other to undo, with the same inefficiency. In the one case, the deed smothers conscience; in the other, conscience the deed. Their actions pertain to the same matter—the murder of the father, the marriage of the mother, the exclusion of the son from the throne. Hamlet is invoked to visit justice upon the man who has done these things; the King is urged by conscience to make them undone. The King refuses; so does Hamlet.

Perhaps there is no passage in Shakespeare equal to this one in grandeur of thought and in clearness and exhaustiveness of statement. The heart is kindled, and the mind is excited to the highest intensity, by its marvelous power. It may be called the Northern or Teutonic interpretation of Christianity, in distinction from the Southern or Romanic. That interpretation insists upon the moral content of religion, as distinguished from its external ceremonies and abstract dogmas. These are considered of no validity unless they make men good—determine their conduct. That a person can be a Christian and immoral at the same time is almost inconceivable to the Northern mind. But if we turn to Calderon, the greatest dramatist of Southern Europe, we shall find quite the opposite interpretation. In his drama called *Purgatorio di San Patricio* there is a direct contrast between these principles. Two characters are portrayed—one of which is good and upright, the other is the most desperate villain that can be imagined, having been guilty of adultery, murder, seduction of nuns—in fact, of quite every conceivable crime. Still, he has Faith, and is ready to lose his life in its defense, and, as a consequence, Heaven has vouchsafed to him many marks of special favor. Both these characters, though morally direct opposites, are still Christians:

> Pues aunque somos Christianos
> Los dos, somos tan opuestos
> Que distamos quanto va
> Desde ser malo a ser bueno.

Here the antithesis is openly stated—it is not necessary to be moral in order to be a good Christian; Christianity and morality are divorced totally. In another drama, *El Principe constante,* there is portrayed the collision between Christianity and Mohammedanism. These two forms of faith are not made the basis of a distinction in character; on the contrary, the Moorish prince possesses all the qualities which command honor and respect in an equal, or even greater, degree than the Spanish prince. Now, it may be fairly stated that this would be no collision at all in Shakespearian art, or for the Northern consciousness. A Spanish audience would, no doubt, applaud the devotion to an abstract dogma, which is represented in this play. But an English or German audience would say: "If Christianity cannot make better men than Mohammedanism, it has no advantage; we would just as lieve be of one as the other." Herein lies the immense difference between Calderon and Shakespeare. The latter brings all religion back to its spiritual basis, and never rests in mere externality. How does it affect the character and conduct of men when they seize these religions as ends in life, and realize them in their actions? asks Shakespeare. His treatment of this theme can be best seen in the *Merchant of Venice,* in the characters of Shylock and Antonio, where there is also portrayed a religious collision—that between Judaism and Christianity. But Calderon's main question is, "Infidel or Christian?" or, perhaps, it is more narrow still—"Catholic or non-Catholic?" If a man only believes in the true doctrine, he possesses the privilege of moral delinquency; for he has the absolute end of man—faith in a dogma. Morality is quite a subordinate, even indifferent, matter. But Shakespeare reverses these elements—dogmatic religion is subordinate to morality, or, rather, it has morality in the highest sense for its content. In the hands of Calderon, the act of formal prayer on the part of the guilty King would have been ample repentance, but Shakespeare demands something profounder than a mere genuflection.

The players have now done their work. The Ghost told the murder, but they have made the King himself, the guilty man, tell it over again. Previously it was unwitnessed, now the whole court can bear witness. The outer dramatic picture of the deed has roused the inner conscience of the doer. A voice from the world beyond it was, now it is a voice in this world. Hamlet glories in his success; Horatio, the well-balanced friend, confirms him. Still the great question remains: Will he now act? Listen to him:

> Now could I drink hot blood,
> And do such bitter business as the day
> Would quake to look on.

Is this loud talk again to smother the rising scruple? Behold, here is the King at prayer: "now might I do it pat—and now I'll do it;" no, he will not; already it must first be "scanned," the reaction sets in afresh, then a reflection, an excuse, and again deferment. So even against the proven guilt—for Hamlet questions not the proof—he does not proceed; he finds a pretext under which he hides his moral hesitation. He is not clear that he ought to revenge the murder, if proven. Long afterwards, when his own life had been attempted by the same guilty King, he can still ask in doubt: "Is it not perfect conscience to quit him with this arm?" This is the trouble now lurking in his soul; so he reacts again internally, and the outer impulse from the scenic representation is paralyzed. But is it the last chance? No, there is one more, and here it is.

The fourth external influence is Fortinbras marching against the Polack. The connection between this occurence and what has just preceded is to be carefully noted. The player exhibited the ideal world of action before Hamlet, but the representation was unable to incite him forward to the deed. There still remains the real world of action, which now appears in the person of young Fortinbras. What influence will this produce upon him? for it would seem to be the climax of incitement. Fortinbras is the man of action, and this element is brought into greater prominence by the small value of its object. The prize is a little patch of ground, not worth a rental of five ducats, yet here is a youth who defies fortune to the utmost for its possession. The contrast strikes Hamlet in the most forcible manner. He has a father murdered, a mother debauched, a throne despoiled—and still he does not act. He resolves anew to perform the deed, but, as the sequel shows, with the same result as before. Here again he states his difficulty with all the energy of self-reproach; it is thinking too precisely on the event, while Fortinbras makes mouths at the invisible event. He confesses that he has strength and means to carry out his end; he can give no good reason to himself for his delay, but is inclined to ascribe it to cowardice—to his anxiety about consequences. It is the strongest example that could be presented to him, and we may suppose that, from the impression which it made upon him, he afterwards selects Fortinbras as the fittest successor to the throne. For we can well imagine that Hamlet now has the highest appreciation of a man of action.

The introduction of Fortinbras has been condemned by Goethe as an unnecessary part of the drama, but its presence can be justified on the strictest artistic grounds. Fortinbras is the man of action, but something more—he is the man of action as the head of the State. He is inspired, in the highest degree, with the sense of nationality. The elder Hamlet had contracted the bounds of his country, which it is the first great object of his ambition to win back, but he is overborne by higher authority. There remains the expedition against the Polack to vindicate some ancient right, or avenge some wrong, from which he returns apparently victorious just at the death of Hamlet. Thus he is seen on all sides asserting his own nationality against external countries which in any way collide with the same; he seeks the full recognition of his people abroad, and is quite ready to subjugate other lands to the strong national spirit which he has aroused. Such a man is a ruler, at least in the most essential sense; he obtains absolute respect for his country without, and strengthens the national spirit within. Herein he stands in direct contrast to Hamlet and the King. They employ their time at home in plotting each other's murder, yet both are afraid to perform the act. The House of Denmark, therefore, goes down in its effete representatives, and the true ruler takes their place.

Thus the play has a positive solution. Most tragedies end with the death of the colliding characters—a merely negative result—which would be the case here were the part of Fortinbras left out. The Danish princes perish because they are unworthy of their dignity, and are succeeded by one who has shown himself to be a sovereign in the highest sense. The play, therefore, begins with Fortinbras (at the second scene), and ends with Fortinbras; his activity is the frame in which its whole movement is set. Thus the poet has portrayed him as the absolute contrast to Hamlet, and made him triumphant, at the close, as the man of action. How much, therefore, must the thought of the poem lose by the absence of this character? When we consider also the additional reason for its introduction—that it forms the culmination of that series of external influences which it is the plan of the drama to unfold—the objection of Goethe would seem to be entirely groundless. For Hamlet must have also the real world of action come up before him to incite him to the deed. Hence this character is an integral and indispensable part of the play.

It would now be advantageous to turn back and review for a moment the four external influences which have been mentioned, and observe their gradation. The hasty marriage of the mother is the first one, wherein Hamlet only surmises. In the second, which is the Ghost, the whole affair is revealed, but in a dreamy, spectral way. The declamation of the actor on the subject of Hecuba, and the subsequent play, constitute the third; it must not be forgotten that the matter is something feigned—not real; the story is a myth; instead of action, it is action represented. The fourth influence—the expedition of Fortinbras—is the deed itself, which now appears before him in its full reality. But neither the representation nor the reality can bring him to the point of action. It is evident that the last and highest effort has been expended, and from now on the nature of these influences and the character of Hamlet must change.

In these four external influences we may find a correspondence to the four internal Hamlets—the instinctive, imaginative, moral, and reflective Hamlets. To the outer world is related an inner world, the two must be seen together. This correspondence, though it may not hold in every detail, is true in general, and is worthy of being noted by the reader who wishes to get all the harmonies out of Shakespeare. The instinctive Hamlet, with his "prophetic soul," foreboded the whole truth from the conduct of his mother. The imaginative Hamlet is he to whom alone the story of the Ghost can be told. The moral Hamlet, with his conscience, is the one to "catch the conscience of the King" through the players. The reflective or intellectual Hamlet is the one to appreciate the deed of Fortinbras, and to make the keen self-introspection, which we find in his— properly fourth—soliloquy. Thus the four internal Hamlets and the four external influences are a correspondence of the inner and outer worlds; moreover both move together in gradation upward to the culminating point which has already been reached.

But what is Hamlet to do now? Kill himself— but that is impossible; he can no more kill himself than kill the King. The question of suicide was settled, as will be remembered, in the well-known soliloquy on that subject. He can only let come what comes, defending himself, perhaps, against the attempts of others; but the great aggressive act, which includes all acts, must remain unperformed. But what is about to come? The consequences of even what he has already done are rapidly returning upon him; the King, goaded by suspicion, has resolved upon his destruction; Laertes, the avenger of Polonius' murder, is near at hand and crying for his blood. The external influences are no longer mere examples brought forward to incite him to action, but he is now involved in their meshes; they seize hold of him and carry him along irresistibly in their movement. At this point he must experience the bitter fact that he is controlled by something outside of his own intelligence, upon which, hitherto, he has had the firmest reliance.

2. We are now to go back and bring up the second set of external influences which come upon Hamlet—those from the Court. They are the Calculable, as the first set was the Incalculable; they come from a limited circle of people, while the first set came from the vast world outside; the one set is the plan of men, the other the plan of Providence, who however, is masked in the guise of Chance. Hamlet is, accordingly, able to meet and foil this second set; here he is not paralyzed, as he was in the first set, but is rather aroused to a wonderful activity, which, however, is not the doing of the positive deed, but the thwarting of the deeds of others.

The conflict between Hamlet and the Court reveals to us chiefly the external Hamlet. Here he acts a part, and takes pleasure in the acting of it; he assumes a mask, the mask of lunacy, which the King seeks in vain to penetrate. The acted Hamlet is the external Hamlet, who thus hides in a disguise the internal Hamlet with his bitter soul-conflicts. The Court is turned loose upon him, as he says, to "pluck out the heart of my mystery;" he throws his mask among them, which breeds an absolute confusion in the courtly mind concerning the question of his insanity. But the courtiers cannot reach his inner secret; they remain caught, more or less, in his outward appearance, in his disguise; many a reader too, of the play has thus been caught.

This conduct of the courtiers is not simply nullified, it is also punished; every person who dares become an instrument of the King has his deed brought back in some shape. Hamlet not merely foils the intruders, but he turns their souls inside out; he becomes a mirror of conscience to his mother and to the King; others he brings to destruction. While they are all trying to ensnare him, he has really ensnared them; he is their fate, and his own too. Let us now follow the courtiers trying to fathom the "something o'er which his melancholy sits on brood."

The first action of the Court against Hamlet is to detain him at home from Wittenberg. Since the death of his father his conduct has excited suspicion, he confesses to have "that within which passeth show;" moreover the King is quite ready to suspect on account of his own guilt. The young Prince is to be watched and his secret is to be found; his response to the King's design is the plan of feigning insanity—the outer garb to mask the inner struggle.

Next, the King sets to work all his instruments. The man of cunning comes first—Polonius, whom Hamlet befools worse than any other courtier, slashing him to pieces with his sarcasm, and, at last, running him through behind the arras, though this was an accident. Love is made an instrument against Hamlet in the person of Ophelia, who, true daughter of Polonius that she is, is ready to betray her lover, but he catches her in the act, and, in terrific scorn, reads home to her the lesson of her infidelity: "Get thee to a nunnery." Though she thinks he is mad, she has herself received the sting of madness in her own soul, and will end in insanity, though this, too, was an accident, that is, not intended by Hamlet. After love, friendship is turned against the Prince, in order to find out his mystery. Rosencrantz and Guildenstern, youthful friends, lie in wait for his soul's secret, but are foiled, made to confess, and, for a final interference, are sent to death by Hamlet in a moment of impulse. He is veritably destiny to the person who interferes with him. The nearest human tie, maternal affection, is also pressed into service against him; his own mother is made to join the instruments of the court in the attempt to probe her son's heart. Yet not his heart, but her own is reached in the trial:

> O Hamlet thou hast cloft my heart in twain!

He is himself a man of conscience, it is his own deepest conflict; he well knows how to set up its mirror in another soul:

> You go not till I set you up a glass
> Where you may see the inmost part of you.

He succeeds, for listen to her outcry:

> O Hamlet, speak no more;
> Thou turn'st mine eyes into my very soul
> And there I see such black and grained spots
> As will not leave their tinct,

Yet not thus will he leave her, but he points the way out of her present condition:

> Confess yourself to heaven,
> Repent what's past, avoid what is to come,

The great duty of repentance is again inculcated; it is the only means of shunning a tragic fate. Here we note the correspondence with the prayer of the King, who also considers the nature of repentance, to which he likewise has been brought by Hamlet, having had a mirror held up to his soul in the little play. Thus, both to King and Queen, Hamlet becomes a conscience which has revealed themselves to themselves; nay, he becomes a call to repentance, which both, however, reject.

II.

We have now arrived at the turning-point of the drama; here begins the Second Movement of the Hamlet Thread. A change takes place both in the external influences or environment, and in the character of Hamlet. The outer world of Chance, the Incalculable, now seizes him, inasmuch as he does not seize it; hitherto it came upon him to drive him to action, but without effect; now it whirls him into its current, and bears him on; if he does not transform the world through his deed, the world will transform him through its happenings. The King has decreed that he must go to England, and he obeys the decree, having his own plan therein; but the Incalculable sweeps in and foils both him and the King, bringing him back to Denmark.

Herewith his conviction changes. He accepts this incalculable element as the final arbiter, and so abjures his own intelligence. He will no longer resist it; accordingly, his inner reaction against external influences quite ceases in this Second Movement. His soul-struggles do not wholly disappear, but they quiet down to the pensive meditation of the grave-yard, for the most part. Impulse can still inflame him, but he hardly attempts to bring himself to do the deed. He resigns himself to the outward power of circumstance, in which he finds his divinity, but to this divinity he immolates his free-will. A great change, certainly; a change which is the forerunner of his tragic destiny. He gives up, as it were; a series of incidents now determine him within and without; he becomes a believer in Fate, nay, in a double Fate, namely, inner caprice or impulse, and outer accident—the Fate in the man and in the world. Previously he resisted external forces, and they could not drive him to action; henceforth they rush forward with him to death.

The second set of influences—those of the court—still continue to be directed against him, but he no longer tries to thwart them. The King still plots, but Hamlet does not counterplot. What is the use? Thus even his negative action—his foiling the work of others—essentially ceases in this Second Movement; he lets the external influence carry him whither it will; for does he not now believe in Fate? Just herewith is coupled his end; the King, no longer thwarted by Hamlet, can succeed in a plot against his life. Laertes, too, appears, in whom Hamlet beholds his own deed returning. Finally, if activity be life, what remains for him but death?

It will be seen that the Second Movement has not, as a whole, the fullness and variety which we saw in the First; it sympathizes with its theme, which is the decline of the man into inaction and nothingness. In this decline we have three different pictures of Hamlet in three different environments. Thus the change of structure in this Second Movement corresponds to the change of thought; Hamlet, no longer reacting inwardly and outwardly, becomes almost passive, and is shown, in panoramic fashion, as the central figure of the three successive pictures.

(1.) First comes the capture of Hamlet by the pirates, and his sudden return. He is upon the high sea, when Chance suddenly puts forth her hand and turns him back. It is a most strange occurrence, and has always given great difficulty. Accident, contrary to the general rule of the poet, seems, in the most startling manner, to determine the course of things, and the whole poem is made, apparently, to rest upon a most improbable event. Hamlet is sent to England; a pirate pursues his ship and grapples with it; he boards the strange vessel, when it suddenly cuts loose with Hamlet alone, and afterwards puts him safely on shore. The whole proceeding is so suspicious that, were such an event to occur in real life, everybody would think at once of collusion. This impression is much strengthened by the confidence with which he speaks of his ability to foil all the machinations of the King in sending him to England.

>   —Let it work,
> For 'tis the sport to have the enginer
> Hoist with his own petar; and it shall go hard
> But I will delve one yard below their mines
> And blow them at the moon.

Indeed, he rejoices in the prospect:

> —O, 'tis most sweet
> When in one line two crafts directly meet.

Note how absolute his trust still is in his intelligence. Such confidence seems to be begotten of preparation. One is inclined, therefore, to explain the occurrence in this way: Hamlet hired the pretended pirate, and gave to its officers his instructions before he left port; indeed, he must have had also some understanding with the officers of the royal ship which was to convey him. Yet this view, apparently so well founded, we must at once abandon when we read Hamlet's account of the affair (Act. V. Scene 2.) In that he ascribes his action wholly to instinct; there was no premeditation, no planning at all. But what is more astonishing, he has come to prefer unconscious impulse to deliberation; he has renounced intelligence as the guide of conduct. Yet, before this event, how he delighted in his skill, in his counterplots, in his intellectual dexterity!

Now, what is the cause of this great change in his character? In the first place, it ought to be observed that the expressions above quoted were uttered by him when there might be still some hope of being brought to action, before the last and strongest influence—the appearance of Fortinbras—revealed to him that his case was desperate. But the great cause of his conversion was this startling event, in which he saw that Accident, or some external power, was mistress over the best-matured plans of men. Here an element appears suddenly that had never been included in his calculations, upon which, heretofore, he had placed so great reliance; suddenly they are swept down by this unknown force. He sees that it is objectively valid in the world, but he knows that he himself is not, for he cannot do the deed; hence he must believe in it more than in himself. Hamlet thus becomes a convert from Intelligence to Fate, from self-determination to external determination. So must every person without Will be, to a greater or less extent, a disbeliever in Will; for his sole experience is that man is controlled from without. Thus it can be seen that the introduction of this accident is based upon the weightiest grounds, and is in the completest harmony with the development of the drama. Accident appears here in a manner which is legitimate in Art—not to cut a complicated knot or to create a sudden surprise, but to determine character.

(2.) Now follows the second picture, showing another most remarkable, yet strictly logical, transition. This man—whose irresolution has become an intellectual conviction; who has even renounced his belief in action and made himself the puppet of chance; who has thus, as near as possible without suicide, stripped himself of a real existence in the world—in what environment next shall we find him? In the grave-yard, alive; for, as before stated, he cannot destroy himself. Thus he is brought to the very abode of death, without entering the door The grave is that bit of earth which contains man when he absolutely ceases to act; he is laid away in it when his body can no longer assert itself, but becomes the prey of the elements. Reality ends there, and possibility begins.

But Hamlet is still alive, and, hence, not yet ready for this final resting-place. Now, for the living, the grave-yard, above all other localities, is the home of meditation; every one feels this influence within its borders; each small mound calls up an infinitude of possibilities. The hum of the actual world is removed, and the future here strikes into the present and absorbs us into itself for the moment. But the future cannot be *realized*, for, when it is real, it is the present. Hence Hamlet, with his subjective, contemplative nature, must find in this spot a most congenial theme for his reflection; he will not be annoyed by the bustling activity of the world, nor pushed on by any necessity to do his deed. All external influences seem removed.

But even the grave-yard—the end of activity—has still an activity of its own, and must also furnish a contrast to Hamlet, which will be seen to disturb him. It is an humble calling, though none the less real—we allude to the grave-diggers. They seem to have an air of indifference and nonchalance which ill accord with the character of the place, and even grate somewhat upon the feelings. But this is just the point; grave-digging is their daily occupation, which they go about unhesitatingly; and again Hamlet beholds men who practically fulfill their calling, however humble and repulsive it may be. Thus the common laborer is also brought in with his lesson; for the low estate of these grave-diggers appears to be strongly emphasized by the poet. To their simple minds the great forms of the world are quite devoid of content or meaning, They talk of Christianity and Law with the most grotesque formality, which becomes the more ridiculous by their attempted adherence to formal Logic. One is inclined to say: A fit place for all such forms when they have lost their inner substance—the grave-yard. It is here shown how the ignorant rabble must regard the highest concrete truth; it loses its entire spirit, and degenerates into an empty formalism. So these grave-diggers exhibit their mode of viewing the great questions of the world, but they soon come down to the more congenial element of banter and jest, and, at last, to the gross appetite in a stoup of liquor. One of them is humming a ditty of youthful love, while at work, when Hamlet appears. O the harsh contrast! "Hath this fellow no feeling of his business, that he sings at grave-making?" No, Hamlet, no; that is his business, which he goes to work at and does without thinking any more about the matter. Still another blow is given to Hamlet by the grave-digger. The man who confounded and befooled the court with his quibbles is now beaten at his own game by one of the humblest of mortals. He has proscribed his own intellect; his intellect proscribes him.

It was stated that the grave-yard is the home of meditation. The mind looks in two directions, and feeds itself upon its own contemplations—forward into the future when it pictures to itself the world to come, and backward into the past when its principal theme will be the transitoriness of human power and glory. The former has been fully considered by Hamlet in the soliloquy on suicide, and, hence, cannot be repeated here. The latter—transitoriness—comes now in its turn, and, consequently, we find Hamlet indulging in those gloomy reflections in which his melancholy and contemplative nature takes so great pleasure. He is in the presence of extinct individualities; imagine what they were—behold what they are. He runs through the scale, dwelling upon the lawyer with sarcastic delight, and loading him with quibbles and gibberish as if to smother him with his own lumber; also recounting with exquisite pathos his boyish remembrances of the clown, Yorick. Mark the difference of style between these two passages, and see how absolutely Shakespeare adapts the form to the subject. Finally, Alexander and Cæsar, the mightiest men of action of the past, are called up, judged merely by their transient bodily existence, and found to be—dust. We need not speak of the positive and eternal principle in these towering individualities—that they are now living, and will live forever, by their deeds in the history of the world; but this is a fact which the contemplation of Hamlet must ignore, since it dwells upon the negative, finite element of humanity. Hamlet has thus passed from the presence of the living hero, Fortinbras, to the presence of the dead hero, Alexander; and a corresponding transition is made in his own character. For, if Fortinbras, with the pressure of the real world, cannot excite him to activity—if his conviction is that man is swayed solely by external forces, then there remains nothing for him but the grave-yard, whither he may go and dwell in contemplation, and, finally, have his deedless body stowed away there in the earth. This last state, we may rest assured, cannot now be far off.

With Alexander and Cæsar he must stop; he cannot go higher; hence, at this convenient moment, there passes by the funeral procession of Ophelia. The old affection rouses in him the dormant man, sudden emotion sways him, and once again we behold the impulsive Hamlet. Moreover, her death is an indirect consequence of his conduct; Nemesis begins to work. But what shall we say to this grave-scene? It is certainly extravagant, but perhaps justifiable, through the participating characters. Laertes, in accordance with his hasty nature, leaps into the grave of his sister and indulges in the wildest grief. But Hamlet follows him, and even surpasses him in extravagance! Hamlet here again acts from his emotions and impulses; the love for Ophelia, and the circumstances of her death, return upon him like the rush of an overwhelming ocean, and bear down all moderation. He for once is mad, as every such man is momentarily mad; he says, he forgot himself. It is our opinion that he does not here feign madness; the motives thereto seem absent; the King knows his secret designs, and he must know that the King knows them. It is the love and death of Ophelia which furnish the cause for this extraordinary spectacle.

There is another contrast in this scene which is too striking to be omitted. Every one speaks with the greatest tenderness and affection of the sweet Ophelia; in the memories of all she is embalmed in love and peace. But there is one exception—the priest. He has no share in the general sorrow; he would even exclude from the rites of decent burial the frail maiden who has lost reason and life together. He is thus placed with the clownish grave-diggers—not only in the character of adherence to empty form, but also in the special subject of conversation, for their discussion is about the Christian burial of one that has committed suicide. Ophelia is laid to rest; Hamlet's acts are beginning to return upon him in his intense sorrow; but a deeper thrust is at hand, for he has already been brought face to face with the avenger.

Thus the impulsive Hamlet has appeared to us again; but in the next scene we are once more introduced to the reflective Hamlet, who intensely self-conscious and introspective, knows and desscribes his new condition. This takes place in the conversation in which Hamlet tells Horatio the circumstances of his escape. He attributes his action wholly to instinct and presentiment, and now, for the first time, he indicates fully the great change which has come over himself. He ascribes to accident, and not to any pre-arranged scheme, the rescue by the pirates; still, in accident, he hints the providential plan. On board the vessel he acted from a secret, irresistible impulse; behold the result. This event has changed his whole view of the world. Hitherto his faith in intelligence was unbounded; his confidence in his own ability to counteract all hostile schemes had never failed; even when he is told that he must go to England, he, with exultation, declares:

> But I will delve one yard below their mines
> And blow them at the moon.

But this strange accident upon the sea has changed his entire way of thinking. Now he believes that often indiscretion serves better than the profoundest deliberation; that destiny rules the hour; that there is an extra-human agency which overrules the activity of man:

> There's a divinity that shapes our ends,
> Rough-hew them how we will.

In a later passage, just before he goes to fence with Laertes, he enunciates the same doctrine in a stronger form. Thus Hamlet abjures Intelligence, which he thinks has been so baneful to him; he resigns himself into the hands of Fate, outer and inner Fate—external chance and internal impulse; he is now ready to obey the first prompting of his soul, as well as to yield to the first impact of the world. We have before attempted to show that this conversion of Hamlet to a belief in destiny was a necessary consequence of his intellectual point of view, for he has now become acquainted with something possessing objective validity, of which his subjective spirit is able to give no adequate account, and which it does not possess. Hence he comes to believe in external determination—in action without forethought. Thus, under impulse, he commits the forgery which sends to death the two royal messengers; but true to his old character, he can still ask the question whether he ought in conscience to slay that King whom, in addition to the other crimes against him, he has just caught laying a snare for his destruction.

(3). But the final consummation, the last transition—that from the grave-yard to the grave—is at hand. Osrick, in the absence of Rosencrantz and Gildenstern, comes to invite Hamlet to fence with Laertes. This courtier is described in full—

more fully, perhaps, than his importance warrants. Hamlet we see here at his old tricks, with his love of sly, obscure satire, which confounds his victim, and comes near confounding his reader. We cannot get his exact meaning, but we do perceive very distinctly the drift; it is directed against the person at hand, who is too dull to comprehend it, as was seen in the case of Polonius. Osrick exhibits the hollowness and formalism into which everything had fallen; it is a drossy age which has lost all substantial worth, contrasting thereby with the deep moral nature of Hamlet. But the match is agreed on, though Hamlet still has presentiments. Here he falls into the trap; and one thinks, if he had been as shrewd now as upon former occasions, he would not have been caught. Undoubtedly the plan against Hamlet is not more profound than many others which he has seen through—why, then, should it succeed? For the reason that Hamlet's view of the moral order of things is changed; he no longer believes that man can determine anything; one act is as good as another for bringing about a result; whether he goes or declines is all the same in the eye of Fate. Hence he resigns himself to destiny, and the cautious Hamlet blindly proceeds to what comes first. He even refuses to obey instinct now, and surrenders himself wholly to chance: "If it be now, 'tis not to come; if it be not to come, it will be now; if it be not now, yet it will come; the readiness is in all."

The two combatants are brought together. Hamlet begs pardon of Laertes, and declares that all the wrongs done by him to Laertes were the result of madness. This means merely impulse—the momentary absence of reason—else we must suppose Hamlet guilty of wanton falsehood, and, besides, destroy the whole meaning of the poem. Here is found the motive for Laertes' generous candor at death, when he discloses the infamous scheme of the King. So they are reconciled, yet they fall by each other's hand; they are incited not so much by *personal* grievances against each other, as they are the avenging instruments of Wrong. Nor must we omit to mention the absolute logical precision and necessity of this mutual destruction; for the poet himself has reminded us of the fact, lest it might escape our notice. Hamlet, the son, is seeking revenge for a father slain. But he slays Polonius, who is also a father, and thus commits the very crime whose punishment is his sole object. In being an avenger he calls up against himself an avenger, who is, therefore, the son of Polonius—Laertes. The execution of his revenge thus involves his own destruction, and, moreover, the special manner of his destruction. But Laertes, too, must perish, for he also has willed murder, and he becomes the instrument of the murderer of a father, though he is himself seeking to avenge a father's murder.

It will be observed that these deaths at the end of the play seem to be accidental, though, to a certain extent, brought about by the plan of the King and Laertes. They, too, are involved—

a result which they did not expect; but the sensuous side must have always an element of accident, because it is externality. What we must look for is the logic of these deaths. Have the persons done that which justifies their fate? Do their deeds imply destruction when taken in a universal sense? In other words, have they only been overtaken by justice, by the irrevocable consequences of their acts? For art must exhibit the deed in its completeness—in its return to itself. If we examine the actions of the various persons swept away in the course of this play we shall find that all have done something which deserved death—that the idea of Retribution is imprinted on every character. Each one has willed that which, by logical necessity, involves his own destruction. Nor has the poet failed to express this thought repeatedly. Laertes seems so impressed with the notion of Retribution that he states it three times:

> *Osrick.*—How is't, Laertes?
> *Laertes.*—Why, as a woodcock to mine own springe,
> I'm justly killed with mine own treachery.

Again:

> —The foul practice
> Hath turned itself on me; lo! here I lie,
> Never to rise again.

Speaking of the King:

> —He is justly served;
> It is a poison tempered by himself.

But even here Hamlet can only act under the spur of impulse; angered by what Laertes tells him, he rushes up and stabs the King, just as he slew Polonius. Hamlet perishes, and we see impulse in its results. Rational action alone can be moral, for it can distinguish its objects. Hamlet confesses that he was wrong in killing Polonius, and regrets it; still, he must bear the consequences of his deed. It is now brought home to him through the son—Laertes.

Hamlet's dying request to Horatio is to report his cause aright, that a wounded name might not live behind him. Thus, at the very last breath, we see a manifestation of that beautiful moral nature, which desires that its motives be set right before the world. Moreover, he gives his dying voice for Fortinbras, the man of action, as the sovereign most suitable for ruling his country. And we hope that it will not seem wholly fanciful to the reader if we point out a deeper signification in this last injunction to Horatio: It means the writing of this drama. For how else can the desire of Hamlet be fulfilled—to have his story told to the world? The poem, therefore, accounts for itself; Horatio is to be poet, and he even states the argument of his work in his conversation with Fortinbras. These are the words:

> And let me speak to the yet unknowing world
> How these things came about, so shall you hear
> Of carnal, bloody, and unnatural acts,
> Of accidental judgments, casual slaughters,
> Of deaths put on by cunning and forc'd cause,
> And, in this upshot, purposes mistook,
> Fallen on the inventors' heads.

Thus ends the greatest of plays, with Fortinbras

and Horatio—ruler and poet—master of the actual world and master of the ideal world; the former is the chief actor, who moulds the reality; the latter is the thinking artist, who transmutes the reality into the transparent forms of Beauty. In this way Shakespeare has given a positive solution to the collision, and has also accounted for his drama; indeed, he has included himself and his part in his work.

CHAPTER THIRD.

The King's Thread.

In the previous chapter the external influences were shown, the object of which was to incite Hamlet to action. In them we saw the character of Hamlet reflected in a great variety of shapes, yet having always the same essential basis. Here is found, undoubtedly, the leading element of the play. But to this action there is a counteraction, which springs from the Court. We saw, in the First Movement, that Hamlet's obstacle was chiefly in himself; that he could not force himself to do the deed, though the most powerful impulsion from without was urging him forward. Then comes the external opposition, which seems trifling compared with the internal resistance. The King and Court are upon his track, yet how easily are they baffled! He could sink them all, were he at one with himself. Hence the internal collision is the main one in the play.

The King is, however, the person with whom Hamlet carries on the external conflict; the others are the instruments of the King. Here we find a series of characters—Polonius and his children, the Queen, Rosencrantz and Guildenstern—who have the same end that the King has, or, at least, all of them are means for the execution of his purpose. Hence they are more or less remotely involved in the same destruction. Hamlet has no such instruments, for the reason that he must first make up his mind to accomplish the deed before he can employ them—which resolution, if he makes it, is out of his power of realization. The only character on his side is Horatio, a friend from the University, and a foreigner, whose chief function is to know the plans and motives of Hamlet, and to be present at the leading events, since he is to be the poet of this drama, and the vindicator of Hamlet's conduct. Thus he hovers over the poem from beginning to end, without much definiteness of character, and without saying or doing hardly anything beyond what is necessary to indicate his presence. He acts principally as a foil to exhibit Hamlet's designs and motives. When the latter has not Horatio to talk with, he has to talk with himself about his affairs; hence the predominance of soliloquy in this play. Hamlet's encomium on Horatio cannot be gainsaid, though it has to be taken largely on faith; it is very interesting, however, as showing what Hamlet admired, if he did not possess:

> For thou hast been
> As one, in suffering all, that suffers nothing—
> —Give me that man
> That is not passion's slave; and I will wear him
> In my heart's core, ay, in my heart of heart,
> As I do thee.

It is otherwise with the King; he can act, and has acted, and, hence, knows the use of instruments. The course of his action is twofold—first, to discover the cause of Hamlet's melancholy; and second, when he has made that discovery, to get rid of the man with such a dangerous secret. The presupposition of his conduct, and, in fact, of the play itself, is a previous crime—the murder of Hamlet's father, by which he came to the throne. The curse is at work from the start; suspicion against the son of the murdered King harasses his bosom, which suspicion is intensified by the strange demeanor of the son. Here the struggle begins. To find out what is the matter with Hamlet—to discover whether he knows the secret of his father's murder—is the first great object of Claudius; for this purpose the characters above mentioned are introduced. But they, too, are to be judged by their deeds; the law of responsibility applies to them also. Hamlet, on the contrary, carefully avoids detection; to cover his thoughts and plans more effectually, he throws over them the night of lunacy. We have already shown, in the first part of the present essay, that this disguise was especially adapted to deceive Polonius, whom, on account of his reputation and position, the King was sure to set on Hamlet's track. It is to be observed that the King was shrewder than his minister. He did not believe that Hamlet was crazy, from the start, though evidently putting a great deal of faith in Polonius. Thus arises that peculiar and dexterous struggle, in which Hamlet seeks to conceal his thoughts and purposes, and the King tries to discover them. The culmination of this counter-movement is when Hamlet, by his "play within the play," shows that he is aware of the great secret. Here is the point where the conscience of the King is aroused; the most fearful struggle rends his bosom; he knows not whether to retrace his steps and repent of his old crime, or to retain his wife and realm by committing a new crime. At last he resolves upon the latter, and, hence, his object now is to get rid of Hamlet. For both these purposes he uses as instruments those persons whose characters are now to be given.

Let us recall the grouping of the characters as it has before been indicated. The first set is the King and Queen, who have a common principle in their conscience-conflict, which has been roused in both by Hamlet. Both, in great distress of soul, are brought to consider repentance; both reject it. Hamlet himself is linked to this set also by his conscience-conflict, though it proceeds not so much from commission as omission. The House of Denmark thus centers spiritually in a common trait: all its members in their guilt show conscience, which goads them to consider repentance, the undoing of the guilt, as the means of escape; but they all reject repentance and perish. Does not this reach to the very heart of the Christian world? It may be fairly placed to the credit of Danish royalty, that it is capable of conscience.

Specially, in reference to the character of the King. He is exhibited in no absolutely depraved light by the drama; he is not a bloody tyrant who proceeds from murder to murder, like Macbeth, but he endures a good deal from Hamlet, so much so, that he gets into trouble with Laertes for his leniency. He drinks too much, in Hamlet's opinion, to which we give our assent. But he seems to desire to live and reign honestly from this time forward, provided there is no reckoning for the past; Hamlet, he has declared, shall be his heir; also, his calmness and self-possession, in very trying circumstances, win our favorable regard. Moreover, he shows, repeatedly, strong compunctions of conscience for his crime; he wishes the act undone, if it occasion no loss to him. He is, therefore, an extreme example of that large class of people who seek to repent of their misdeeds, yet desire to retain all the profits thereof. Still, he has good personal reasons for not proceeding with open violence against Hamlet, namely, his fear of the people, who idolize the young Prince, and the affection of the Queen for her son.

Thus the King also has two collisions—the external one with Hamlet, and the internal one with himself. The latter is most powerful; he has committed a crime which he seeks, yet is unable, to make undone without its undoing himself; repentance involves his death, since he must confess his crime to the world and surrender all its advantages, namely, his kingdom and his queen, and then submit to the penalty of the law. Repentance thus seems to him to annihilate the very end for which it exists, and to become self-contradictory; for, if it destroys men, thinks he, what is the use of their repentance? To repent is death; not to repent is death; he wills to do, yet not to do. But he cannot stand still; his deed is upon him; he has to bolster it up by a new act of guilt. He now commences plotting against the life of Hamlet, who, at last, falls through his machinations. Thus crime begets crime. His retribution, however, comes in full; he perishes by the hand of him whose death he has sought and whose father he has slain.

The Queen has been disloyal to her husband, but probably not a direct participant in his murder. She has violated the very principle of womanhood, and has destroyed the ethical basis of female character. Excepting the charge of infidelity made by the Ghost and the intimations of Hamlet, we have no declaration of the exact nature of her crime. Considering the important part she plays in the action, and the great influence which the King confesses she has over him, one is inclined to see in her a principal in the murder—a second Clytemnestra. But it must be confessed that the poet has left the precise nature and degree of her offense in great uncertainty, and assuredly with design; yet few readers, perhaps, have any doubt about her being an accessary, in some way or other, in the murder of her husband. The reason why the poet has thrown a veil over her guilt is that he was unwilling—in fact, unable—to make Hamlet play the part of Orestes, the slayer of his own mother. It would not comport with the character of Hamlet, nor would it suit a modern audience; and, still more, it would disturb the course of the play, which demands the concentration of his revenge upon the King. If he could not kill the King, much less could he kill his own mother. His revenge is to call up her conscience and emotional nature —to show the tremendous chasm between herself and the truly ethical woman; for thus she would be harrassed by her own feelings more than by any punishment, since it is emotion which forms the leading characteristic of her nature. The Queen dies; for she has violated the principle of her rational existence—fidelity to the family relation. The man who corrupted her purity mixed the draught which deprived her of life; and the former was more truly destructive than the latter. But she loves Hamlet with the affection of a mother; the maternal relation is more powerful than the marital.

In connection with the Queen a question of some interest arises concerning the reason why she does not perceive the Ghost when it is seen and addressed by Hamlet (Act III, Scene 4). The common supposition seems to be that the poet desires to indicate that it is merely a subjective ghost, and some critics have gone so far as to recommend its entire banishment from the stage in this scene. The poet, however, introduces it, and makes it address Hamlet in this very passage. We cannot think, therefore, that he intends to destroy all the work which he was so careful hitherto in doing, namely, the preservation of the objectivity of the Ghost. It seems to us that he merely intends to show that it does not lie in the character of the Queen to see ghosts. But Hamlet sees them, and this forms one of the great distinguishing elements of his nature. Nobody besides himself ever sees the Ghost, if we except the soldiers and Horatio in the First Act, and they are made to see it for the purpose of rendering it real to the audience, and not to exhibit any fundamental principle in their character. The difficulty is to preserve the objectivity of the Ghost to the audience, and, at the same time, not to let it appear to those whose characterization would be thereby distorted. That the Ghost lies wholly in Hamlet's imagination, if the Queen, though present, does not see it, is a very natural inference; but the point is that the poet, instead of intending to call up that inference in the minds of his audience, would have every eye behold the Ghost in its reality, as being Hamlet's great problem. The Ghost is certainly inside of Hamlet, and outside of him too, but there is required a ghostly eye and ear to see it and to hear it. Such the Queen does not possess.

The second group of characters is made up of the family of Polonius, father, son, daughter.

They have a common trait which binds them together, as well as contrasts them with the royal family. This trait goes back to the moving thought of the drama—conscience. Polonius and his children show no inner questionings, no qualms of guilt, no tendency to repentance, such as we have noticed in the royal personages of the play. We may call them the conscienceless set; the great spiritual movement of the time has not entered into them; once or twice only can we see that it brushes them a little uncomfortably. They show no pang for the deed, they offer themselves as ready instruments to the guilty King, without inner conflict or reaction. Of all three this is true, though their characters in other respects are different.

The father, Polonius, is the leading instrument of the King against Hamlet; his life has, apparently, been devoted to reading the secret thoughts of others, and concealing his own. In him we see the shrewd diplomat; and we cannot help thinking that the poet drew this character from the Italian diplomacy of his own and preceding ages. Base motives Polonius appreciates; but he does not recognize the moral law in himself, nor in others, nor in the world. For this reason he totally misunderstands Hamlet, whose moral nature is the essential part of him.

The fundamental characteristic of Polonius is cunning—cunning as the absolute basis of conduct. Now, cunning is not to be eschewed within its proper limitations; but, when it is made the highest rule of action, it must necessarily assail, and attempt to subordinate, the ethical principles of the world. For, if it is the highest, Right, Morality, Religion, are inferior, and must be disregarded. Such, in general, is the character of Polonius, which age and long habit have so confirmed that it is seen in the most trivial affairs of life, and makes him often have a decidedly comic tinge. Cunning thus becomes anything but cunning; it destroys itself. He does not believe in an ethical order of things, or, rather, is totally ignorant of the same. The world is governed wholly by adroit management, according to him; the externals of life—conventionalities—are the most important element of knowledge. This is seen in the parting advice given to his son: excellent precepts for external conduct, but, on the whole, a system of selfishness, whose germ is "to thine own self be true," which here means the narrow individual. Note that there is no allusion to moral principles as the guides of human conduct; in fact, we learn, in another place, that he would even be pleased to learn of the moral derelictions of his son, as the "flash and outbreak of a fiery mind." Moreover, he has no faith in the sincerity of Hamlet's love for Ophelia, or, really no faith in love at all; in his judgment it is lust, with ulterior designs.

Such a man stands in direct opposition to Hamlet; the latter, therefore, has for him, not only dislike, but also the most unqualified contempt. Polonius has no comprehension of such a character. Hamlet worries him by dark sayings, which have always a secret sting, and utterly confounds him at his own game. It would almost seem as if the poet meant to show the folly of cunning—how it completely contradicts and destroys itself. Polonius sends Reynaldo to Paris to look after his son, and gives some very shrewd instructions. At first one is inclined to ask, if he cannot trust his own son, why should he trust his servant, and who is to watch the latter? For the basis of his conduct is distrust. But what is the use of the information when he gets it? None at all; for he allows to his son those very vices which he sent Reynaldo to observe. Also, in the play we hear no more of the matter; this scene is, therefore, simply to show the leading trait of Polonius.

His object, then, is espionage, for its own sake; management—not for any end, but to be a managing; he thus plays with his own cunning. Polonius has now reached that interesting stage of mind when he delights in cunning for its own sake, and seeks the most tortuous path when a straight one is at hand. This crookedness extends also to his language, which, before it comes to the point, takes a dart to one side and loses itself in its own prolixity. Now, such a man is set to work to ascertain the secret of Hamlet, whose nature lies outside of his intellectual horizon. How completely he is befooled is evident enough; the old fellow is compelled to confess that his cunning has overreached itself in thinking that Hamlet's love for his daughter was fictitious; and he feels sorry that he had not "quoted him with better heed and judgment," for, after all, he was very willing for Hamlet to be his son-in-law. In this respect it is also curious to observe his duplicity towards the King, for to the latter he professes to have broken off the match for reasons of State. Finally, it is his own cunning which brings him to sudden death, through his concealment behind the arras. Cunning thus destroys itself.

This brings us to consider the ground of his death, which is often thought to be harsh and repulsive, and, in addition, an unnecessary incident in the play. The first question to be asked is, has he done anything to merit such a fate? Undoubtedly; for he has shown himself the willing instrument of the King in all the schemes against young Hamlet; and it is hinted that his present influential position is owing to the hand he had in the conspiracy against the elder Hamlet. Polonius has, therefore, merited the retribution which has come. But is Hamlet justified in killing him? Undoubtedly not. Hamlet acts upon impulse; makes a mistake which brings, ultimately, retribution upon himself at the hands of Laertes. Though Polonius may deserve death, yet Hamlet cannot rightfully be the executioner; hence guilt falls upon him. All this is expressed by Hamlet himself, who fully appreciates his situation, and declares his repentance for the act:

—For this same lord
I do repent, but Heaven hath pleased it so
To punish me with this and this with me,
That I should be their scourge and minister.

Here he states that he was the instrument for the punishment of Polonius, and that the murder of Polonius was the instrument of his own punishment. The death of Polonius is, therefore, not an accident in the play, in the sense that it is not motived beforehand; it also shows how Hamlet can act from impulse before reflection sets in, and that such action plunges him into the deepest guilt. Acting from impulse, he slays the wrong one, but, as a rational being, he must be held responsible for his deed. Another distinction should be kept in the mind: Polonius is a subject, and, hence, amenable to law; while the King, as the fountain of justice, is above law, and, hence, can be punished only by murder.

Punishment must now be inflicted on Hamlet—but by whom? Here appears the avenger Laertes, the son of Polonius, in accordance with the strictest retribution; for Hamlet is seeking revenge for a father slain, yet has himself slain a father, whose son, according to his own logic, must now rise up and try to kill him. Laertes is a chip of the old block, with the difference of age. For what the young man tries to carry by storm and impulse, the old man tries to obtain through cunning. Both are equally devoid of an ethical content to their lives. How much they are alike, and how completely Hamlet's character lies outside of their comprehension, may be seen in the advice which both give to Ophelia concerning Hamlet.

The first fact which is brought to our notice about Laertes is his request to return to France, which fact is an offset to the desire of Hamlet to go back to Wittenberg. We have already shown the importance of this stroke in the life and character of Hamlet. Equally important and suggestive is the statement concerning Laertes. It indicates that he sought and possessed the French culture, in contrast to the German culture of Hamlet. The French have been in all times noted for the stress they lay upon the externalities of life. In whatever pertains to etiquette, polite intercourse, and fashion, they have been the teachers of Europe, and have elaborated a language which most adequately expresses this phase of existence. But it must be said that the perfection of the External has been attended with a corresponding loss of the Internal—that the graces have too often not only hidden, but extinguished, the virtues.

In this school Laertes has been educated, and herein shows a striking contrast to the deep moral nature of Hamlet. He has, therefore, the advantage of not being restrained by any uncomfortable scruples, and here again the contrast with Hamlet is prominent. Laertes can act. Yet he proceeds from impulse, though he has sufficient cause for anger; hence he, too, is on the point of killing the wrong one, just as Hamlet did in the case of Polonius. That Laertes is ready to destroy the whole ethical order of the world in his revenge—that his nature is quite devoid of the great moral principles of action, is shown in the following words of his:

> To Hell, allegiance! vows to the blackest devil!
> Conscience and grace to the profoundest pit!
> I dare damnation. To this point I stand—
> That both the worlds I give to negligence,
> Let come what comes, only I'll be revenged.

No doubt he is now in a high passion, but this is just his characteristic. Here he openly abjures conscience, religion, fidelity—the very basis upon which the moral system of things must rest. Yet we find that, in the end, he does acknowledge one controlling principle, the emptiest and most worthless of all—honor, which, however, does not prevent him from entering into a rather dishonorable conspiracy with the King against Hamlet. Such is Laertes; yet he is not without a generous, gallant element in his character. Witness at his death the forgiveness which he asks of Hamlet. He dies because he has willed the death of Hamlet, which, though merited, he cannot inflict as an individual. Moreover, he assails his own principle in becoming the instrument of the King against Hamlet; for he, the avenger of a father, is aiding the murderer of a father against just such an avenger as himself. His act, therefore, logically involves his death; also, he is a subject, and must resort to the court of justice; he has not the excuse of Hamlet for the murder of Claudius, since the King, being the source of justice itself, cannot well be subsumed under his own creature.

Ophelia too becomes an instrument against Hamlet, through her father. She is one of the fairest of our poet's creations, whose very beauty lies in her frail and delicate nature. We feel from the first that she is too weak to endure the contradictions of life; that a flower so tender must perish in the first rude storm. She has little individuality of her own; she is wholly wrapped up in the father and lover; her reliance upon others is absolute. Now comes the rudest shock which can assail a woman; both props are torn from under her, and there remains nothing for her support. Her lover goes crazy—for that is her belief—and slays her father. Her mind has no longer any center at all, because it has none in itself; insanity during a short time follows, and, ultimately, death by accident; for she was dead in thought, but could only perish by accident, since she was crazy, and, hence, irresponsible. Her snatches of old songs exhibit the working of memory and imagination, without the controlling principle of reason; she runs into licentious fancies, superinduced, no doubt, by the previous conversations of Polonius, Hamlet and Laertes. Here we have an undoubted case of destruction without guilt; but, as before remarked, in the case of Hamlet, a certain degree of individuality is the very condition of existence; no one can live who cannot endure the conditions of life. Ophelia perishes through her beauty; that which constitutes the strongest charm of her character is what makes her greatest weakness. We may contrast her with Portia, who possesses the side of strong individuality without losing her ethical character or true womanhood. But Ophelia is all trust, all dependence; there is in her hardly a trace of selfishness or self-reliance even; she can think of herself only in her losses. Hence the sweetness, beauty, and loveliness of her character; but, alas! hence also its utter frailty.

Still, we must see that Ophelia is a true daughter of Polonius, a decided sense of duty is not her possession; she belongs, by birth and character, to the conscienceless set. She allows her father and brother to dishonor the fair name, and sully the motives, of her lover, without active protest on her part, though she knows well that "he hath importuned me with love in honorable fashion." She manifests no assertion of love as a duty, which is its triumph; for there is a conscience in love, which the best men and women recognize and follow, against obstacles heaven-high. Here the obstacle is the parent, over whom Shakespeare always makes the strong-hearted daughter victorious, if there be no other element of conflict. Doubtless she loves Hamlet; but hers is the passion of love without its conscience. Moreover, she loves him for his externals; he is "the glass of fashion and the mould of form;" he has "the courtier's, scholar's, soldier's, eye, tongue, sword;" though she speaks of his "sovereign reason," which, she thinks, is overthrown, she has no appreciation of his deep soul-struggles, which are hid under that cloak of insanity. His moral nature finds no response in her; she permits him to be wrongfully besmirched, sends back his tokens, and, finally, betrays him while loving him. Yet all this she does in obedience to parent, which thus becomes the test of her character. Still Ophelia is not bad, she is weak, obedient and beautiful.

Once more let us summon before ourselves the total movement of the play. Its presupposition is the crime of Claudius, who has murdered the King, corrupted the mother, and usurped the realm. This calls up the son, who is to requite both the murderer and the faithless mother. It is the object of the son, first, to discover the truth of the guilt, and, secondly, to avenge the same when discovered. It is the object of the King to find out the plans of Hamlet, and then to make way with him when he has found them out. Hamlet has the assistance of one friend—Horatio; the King has the assistance of a number of persons connected with his court. The previous crime is the central point from which the two counter-movements of the play take their origin; the action of the King and Hamlet respecting this crime gives the essence of their conduct and character. Both exhibit negative phases of the ethical deed; the one refuses to do it at all, and, hence, never reaches any positive act; the other commits a crime—that is, destroys the Ethical—and then refuses to make the crime undone. It is at this point that we can see that the delinquency of both is the same: each refuses to perform the ethical deed—the one, because he will not act; the other, because he will not repent; or, to use a figurative contrast—the one, because he will not go forward; the other, because he will not go backward. Nor must we forget the other side, which gives the internal collision. Both have a justification for the course which they pursue—the one, because through action he would be compelled to commit a crime; the other, because through repentance he would have to sacrifice his life. To force Hamlet to action the External, in the form of a series of influences, is brought to bear upon him; to force the King to action the Internal—Conscience—wields her power. But, in the one case, the External is baffled by the Internal, in the shape of Reflection and Conscience; in the other case, the Internal is baffled by the Exterternal, in the shape of worldly power, possessions, and ambition.

But now the reader himself must undertake to complete these interesting contrasts, and to work out the further details of the drama. It is, no doubt, the profoundest of Shakespeare's plays in respect to its thought, and its collision seems to touch the very core of modern spirit. The Theoretical and the Practical, Intelligence and Will, are here exhibited in their one-sidedness, and it is shown that neither is sufficient by itself. If the play has any moral, it would seem to be that the man who refuses to translate his thought into deed is as great a criminal, or, at most, possesses as little power of salvation within himself, as he who will not undo his own deed when it is wicked.

Moreover, this play stands alone in the fact that it quite touches the limits of the Drama itself. For the essence of the Drama is to portray some form of action; but here that form largely is non-action; hence the plan of the play, and the necessity for those external circumstances which were detailed in a previous section; for they must be external, since the character is essentially passive. The work thus marks the outlying boundary of Shakespeare's poetical activity, and exhibits the broadest range of his genius. The rest of his dramas depict collisions of various kinds, but it is the nature of the collision to be between higher and lower forms of Will. But here he quite sweeps the whole field of the Will, and makes it one of the colliding principles. He thus produces the most comprehensive of all dramas, and seems to exhaust the very possibilities of Dramatic Art.

Let us beware, then, of making Hamlet too limited, too finite. We must have noticed that the horizon of his character is so vast that one is apt to get lost in it, or to take some fragment of it for the whole. But, what is even more difficult, it is full of antithetic tendencies; it cannot be confined to one direction; every trait seems to be re-acting against itself, and changing to its own opposite. No sooner do we see some limit to his character, than we find him storming against that limit, and trying to get beyond it. To take our old example, when conscience puts its restraint upon him, he turns to revenge; but when revenge becomes a limit, he goes back to conscience. It is true that most of Shakespeare's great characters have this same double tendency; they are shown as limited in some direction, but that is not the whole of them, they are also limit-transcending, striving after the beyond; they are, indeed, finite, but have in themselves the opposite of the finite—the infinite. But above all Shakespeare's characters, Hamlet is the limit-transcending spirit, which can never rest in its own bounds. He is the thinking man, and it is the nature of thought to be, not a part, but the whole, to be not the limited, but the unlimited. The Finite and the Infinite are thus commingled in Hamlet, as in every human being; but the Infinite is by far the stronger tendency; earthly bounds satisfy him not, the limited deed here vanishes into the unlimited thought beyond. The Ghost coming from that world beyond and holding communication with him is the deepest symbol of his character. It is no wonder that it will speak to nobody but him. Hamlet, though he has definite tendencies, which are to be marked, must not be reduced to the definite simply, for his nature is to throw down his limits and be as infinite as Thought.

www.ingramcontent.com/pod-product-compliance
Lightning Source LLC
Chambersburg PA
CBHW020834020526
44114CB00040B/758